International Labour Mobility

Valentina Vasile • Elena Bunduchi
Daniel Stefan • Calin-Adrian Comes

International Labour Mobility

How Remittances Shape the Labour Migration Model

palgrave
macmillan

Valentina Vasile
Institute of National Economy
Romanian Academy
Bucharest, Romania

Daniel Stefan
Institute of National Economy
Romanian Academy
Bucharest, Romania

Faculty of Economics and Law
George Emil Palade University of
Medicine, Pharmacy, Science, and
Technology of Targu Mures
Targu Mures, Romania

Elena Bunduchi
Institute of National Economy
Romanian Academy
Bucharest, Romania

Faculty of Economics and Law
George Emil Palade University of
Medicine, Pharmacy, Science, and
Technology of Targu Mures
Targu Mures, Romania

Calin-Adrian Comes
Institute of National Economy
Romanian Academy
Bucharest, Romania

Faculty of Economics and Law
George Emil Palade University of
Medicine, Pharmacy, Science, and
Technology of Targu Mures
Targu Mures, Romania

ISBN 978-3-031-18682-0 ISBN 978-3-031-18683-7 (eBook)
https://doi.org/10.1007/978-3-031-18683-7

This Palgrave Macmillan imprint is published by the registered company Springer Nature Switzerland AG.
The registered company address is: Gewerbestrasse 11, 6330 Cham, Switzerland

Contents

About the Authors

Valentina Vasile, PhD in Economics, a full professor and a senior researcher first degree, is working as Director of the Institute of National Economy, Romanian Academy, and is teaching at Nicolae Titulescu University of Bucharest. She is also a PhD advisor and Deputy Director of the doctoral school SCOSAAR of the Romanian Academy, Department of Economic, Law, and Sociological Sciences. She has a wide experience as a researcher in economics, who participated in internal and international interdisciplinary research projects, main topics of which being labour economics, migration, human capital, digital economy and employment, social policies, education, and macroeconomics, sustainable development, resilience and circular economy. She has a good international cooperation as coordinator and is a team member in interdisciplinary research projects financed from European funds, Horizon2020, SEE Program, Black Sea Basin ENI CBC, CEDEFOP, ILO, Eurofound or other sources like projects financed by universities (i.e. Hitotsubashi University, Tokyo, Japan, etc.). Her articles have appeared in scientific papers and books indexed in Web of Sciences, Scopus and other international databases and acts as a reviewer for several scientific journals.

Elena Bunduchi received the BS degree in Finance from the Academy of Economic Studies from Chisinau, Republic of Moldova, in 2011. In 2019 she received her PhD from the Institute of National Economy, Romanian Academy. Since 2016 she was a teacher assistant at "Petru Maior" University from Tîrgu-Mures. From 2020 she is a lecturer with the University of Medicine, Pharmacy, Sciences and Technology of Tîrgu-Mures, Mures County, Romania. Now she is a postdoctoral student at the Institute of National Economy, Romanian Academy. Her research interests include the impact of international migration and remittances on economic growth, direct investment decision, data analysis and impact of digitalization on economies and societies from a macro- and microeconomic perspective. Elena Bunduchi was the manager of several national research mobility programmes and a team member in different international and national projects, author and co-author of peer-reviewed international publications, respective author and co-author of several national publications.

Daniel Stefan received the BS degree in Finance from "Babes Bolyai" University, Cluj Napoca, Romania, in 1999; the MS degree in Financial Strategies for Business from "Babes Bolyai" University, Cluj Napoca, Romania, in 2000; and the PhD degree in Finance at "Babes Bolyai" University, Cluj Napoca, Romania. In 2012 he graduated post-doctoral studies at the Institute of National Economy of Romanian Academy. From 2002 to 2022, he was an assistant professor, lecturer and associate professor at "Petru Maior" University of Targu-Mures, Romania, currently "George Emil Palade" University of Medicine, Pharmacy, Sciences and Technology Targu-Mures, Romania. His research interests include the FDI, emerging markets, direct investment decision and decision systems. Stefan is the President of Romanian Research Group for Corporate Finance and has been the guest editor of *Optimization*, Taylor & Francis, *Procedia Economics and Finance*, Elsevier.

Calin-Adrian Comes received the BS degree in Business Information Systems from Babes-Bolyai University, Cluj-Napoca, Romania, in 2000 and the PhD degree in Cybernetics and Statistics from Babes-Bolyai University, Cluj-Napoca, Romania, in 2012. From 2014 to 2016, he was a post-doctoral researcher at Romanian Academy, Research Institute of Quality of Life. Since 2001, he has been an assistant professor, lecturer, associate professor with the Financial and Accounting Department, Faculty of Economics and Law, "Petru Maior" University of Târgu-Mures, Romania, actually "George Emil Palade" University of Medicine, Pharmacy, Sciences and Technology of Târgu-Mures Romania. He is the author of 1 book, more than 20 peer-reviewed articles and 15 peer-reviewed conference papers. Mr. C.-A. Comes is a guest editor, editor and reviewer for numerous peer-reviewed journals in Elsevier, Springer and Taylor & Francis. His research interests include statistics, econometrics, data mining and Big Data.

List of Figures

List of Tables

CHAPTER 1

Introduction

Valentina Vasile and Elena Bunduchi

Migration has become a large-scale phenomenon, which affects all states of the world, regardless of their geographical area or level of economic development, and the ever-increasing number of international migrants has exceeded the growth rate of the world's population. Therefore, understanding the role and impact of migration in countries of origin and destination is an important step in ensuring sustainable economic development and the achievement of the Sustainable Development Goals. As a result of the increasing attention paid to migration, we consider it very topical to study the impact of the phenomenon on all the countries involved, both those of origin and destination.

Mobility for work is a natural process that allows a better match between the individual's work potential and the employer's need for work. As a production factor, the workforce influences production and economic growth at the company level and generates budget revenues through taxes and fees. In the classical sense, mobility for work can be geographical and/or occupational, it can be temporary/for a defined term, multi-year/for an indefinite term or definitive migration, which also implies the relocation of the household in the vicinity of the workplace. The digital transformation of the business environment has increased the importance of remote work and hybrid work, which deepens the segmentation of the traditional migration model and gives way to the development of "digital migration", without a change of residence but with an increase in money transfers from

V. Vasile et al., *International Labour Mobility*,
https://doi.org/10.1007/978-3-031-18683-7_1

work abroad. From the perspective of this work, geographic mobility becomes significant if it is associated with movement across national borders, respectively external mobility, whether it is temporary or definitive, known as international mobility for work. Mobility for work, as an opportunity supported by globalization, is always operationalized by the individual's motivation, and the freedom of labour movement represents the facilitating framework, with effects on the (re)allocation of the effective labour force. According to International Labour Organisation (ILO, 2022) "Migrant workers contribute to growth and development in their countries of destination, while countries of origin greatly benefit from their remittances and the skills acquired during their migration experience."

Although specialized literature and some political actors tend to emphasize the positive effects generated by migration, and implicitly, remittances, this research aims to identify the real economic and financial externalities of the mobility of labour resource, mainly from the perspective of the countries of origin, which benefit from remittances, by testing the favourable hypotheses already formed worldwide. Like any economic phenomenon, external migration also generates negative externalities, but specialized literature has emphasized the net positive effect of external mobility for work.

In order to fulfil the proposed general purpose, we have identified a series of specific objectives:

- The conceptual approach to the migration phenomenon and its results—remittances, from the perspective of scientific theories and currents that are the basis for explaining the premises of the emergence and development of migration and the role of remittances in this process
- Identifying the role of remittances among external financial flows and the impact generated by them on the economic growth of the beneficiary states by performing an econometric analysis applying a panel data model
- Multidimensional analysis of the effects of remittances from a macroeconomic and microeconomic perspective at the level of the origin countries
- The identification of migration policy measures, which allow an efficient management of the flows of people and the correct direction of remittances, so as to contribute to sustainable economic growth

This book is structured into 11 chapters, which address the theoretical and practical parts of the research topic.

In Chap. 2, conceptual aspects of remittances are presented, as well as the definition of these financial flows from the perspective of harmonization with the indications of the International Monetary Fund. At the same time, the problem of quantifying the volume of remittances from the perspective of official and unofficial transfer channels was addressed and measures adopted by the countries of origin regarding the management of remittances were identified, with emphasis on the cost of remittances.

In Chap. 3, the theories of migration are presented, being analysed primarily from the perspective of remittances and their role in defining the behaviour of migrants.

Chapter 4 is dedicated to the historical evolution and current trends of migration and remittances at the global, European and national level. Thus, we find that the migration phenomenon is growing rapidly in recent years, encompassing the world's population, regardless of the geographical area or economic status, changing the traditional pattern of migration from poor states to rich ones.

Chapter 5 aims to analyse the effects of remittances and FDI on the economic growth of the beneficiary states (EU-28 member states + Moldova, Ukraine and Serbia, which were grouped according to the mobility rate external of persons). Within each group, subgroups were formed depending on the level of GDP/capita. The obtained results support the idea that countries with a lower level of economic development are more dependent on these external financial flows compared to developed states.

In Chap. 6, the idea of analysing remittances in the countries of origin is continued, but we have carried out a multidimensional analysis at the macroeconomic and microeconomic level in Romania and the Republic of Moldova. In the case of Romania and the Republic of Moldova, at the macroeconomic level, is presented the impact generated on the labour market indicators, and the financial effects on the balance of payments. At the microeconomic level, this research highlights the impact on the change in current consumption expenditures, the quality of life (reflected in health expenditures), of the formation of human capital (education expenditures) and the households' degree of modernization and endowment with technologies.

In Chap. 7 we analyse migration and remittances from a social point of view of the country of origin and destination, identifying the macro- and microeconomic, positive and negative effects felt by both countries involved in the migration process.

In Chap. 8 an analysis of migration strategies at the level of the European Union and Romania is carried out, at the same time, being documented examples of good practices of efficient management of remittances, so as to contribute to the economic growth of the country of origin through the development of entrepreneurship.

In Chap. 9, the boomerang effect of the management policies of the phenomenon of emigration in Romania is analysed, from policies encouraging Romanians to migrate for work to negative attitudes of the population and the authorities with the return of migrants during the COVID-19 pandemic.

Chapter 10 presents the definition of the status of migrants as critical workers during the COVID-19 pandemic, as well as the presentation of the paradigm shift and the treatment of migrants within the destination countries. At the same time, the impact of the pandemic on the migration phenomenon and its future implications is emphasized.

In Chap. 11, the final conclusions of this research can be found, stating the main results obtained, the elements of novelty and personal contribution, as well as future research directions.

Remittances remain an important financial inflow in less developed countries. According to the World Bank database, remittances proved to be more resilient during COVID-19 crisis and surpass the sum of foreign direct investment and overseas development assistance, registering a robust 7.3% growth in 2021 against 2020 (World Bank, 2021). Therefore, the multidimensional analysis of remittances and highlighting the impact in the countries of origin will be a necessary approach in the future, facilitating, from multiple perspectives, the achievement of the SDGs' objectives. The current work is a point of reflection for (re)defining policies to support the effective valorisations of human capital, through employment and productivity, but also as a lever to support the increase in the quality of life of the beneficiaries of remittances, together with business environment in the country of origin.

References

ILO. (2022). *Labour Migration*. International Labour Organization. https://www.ilo.org/global/topics/labour-migration/lang%2D%2Den/index.htm

World Bank. (2021). *Remittance Flows Register Robust 7.3 Percent Growth in 2021*. The World Bank. https://www.worldbank.org/en/news/press-release/2021/11/17/remittance-flows-register-robust-7-3-percent-growth-in-2021

CHAPTER 2

Theoretical and Conceptual Framework of Remittances

Valentina Vasile and Elena Bunduchi

Remittances: Conceptual Overview

Remittances were considered current transfers made by migrant residents employed in a foreign country (IMF, 2004), but since 2009 (IMF, 2009), the notion of personal transfers replaces the element of remittances of workers. Unlike remittances, personal transfers are independent of the income source of the transmitting household, of the relationship between households and of the purpose of the transfer, even if it is recognized that personal transfers are usually intended to support relatives in the country of origin of migrants.

According to Fig. 2.1, remittances have the following components:

$$\text{Personal remittances} = \text{Personal transfers} + \text{Employee compensation} + \text{Capital transfers between households}$$

- Personal transfers are all current transfers made or received by resident households to or from non-resident households (IMF, 2009).

Thus, personal transfers include all current transfers which take place between resident and non-resident individuals.

V. Vasile et al., *International Labour Mobility*,
https://doi.org/10.1007/978-3-031-18683-7_2

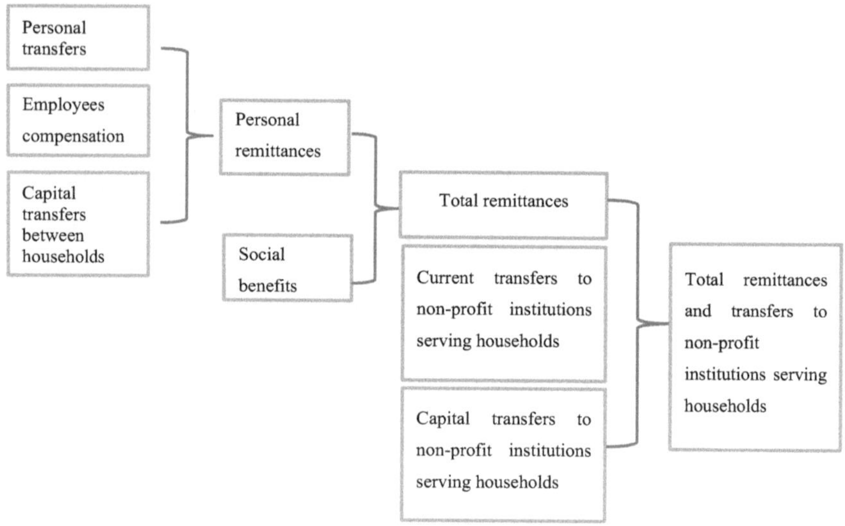

Fig. 2.1 International Monetary Fund presentation of the definition of remittances. Source: Based on (IMF, 2009)

- Employee compensation refers to the income of frontier, seasonal and other short-term workers who are employed in a non-resident economy and of residents employed by non-resident entities (IMF, 2009).
- Capital transfers between households reflect the amount of wealth held by migrants when they change their place of residence from one state to another, thus leading to a change in the assets/liabilities of both countries.

$$\text{Total remittances} = \text{Personal remittances} + \text{Social benefits}$$

- Social benefits[1] include social security and social assistance benefits. These are current transfers received by migrant households meant to

[1] EU law stipulates equal rights for EU migrants in relation to natives in terms of social benefits. In order to benefit from the social benefits offered by EU countries, an EU migrant must be employed, a student or actively looking for a job. In addition, the following factors are taken into account: length of stay; source of income in the case of students; marital status; at the same time, the migrant must demonstrate a degree of attachment to the country of destination.

cover needs arising from certain events or circumstances, for example, illness, unemployment, retirement, housing, education or family circumstances.

$$\begin{aligned} &\text{Total remittances and transfers to non} \\ &\quad \text{profit institutions serving households} = \text{Total remittances} \\ &\quad + \text{Current transfers to non profit institutions serving households} \\ &\quad + \text{Capital transfers to non profit institutions serving households.} \end{aligned}$$

- Current transfers to non-profit institutions in the service of households consist of cash transfers received by non-profit institutions in the service of households from other non-resident institutional units, in the form of contributions, voluntary donations, etc. (IMF, 2009).
- Capital transfers to non-profit institutions serving households (NPISHs) consist of cash transfers received by non-profit institutions serving households from other non-resident institutional units, in the form of development aid programmes, cross-border sponsorships, etc. (IMF, 2009).

The current definition of remittances was introduced with the IMF's implementation of a new Balance of Payments (BPM6) methodology, which allows clear concepts to be established regarding the composition of remittances and the comparability of international statistics.

Both Romania and the Republic of Moldova detail the components of remittances according to BPM6 (Table 2.1). Even if the components of remittances are comparable between the two states, we note that in the balance of payments of the Republic of Moldova, "other accounts" is more detailed, compared to Romania, being also mentioned "population households", which includes personal transfers, employee compensation and social benefits.

Although BPM6 has improved the way remittances are recorded in the destination states, there may be errors caused by incorrect measurement. For example, compensation of employees impacts GDP, the primary income account and disposable income in the origin country. Thus, if it is measured incorrectly, the value of the savings in the country of origin will be wrong, due to the fact that it is calculated as the difference between disposable income and final consumption expenditure. Personal transfers,

Table 2.1 Source of registration of remittance components

Elements	*BPM6*	*BP Romania*	*BP Moldova*
Personal remittances: a+b+c			
a. Personal transfers	Secondary income account, standard element	Secondary income account, other sectors	Secondary income account, population households
b. Employee compensation	Primary income account, standard element	Primary income account, standard element	Primary income account, standard element
c. Capital transfer between households	Capital account, additional element	Capital account, other sectors	Capital account, population households
Total remittances a+b+c+d			
d. Social benefits	Secondary income account, additional element	Secondary income account, other sectors	Secondary income account, population households
Total remittances and transfers to NPISHs: a+b+c+d+e+f			
e. Current transfers to NPISH	Secondary income account, additional element	Secondary income account, other sectors	Secondary income account, population households
f. Capital transfers to NPISH	Capital account, additional element	Capital account, other sectors	Capital account, population households

Source: Based on data from BPM6, NBR and NBM

on the contrary, do affect disposable income and savings and are not reflected in GDP or in the primary income account. Capital transfers are not reflected in GDP or in the income account, but they lead to changes in the balance of payments of both economies, distorting them as a result of incorrect measurement. With the new version—BPM7, to be released in 2025 (IMF, 2022), these possible errors will be avoided.

Transfer Channels

Remittance flows can reach countries of origin through several channels, considering the availability of financial services, the issuer's preference and the institutional environment. A channel can be considered official in one state and informal in another, given the legislative regulation.

Channels authorized to carry out transactions in the field of money transfer in one country/region/locality to another are considered official, including:

- Banks, which are a key element in the transfer of remittances, as a result of extensive networks in both destination and home countries.

Commercial banks that are present in several states transfer remittances through their own branch network, while banks that are not territorially represented in the remittance recipient country either use transfer services provided by a global operator or use the services of a correspondent bank. In order to transfer through banks, the sender and the recipient have to be customers of those banks and have active accounts in those banks; this condition, however, determines the reduction of customers, even if this is a security measure taken due to the trading of large sums of money.

- Money transfer operators are financial institutions, other than banks, that undertake to transfer money received from customers using their internal transfer system or an international banking network (Western Union, Money Gram, Unistream, Strada Italia, etc.).

Funds received from customers reach the country of origin in the form of money, checks or bills of exchange. Operators usually have networks developed in the country of origin. In order to send or receive the money, one of the two subjects is not required to be the holder of cards or bank accounts, it is not even necessary to present proof of the citizenship of the state from which the transfer takes place. The transfer of cash takes place through the banking system of the country receiving the remittances. Large operators can transfer money anywhere, even by delivering the transfer amount to the destination. Money transfers through specialized operators are often used by new migrants, who remit small amounts of money. At the same time, their popularity is growing in countries where, for one reason or another, the banking system and informal channels are not developed.

- Post offices provide their own transfer services or act as an intermediary for other international transfer companies. Remittances can be transferred by simple letters, postal order or urgent postal services.

There is usually a limit on the amount that can be sent, and the transfer fee is paid by the sender either in cash at the time of transfer, or is settled from his account opened at the post office. Although post offices have a wide geographical distribution, they are not very popular among migrants, due to the limitation of the amount that can be sent, the liquidity challenges in the post offices in the origin countries and the delay in transfers.

- Credit unions facilitate remittance transfers by providing bank bills of exchange or by immediate electronic money transfers.

Transfers take place either through the union's own transfer network or through the International Remittance Network, a programme developed by the World Council of Credit Unions (IMF, 2009).

Under this platform, transfers are processed via an automatic clearing facility, through which remittances are transferred to an intermediary partner bank. After which the bank transfers funds to its branch in the beneficiary country.

- Telephone companies use their mobile networks to provide remittance transfer services.

The transfer mechanism consists of prepaid telecommunications services, which in most cases cannot be resold. Therefore, the maximum value of these transfers can be equal to the amount that the beneficiary would have to pay for the use of the mobile network.

An innovation for this channel has become the possibility of the bank notifying the beneficiary about the time and place from where he can withdraw the remittances to be collected. When the sender sends a sum of money to the bank in the destination country, it notifies the partner bank in the sender's country of origin, and with the message received on the mobile phone, the beneficiary can withdraw the money from a bank or ATM.

Although official channels are developing, especially with the digitization of the population, unofficial channels are still preferred by migrants, namely:

- Hawala is the most developed informal system in the Middle East and South Asia and includes several subjects. A normal transaction involves contacting a hawala operator in the state of destination by the sender of remittances. In order to carry out the money transfer, the operator in the country of destination instructs the hawala operator in the country of origin to pay the amount agreed with the sender to his family, after careful identification and verification of the beneficiaries. Hawala operators can function in travel agencies or even grocery stores (Jost & Sandhu, 2000). Subsequently, transactions are settled between operators in the two states involved in the process, bilaterally or multilaterally, if another operator from a third country has been involved.

- Hundi is considered one of the oldest credit instruments in India. From a technical point of view, hundi is an unconditional written order by which the migrant transfers a sum of money in foreign currency to a local agent, and he hands over to the migrant's family or beneficiaries the equivalent of that amount in local currency at an exchange rate previously agreed with the migrant. This unofficial channel is very popular especially in areas away from big cities.
- Chops is a system similar to hawala, through which the sender contacts a broker in the destination country to make a transfer, mentioning the relevant information about the transaction and the beneficiary. The broker of the destination country transmits that information to the agent of the origin country and at the same time uses a train ticket or a playing card, on which he writes a number, breaks this ticket in half and gives a part of it to the sender, while the other to the agent in the country of origin. When the recipients of the transfer go to collect the amount remitted, they must present to the broker in the country of origin half of the ticket, which was sent to them by the sender.
- Carriers (transport operators) are also involved in the transfer of remittances to the country of origin. Migrants choose transport operators, either for the transfer of declared or undeclared money, or for the low costs involved and speed. Senders leave their contact details and receive a number or password for the package shipped, then these security features are requested by the carrier from the beneficiary in the country of origin. This channel enjoys popularity in many underdeveloped or developing countries (Chisasa, 2014).
- The personal transfer by the migrant or through friends and relatives is a physical way of transferring remittances to the migrant's country of origin, at the time of his return or when he is visiting; the cost of the transfer is found in the transport of that person.

Even if the transfer of remittances using informal channels involves risks, they are preferred by migrants as a result of the related advantages. Although there are not many studies that have addressed the informal remittances, Freund and Spatafora (2005) have analysed informal transfers for more than 100 developing countries, and the results suggest that they amount to 35–75% of total formal remittances. At the same time, the volume of unofficial remittances received varies from one region to another and also takes into account the economic growth of the beneficiary country. Thus, Eastern Europe and Sub-Saharan Africa recorded a higher volume of remittances through informal channels compared to the states of East Asia and the Pacific. The reason why migrants from less developed countries choose to remit through informal channels is found, especially, in the high cost of remittances generated by official, formal channels (Martins, 2022). Additionally, the technologies implemented in the banking sector and transfer agencies are much more advanced compared to developing countries. Banks usually do not have geographical representation in poorer or isolated areas. Another reason would be the low level of education of the people in those areas, which prevents them from opening a bank account, and illegal migrants do not have access to such services. Besides these factors, in some countries there is still an attitude of suspicion and mistrust of banks.

However, informal channels also have a number of risks attached to them, such as the danger of losing/stealing money, money laundering attempts and terrorist financing (Table 2.2). Hence, safe and reliable official, formal remittance transfer channels need to be further developed, albeit at higher costs.

The Cost of Remittances

National authorities have an important role in the market for economic transfers. The main goal of some governments in their countries of origin is to boost the remittance inflows, to redirect them into productive sectors and to protect the participants from coercion, exploitation and theft. To accomplish these goals, a number of legal, incentive and counselling policies and programmes have been developed (Orozco & Yansura, 2015). However, not all government involvements are minimally intrusive or less disruptive.

Although the volume of remittances is increasing, according to World Bank (2022a) the costs are still high with a modest downward trend. Although on average the trend is decreasing, there are still considerable differences in different geographical regions (Table 2.3).

Table 2.2 Advantages and disadvantages of official and unofficial remittance transfer channels

Transfer channels	*Transfer mechanism*	*Advantages*	*Disadvantages*
Officials:			
Banks	Electronic transfer—lack of cash flow	– Speed of transfer – Transfer security, especially for large sums of money	– The need for a banking system with a developed territorial network – The obligation to have cards and accounts in the respective bank, both for the sender and for the beneficiary
Money transfer operators	Electronic transfer—lack of cash flow	– Delivery of remittances even in hard-to-reach regions – Transfer speed – Lack of restrictions on customer identification and of the need to hold cards or bank accounts – Transfer security	– The lack of a platform on remittance transfer and the use of the banking systems in the country of origin generates an increase in cost
Credit unions	Electronic transfer—lack of cash flow	– Transfer speed – Transfer security	– The transfer depends on the banking system of the beneficiary country
Postal offices	Electronic transfer—lack of cash flow	– Transfer security	– Existence of a limit on the amount remitted – Delayed transfers
Telephone companies	Electronic transfer—lack of cash flow	– Transfer security – Transfer speed	– Impossibility to transfer a sum of money, as a result of the limitation of the amount remitted to the value of the beneficiary's invoice for the states where there is no option to withdraw remittances through the message received from the bank in the destination country
Informal:			
Hawala	Transmission of payment instructions—lack of cash flow	– Low costs – Possibility of remission, even in less developed areas – It does not depend on the level of development of the financial sector and the territorial expansion of banks	– Trust-based system

(*continued*)

Table 2.2 (continued)

Transfer channels	*Transfer mechanism*	*Advantages*	*Disadvantages*
Hundi	Transmission of payment instructions—lack of cash flow	– Low costs – Rapidity of the transfer, the beneficiaries receive the amount remitted on the same day as its transfer – Delivery at home – It does not depend on the level of development of the financial sector and the territorial expansion of banks	– Insecurity of the transfer made
Chops	Transmission of payment instructions—lack of cash flow	– Low costs – It does not depend on the level of development of the financial sector and the territorial expansion of banks	– Insecurity of the transfer made
Carriers (transport operators)	Physical transfer—the presence of cash flow	– Low costs – It does not depend on the level of development of the financial sector and the territorial expansion of banks – Transfer speed	– Insecurity of the transfer made
Relatives/ friends/ personal transfer	Physical transfer—the presence of cash flow	– Costs that amount only to transportation expenses	

Regarding the cost borne by Romanian migrants in order to transfer remittances to the country of origin, we note that the latest available data from the World Bank presents Spain as the state with the lowest average cost of remittances arriving in Romania through banking institutions, where for the transfer of \$200 an average interest rate of 4.74% is applied, i.e., \$6.64 paid for \$200 transferred. In addition to Spain, we see a reduction in the average cost in the UK, from about \$15 to \$9 for the transfer

Table 2.3 The cost of remittances borne by Romanian migrants for the transfer of $200 in the first quarter of 2017–2022

The country from which remittances are sent	*Bank fees, $*	*Exchange rate margin, %*	*Average cost, %*	*Total average cost, $*
Italy				
Trim I year 2022	6,93	0,99	4,46	8,92
Trim I year 2021	7.27	1.46	5.09	10.19
Trim I year 2020	7.10	1.10	4.65	9.30
Trim I year 2019	8.47	0.91	5.15	10.30
Trim I year 2018	7.83	0.88	4.80	9.60
Trim I year 2017	8.25	0.64	4.96	9.52
Spain				
Trim I year 2022	3.25	2.42	4.74	6.64
Trim I year 2021	5.73	1.90	4.77	9.54
Trim I year 2020	6.30	0.79	3.94	7.88
Trim I year 2019	6.98	0,39	3,88	7,75
Trim I year 2018	9.10	0.00	4.55	9.10
Trim I year 2017	9.96	0.00	4.98	9.96
Germany				
Trim I year 2022	7.54	1.26	5.03	10.05
Trim I year 2021	5.11	1.18	4.83	6.76
Trim I year 2020	7.18	1.22	4.81	9.63
Trim I year 2019	7.47	0.55	4.28	8.57
Trim I year 2018	7.62	0.74	4.55	9.09
Trim I year 2017	7.85	1.49	5.41	10.83
United Kingdom				
Trim I year 2022	5.11	2.09	4.64	9.28
Trim I year 2021	6.00	2.19	5.19	10.39
Trim I year 2020	7.10	2.91	6.46	12.91
Trim I year 2019	7.86	2.21	6.15	12.29
Trim I year 2018	8.04	2.16	6.18	12.36
Trim I year 2017	9.69	2.88	7.72	15.45

Source: Based on data Remittances Prices Worldwide (World Bank, 2022b)

of $200 to Romania. On the other hand, the average interest rate increased in Germany during the analysed period.

Internationally, the total global cost of transfers is about $30 billion per year (Cecchetti & Schoenholtz, 2018). Directly, the cost of remittances is borne by the migrants and the beneficiary family, but indirectly this cost also falls on the countries of origin. The policies to encourage remittances promoted by many of the countries of origin must be supplemented with measures to reduce remittance costs. One measure could be for the authorities to offer alternative means of financing investments in case transaction costs are high.

In this context, in July 2009, the most advanced economies (G8) pledged to lower remittance costs to 5%—a commitment included in the UN Sustainable Development Goals in 2015 (United Nations, 2015). However, after about ten years, the overall average is about halfway to the proposed goal.

According to Cecchetti and Schoenholtz (2018) there are two main methods to reduce costs: education and competition. World Bank has calculated the "Smart Remitter Target" (SmaRT)—a competitive benchmark calculated as the mean of the three remittance service providers with the lowest costs in each corridor. At the beginning of 2022, the average global SmaRT interest rate was 4.92% (World Bank, 2022a).

Returning to competition, Beck and Peria (2009) stated that countries with a higher number of migrants and more competition have lower costs. In fact, in December 2022, the World Bank (World Bank, 2022a) reported that remittance costs vary considerably depending on the used transfer channel, with money transfer operators costing an average of 5.28%, compared to 2.87% — the cost of electronic transfer via mobile phones.

In addition to the mechanisms described, we believe that state authorities should take the following measures to reduce the cost of remittances:

- Streamlining the infrastructure of the payment system in order to eliminate the inefficiencies of the cash flow.
- Transparency and availability of information on remittance pricing and transfer conditions, which can increase consumer awareness and enable them to make informed decisions. In addition, sound consumer protection, good governance and the implementation of good risk management practices can increase consumer confidence in the system.
- Creating a favourable environment for promoting innovation and market access, while protecting customers and systems from possible financial risks.
- Increasing synergies at national and local level.

Focusing efforts in these areas could reduce remittance prices and increase the amounts that reach migrant workers' families each year by millions of dollars.

Instead of Conclusions

The remittances concept is among the more difficult economic constructions to define and interpret. While the new guidelines developed by the IMF have done much to clarify the concept of remittances, its complexity still needs to be fleshed out.

Technological development and innovations have not yet succeeded in reducing the volume of remittances sent through unofficial channels. Thus, the 5% target set by the developed economies has not yet been reached, the global average cost of remittances being 6.09% (World Bank, 2022b). Only a coordinated and harmonized policy with direct mechanisms of influence on the cost of remittances can have the expected effects.

References

Beck, T., Peria, M. S. M. (2009). *What Explains the Cost of Remittances? An Examination Across 119 Country Corridors*. Policy Research Working Paper Series.

Cecchetti, S., & Schoenholtz, K. (2018). *The Stubbornly High Cost of Remittances*. https://voxeu.org/article/stubbornly-high-cost-remittances.

Chisasa, J. (2014). Nature and Characteristics of Informal Migrant Remittance Transfer Channels: Empirical Study of Remittances from South Africa to Zimbabwe.

Freund, C., & Spatafora, N. (2005). *Remittances: Transaction Costs, Determinants, and Informal Flows. Policy Research Working Paper; No. 3704*. World Bank.

IMF. (2004). *Working Abroad: The Benefits Flowing from Nationals Working in Other Economies*. IMF.

IMF. (2009). *International Transactions in Remittances Guide for Compilers and Users*. IMF.

IMF. (2022). *Update of the Sixth Edition of the Balance of Payments and International Investment Position Manual (BPM6)*. IMF. https://www.imf.org/en/Data/Statistics/BPM.

Jost, P., & Sandhu, S. H. (2000). *The Hawala Alternative Remittance System and its Role in Money Laundering*.

Martins, A. A. (2022). Nigerian Migrants' Remittances: The Unofficial Channel. *European Journal of Business and Management, 13*(23):2021. https://doi.org/10.7176/EJBM/13-23-05. www.iiste.org issn.

Orozco M., & Yansura, J. (2015). *Remittances and Financial Inclusion: Opportunities for Central America*.

United Nations. (2015). *Transforming Our World: The 2030 Agenda for Sustainable Development A/RES/70/1*.

World Bank. (2022a). *Remittances Prices Worldwide Quarterly. An Analysis of Trends in Cost of Remittance Services*. World Bank.

World Bank. (2022b). *Remittance Prices Worldwide*. The World Bank. https://remittanceprices.worldbank.org/.

CHAPTER 3

Migration Theories and the Role of Remittances

Elena Bunduchi and Valentina Vasile

Migration, especially job mobility, creates macroeconomic and household/individual effects, both in the country of origin and in the country of destination.

Over time, however, a number of theories have been developed, approaching the concept of migration from various perspectives, both macro and microeconomic, in order to explain the root causes of migration and the determinants of the remittances.

The Push-Pull Theory

A representative of push-pull theory is Ravenstein Ernst Georg, who used data from England and Wales from 1885 to 1889 in order to draw up "The Migration Laws". Currently, these laws still apply, but with some modifications (Table 3.1).

Ravenstein's laws are the basis of the push-pull theory, which analyses migration from the perspective of a set of factors that determine or prevent the population from migrating, factors that are found both in the country of origin and in the country of destination. The factors that stimulate (push) the population migration are: high incidence of poverty, high unemployment rate, fast population growth rate, reduction of agricultural land area, political instability, lower social status, presence of military

V. Vasile et al., *International Labour Mobility*,
https://doi.org/10.1007/978-3-031-18683-7_3

Table 3.1 The actuality of Ravenstein's migration laws

Migration laws	*Is it still a fact?*			*Comment*
	Yes	*Partial*	*No*	
People migrate mainly short distances from their country of origin, and those who choose to travel longer distances are motivated by large industrial and commercial centres		X		The criteria that are taken into account in choosing a destination state country are not only represented by distance, but also by financial opportunities, by political and environmental stability
Most migrants come from agricultural countries and move to industrialized ones	X			Migrants also come from high-density states
Large cities see an increase in the number of inhabitants due to migration and not an increase in the birth rate	X			The large cities preferred by migrants register reductions in the birth rate, and the migration phenomenon determines the increase in the population
The number of migrants in the country of destination increases with the development of industry, trade and infrastructure	X			The developed states are preferred by migrants
Each migration flow also generates a return migration flow	X			OECD studies (2016) show that 20–50% of migrants return to their country of origin
In the case of short-distance migration, women predominate, whereas men predominate in long-distance migration			X	The profile of the woman migrant has changed, nowadays women represent 48% of the total migrants and long distances are no longer representative only for men
The main factor generating migration is the economic one		X		Political instability and military events are the main causes of migration for some states

Source: Based on Ravenstein's migration laws (Ravenstein, 1885, 1889)

actions, etc. Discouraging factors in the host country are: discriminatory legislation for migrants, lower income compared to natives, language difficulties, religious differences, xenophobia, etc.

However, many consider Ravenstein's laws as empirical generalizations rather than laws. Samers (2015) describes them as more valid for domestic migration than for international migration. Although Ravenstein's laws were fully applicable for the period 1885–1990, today, as a result of the changing economic, political and social conditions of the world, their applicability is partial.

Dual Market Theory

The dual labour market theory was developed during the 1970s and argues that the population's decision to migrate stems from the growing demand for labour coming from modern industrial societies.

The promoter of the dual labour market theory is Piore (1979), who argues that international migration is caused by migrants' permanent demand for labour, which is indispensable to the economic structure of developed countries. According to him, migration is not caused by factors of rejection in the country of origin, but by factors of attraction in the countries of destination. This demand for migrant labour stems from the following characteristics of developed countries:

- Structural inflation, following a raise in wages as a consequence of attracting native workers. In order to avoid inflation, employers prefer migrants, who accept lower wages compared to natives.
- Motivational issues are another characteristic of natives in developed countries. Natives of developed countries view employment not only in terms of wages, but also in terms of gaining and maintaining social status, and unskilled labour is viewed with contempt (Massey et al., 1993), whereas, in the case of migrants, the main motivation is to increase their income, which would lead to improved living conditions, the possibility of purchasing real estate, access to education for their children, and the purchase of consumer goods and products. Although they perform unskilled work, the fact that their wages in the country of destination are higher than the wages in the country of origin for skilled work motivates them to accept those jobs;
- Economic dualism is reflected in the segmentation of the workforce into a highly skilled labour force and a medium-skilled or unskilled labour force, which is found especially in developed countries. Highly qualified natives and migrants have jobs that require highly qualified staff, a high level of wages, the provision of high-performance equipment and machinery, and good working conditions. As a result of the employers' investments in their staff, in their continuous training, the costs incurred in case of possible resignations would be high.
- On the other hand, jobs that require medium-skilled or unskilled personnel have the following characteristics: instability, a limited career path and low wages. In crisis situations, medium-skilled or

unskilled employees are most likely to be fired. Thus, it is very difficult for employers to attract native workers for these jobs, as the latter prefer high wages, job security and the possibility of advancement. For this reason, employers are forced to employ migrants to fill vacancies, thus increasing the demand for migrants.
- The demographic changes of the labour supply appeared, according to this theory, with the increase of the role of the woman both in the family and in the society. By the early 1970s, the demand for medium-skilled or unskilled labour was supplemented by teenagers and women (Massey et al., 1993).

According to the dual market theory, teenagers are constantly changing jobs, and their goal is to earn extra income and gain experience, while being aware that they will have better jobs in the future, immediately after finishing their studies and gaining work experience. From the perspective of teenagers, their job does not determine their social status, being only a source of income.

Piore (1979) underlines that socio-demographic changes in the 1970s, such as declining birth rates and educational expansion (Meyer & Rowan, 1977), have resulted the growing importance of women in society. Their jobs are seen not only as a source of income, but as a possibility to obtain a social status. Likewise, the increase in the divorce rate results in the transformation of the women's income from extra to main income, in order to support them and their children.

The imbalance between the demand and the limited labour supply of the natives leads to the increase of the demand for the labour force of the migrants, thus contributing to the amplification of the migration phenomenon. Increasing demand for migrants is a factor in attracting migrants to the destination country and even if, in the post-war period, this theory was the basis for explaining migration trends to Europe and the United States, we consider that explaining the migration process only in terms of increasing demand for migrants cannot be considered sufficient, and a deeper analysis of migrants' decision-making is needed.

Rational Choice Theory

The most important features of rational choice theory are the perspectives of the subjects of the migration process and the link between the micro- and macroeconomic levels (Opp, 1999). The perspectives of the subjects explain the behaviour of the individuals, and the micro-macro modelling shows us that the sum of the decisions taken by the individuals results in a change at the macroeconomic level.

From the perspective of the rational choice theory, individuals are seen as subjects that can choose from several options, and the constraints in the country of origin and the possible opportunities in the country of destination impose restrictions on their decision. At the heart of the decision-making process is the cost-benefit approach.

Thus, migration is seen as a rational decision, which aims to maximize the benefits of individuals. de Jong and Fawcett (1981) believe that the individual's decision to migrate depends on his choosing the one alternative that offers maximum utility out of a multitude of alternatives. De Jong's model defines the individual's intention to migrate as a result of summing up the value expectancy in areas such as health, status, comfort, independence and morality. However, certain characteristics can influence in one way or another the value of the expected utilities, such as: the specific characteristics of the individual or of the household resulting from demographic or socio-economic variables; social and cultural standards; risk tolerance.

In order to assess the utility of the destination country, Brown and Moore (1970) introduced the concept of the place utility. It is very important for an individual that the reference goods which are essential for him be traded in the country of destination, so that the migration may not deprive him of those goods or services with which he is accustomed.

Thus, according to the theory, following the analysis and comparison of the benefits offered by the country of origin and the country of destination, the individual will rationally choose the most attractive option from all points of view.

Rational choice theory includes different dimensions of utilities and takes into account different costs and benefits. Unfortunately, in the rational choice theory, the share of the utility of the factors taken into account by the migrant and the link between monetary and non-monetary factors remain unspecified. It is difficult to generalize the factors that have the greatest weight in the decision to migrate, due to the fact that each individual perceives utility differently. The decision to maximize benefits depends on the accuracy of the information available to the individual and their quantity, and it is possible that some people may not have the ability to analyse the cost-benefit elements. Another shortcoming is that the theory does not show the factors that determine the decision to migrate, and does not explain the share of deterrents in the destination country.

World-Systems Theory

World-systems theory appeared was developed in 1974 with the publication of the first volume of I. Wallerstein's tetralogy. Wallerstein introduces the notion of the world-system and considers that world states fall into three broad categories: the core countries, which include the most economically developed states, called the dominant powers; semi-periphery countries, which include less developed states; and periphery states, with underdeveloped states which are considered areas outside the world system, or the so-called poor nations (Wallerstein, 1974). The most important concepts of world-system theory are:

- The role of a state in the world-system, which refers to the nature of a state's relations with the rest of the world and the international division of labour.
- The degree of dependence of a state, which refers to how much a country is affected by possible fluctuations that take place within the system.
- The degree of development, which shows the position of a state within the system from the perspective of the level of economic development.

Sassen (1988) adapts the theory of the world system to explain the migration process, noting that migration is a side effect of the capitalist system. According to the theory, the dominant powers in the core of the world-system exploit the poor nations. In the wake of rising wealth, owners and managers of profitable multinational companies tend to expand into underdeveloped countries in search of land, raw materials, cheap labour and new markets (Wallerstein, 1974). The result of the expansion of the dominant powers in the states on the periphery of the world-system is found in the increase in the number of people who choose to migrate to economically developed countries. The factors that generate migration can be found in the following aspects:

- Modernization of agriculture, which reduces the need for labour in the respective economic sector and creates a surplus of labour in rural areas.
- The extraction of raw materials requires cheap local labour, mainly made up of former farmers, which are removed from their traditional environment.

- International corporations tend to offer low wages to employees in underdeveloped countries, offering them short-term jobs.

The forced development of transport and telecommunications in underdeveloped countries, without which corporations would not be able to carry out their investments, along with access to media sources that reflect the values and lifestyle of the developed countries of the world system, amplify the desires of the population to migrate to the core countries.

At the same time, in the case of the former colonies, another important factor that boosted the migration was observed, namely, the familiarization of migrants with the language, culture and customs of the state that invested in their country of origin.

The big cities in the core states of the world-system are a favourite destination for third-world migrants, due to the high demand for labour at the extremes of the occupational hierarchy.

The world-systems theory treats migration as a mechanism for balancing labour supply and demand globally, not at the level of the national economy. According to the world-systems theory, the phenomenon of migration has grown as a result of the development of the global market and global political and economic organizations, a concept developed by Massey (1999):

1. International migration is a natural consequence of the emergence and development of the capitalist market in underdeveloped countries, so that the reach of global economies into third-world countries has been a catalyst for the emergence of migration.
2. The migration of the population takes place especially from the former colonies to the former colonial powers, as a result of the cultural, linguistic, administrative, investment, infrastructure and communication links that were established during the colonial empires.
3. Since international migration is due to the globalization of the market economy, the only solutions for home governments to influence migration would be to regulate the foreign investments of large international corporations and to control financial and trade flows. However, these measures are very difficult to implement and their imposition could lead to international trade disputes, the likelihood of economic crises, and due to the fact that multinational companies have financial resources and international political support, they can block any such measures undertaken by poor states.

4. The political and military interventions of the governments of capitalist states made in order to protect their investments abroad and the interventions of the governments that militate for the concept of global market can generate the appearance of serious military conflicts, thus causing another form of migration, namely refugees.
5. Population migration does not have a direct influence on the level of wages or on the differences in working conditions between states, all of which result from the dynamics and structure of the global economy.

The factors that determine migration from the perspective of world-system theory are undoubtedly of major importance in explaining the increase in the number of migrants, but they rather present the reality and do not provide an explanation for the occurrence of the migration phenomenon. At the same time, the theory does not analyse the migrants once they arrive in the country of destination, nor the reason why some choose to return to the country of origin, where the determinants of migration have remained unchanged. In addition, the theory does not explain why a large part of the rural population in underdeveloped countries chooses internal migration. Nor does it take into account the migration that takes place between economically highly developed countries, relying only on migration flows from poorly developed to developed countries.

The Theory of Neoclassical Economics

The theory of neoclassical economics was developed between 1930 and 1970, in order to explain the internal movements of the population as a result of the process of economic development (Hicks, 1932). Although the theory initially explained the specifics and causes of internal displacement, it has become one of the most popular theories of international migration. The neoclassical theory of migration places in the foreground the role of economic factors in explaining the emergence of migration flows and of the decision to migrate. The authors of this theory (Hicks, 1932; Harris & Todaro, 1970; Stark & Taylor, 1989) investigate both domestic and international migration from a macro- and microeconomic point of view.

Harris and Todaro (1970) are the promoters of the theory of neoclassical economics from a macroeconomic perspective, according to which international migration is caused by geographical differences in labour supply and demand, differences that are reflected in the size-wage, as follows: in underdeveloped countries, where labour supply exceeds demand, wage levels are lower compared to developed countries, where labour demand is higher than the supply. These wage differences cause people to migrate to countries where the wage level is higher than in the country of origin. As a result of the migration of the population to developed countries, a balance of the labour market emerges: in underdeveloped countries, there is an increase of wages due to the reduction of labour supply, and in the destination states the phenomenon is reversed. Thus, the theory of neoclassical economics presents migration as an indispensable part of the process of economic development.

In the early 1960s, population migration began to be analysed through the theory of neoclassical economics at a microeconomic level. Sjaastad (1962) examines the individual who makes the decision to migrate, analysing and comparing the costs and benefits of migration. In assessing the benefits of migration, the potential migrant first considers the possibility of finding a job in the region where he or she intends to migrate, in addition to the wage differences and the expenses required to travel.

The neoclassical theory focuses only on economic factors, arguing that the population migrates only because of the level of employment and the wage gap between the country of origin and the country of destination. However, economic factors are not the only motivation for migration, as the current social and political situation, which generates the amplification of the migration phenomenon, is very different compared to the period 1930–1970. This theory was developed during the industrial period of the migration of the European population to the United States of America and Australia, its applicability being reduced almost entirely at present.

Neo-Marxist Theory

The neo-Marxist theory has its origins in the 1970s–1980s and comes as an answer to the approach to migration from the perspective of the theory of neoclassical economics.

The main idea of the neo-Marxist theory is the inequality of the distribution of economic and political power between developed and underdeveloped states, and the fact that the population does not have equal access to resources, while the rise of capitalist power deepens these inequalities (de Haas, 2010). Thus, developed states or regions exploit less developed states or regions. The inequalities between the two sides are the driving force behind migration, because poorly developed countries will not be able to keep up with the level of economic development of developed countries, thus becoming cheap labour providers for developed countries.

Due to the fact that poorly developed countries are providers of cheap, highly skilled labour, they will not see an increase in the level of development following brain drain, always remaining the states that supply the labour market in developed countries. In this way, migrants meet the needs of developed countries, neglecting the needs of their country of origin. Even the fact that the country of origin is the beneficiary of remittances from developed countries does not contribute to national economic growth, as those capital inflows are not directed to the productive sector, but mainly to consumption, especially the consumption of imported products. Productivity in underdeveloped countries cannot register positive results due to the fact that highly qualified individuals, who should be the promoters of economic growth, migrate, while people with a low level of education stay in the country (Moyo et al., 2012). Thus, according to neo-Marxist theory, migration has only negative consequences for the country of origin, due to the fact that it is exploited both in terms of labour and resources. At the same time, the theory of dependence initiated by Frank (1966), which is one of the main Marxist economic theories, argues that migration hinders economic development. Thus, migration is not only a consequence of the inequalities of economic development, but it is also a factor that contributes to their accentuation.

We cannot agree with the fact that the current migration phenomenon can be explained by neo-Marxist theory. Although migration has negative effects on the countries of destination and origin if it is not managed effectively, its importance and positive effects have been recognized by experts in the field. Among the positive effects generated by migration in the country of origin, we can list reduction of the unemployment rate, increase of consumption and exports, combat of poverty through remittances received. The applicability of this theory is currently limited, with increasing emphasis on the positive impact that migration can have on the country of origin and destination.

Migration Network Theory

The concept of migratory network is known to the literature starting with the research done by Thomas and Znaniecki (1918, 1920).[1] In the 1980s, in order to explain and bring under debate the effects of rural-urban migration, the migratory networks theory was outlined. Migration networks are interpersonal links between current migrants, people who have been involved in the migration process in the past and people who are not connected to this phenomenon, links that are reflected in kinship, friendship and territorial affiliation.

The migration networks theory accepts the idea that migration is an individual or family decision-based process, but over time people who decide to migrate are influenced by the number of close people who have already migrated. From the perspective of network theory, the phenomenon of migration has the following characteristics (Massey, 1990):

- Once begun, the migration process extends over time, until the migration networks are so widespread in the country of destination that people in the country of origin do not encounter difficulties at the time of migration; then the flow of migrants decreases.
- The size of the flow of migrants between countries of origin and destination is not strictly related to the wage gap or employment opportunities between the two states, due to the fact that the effects of these variables are overshadowed by reduced costs and risks resulting from the extension of migratory networks over time.
- Due to the fact that international migration is expanding as a result of the formation and development of migration networks, it becomes, over time, independent of the initial cause factors.
- As migration networks expand and migration costs and risks decrease, migrants become less selective about their country of destination.

[1] Thomas, W.I., Znaniecki, F., *1918–1920. The Polish Peasant in Europe and America*—is considered one of the best sociology books on migration, having been published in 5 volumes between 1918 and 1920.

- The authorities of the countries of destination have difficulty in trying to control the number of people crossing their borders, due to the fact that the process of forming migration networks cannot be controlled and occurs regardless of the political regime implemented.

Although the theory of migratory networks took shape in the first quarter of the last century, interest in this theory has intensified especially in the last quarter of the century, due to awareness of changes in the phenomenon worldwide, such as: the importance of family reunification, the extent of clandestine entry methods, the impossibility of stopping the flow of migration by political factors. Even though this theory is still applicable today, we have found that it has proved difficult to demonstrate empirically that migrant information and assistance networks are the most important factors driving migration.

The Institutional Theory

The approach of migration from the perspective of institutional theory, which emerged in the decade 1980–1990, focuses on the analysis of institutions that arise as a result of the migration phenomenon, private institutions and voluntary organizations designed to meet the demand created by the imbalance between the number of people willing to migrate to a host country and the number of visas issued by the authorities of those states. This imbalance has led to the creation of a market for these institutions, which promote migration for profit, through legal or illegal actions.

Private institutions offer potential migrants services to facilitate access to the labour market by concluding contracts between employers and migrants, arranging fake marriages between migrants and natives, and even providing credit assistance.

On the other hand, voluntary organizations help migrants by providing social services, counselling, legal advice on the means of legalizing migrants' residence, shelter and even material assistance.

Recognition of the growing importance of private institutions and voluntary organizations aimed at facilitating access to the destination country, whether illegal or legal, leads to the emergence of migration hypotheses, different from those provided by micro-level theories:

- Due to the fact that institutions that provide support, advice, as well as those that promote international migration, are developing, migration becomes much more institutionalized and independent of the initial drivers.
- Governments of destination states have difficulty trying to control the size of the flow of migrants.

Given the fact that private institutions make very high profits from the services provided to migrants, the measures taken by governments against migrants will lead to the creation of a black market, which will in turn lead to an increase in illegal migration. At the same time, harsh measures against migrants are met with hostility by humanitarian organizations.

The theory is still significant and relevant today, when more and more people turn to institutions that provide support to migrants as a result of recent political and military events. The development of the institutional side in states with a well-defined migration network gives independence to the migration process in relation to the environment in which it takes place.

Cumulative Causation

Cumulative causation is not necessarily a theory of migration, but rather a perspective on it. The promoter behind this perspective on migration is Myrdal (1957). Causation is cumulative in that each act of migration alters the social context in which future (subsequent) decisions are made in a typical way, making additional displacements more likely (Massey et al., 1993).

Taylor (1992) highlighted six socio-economic factors that are influenced by migration from the perspective of cumulative causation:

- *Uneven income distribution* in underdeveloped countries is rare (Stark & Taylor, 1991), but when members of some households migrate to a developed destination country and remittances received lead to an increase in the standard of living of the household in the origin country, income inequality occurs. The increased living standard of some households, as a result of remittances, leads to the appearance of the desire to migrate among other households, which in the future will generate an income gap in the country of origin, which, in turn, will also drive the migration process.

- *Ownership of land* among migrants from rural areas is an important goal (Rhoades, 1978). However, for migrants in urban areas, land is more of a source of income in retirement, not a productive investment.
- *The organization of the agricultural production* refers to the way the agricultural land is processed. Thus, migration generates the technologicalization of agriculture, which means that the need for agricultural labour is reduced, and being replaced by machinery. So, the larger the migration phenomenon, the more technological agriculture is, which in turn generates the increase of migration as a result of the increase of unemployment, due to the substitution between labour and capital;
- *The culture of the migrant population* changes, and as the phenomenon of migration spreads in a region, it leads to changes in culture and values that facilitate the likelihood of future migration (Massey et al., 1993). After a period of time, there is a change in the perception of things, preferences and values among migrants (Piore, 1979). At the same time, Massey (1986) pointed out that once a person has migrated and returned to their country of origin, there is a very high chance that they will migrate again, and the chances increase with the number of departures already made.
- *Regional distribution of human capital* results from the selectivity of the migration process; initially highly qualified people with higher education migrated, motivated by the desire for higher wages; since the formation and development of migration networks, which led to reduced costs and risks, migration became less selective.
- *The social status* of the natives is affected by the flows of international migrants. When certain jobs in the destination country are mainly occupied by migrants, they receive the label of migrant jobs (Piore, 1979). The natives believe that accepting a job for migrants would have a negative impact on their social status, thus increasing the demand for foreign labour.

Analysed from the perspective of cumulative causation, migration has some common points with the theory of migratory networks, namely:

1. The social, economic and cultural changes that are generated by migration, both in the country of origin and in the country of destination, offer migrants resistance to the regulations of the authorities, since the mechanism of cumulative causation is not available to governments.
2. It is difficult for state authorities to reduce labour mobility by recruiting natives for those jobs that were held by migrants as a result of social labels.

Although the theory of cumulative causation is a complex one, different from explanatory models that focus on a single factor, we find that it has some limitations. First of all, the theory does not have a theoretical analysis of the impact of migration on developed countries, which today have the role of country of origin, focusing only on underdeveloped countries, in which agriculture predominates. In addition, the verification of the theory is difficult to perform due to the need for longitudinal data, which are not always available to users.

The increase in the number of international migrants and the difficulty of controlling those flows have led to the development of migration theories, which play the role of explaining and analysing the process of international migration. The theories developed so far mainly analyse the impact of migration on developed countries, or work only from the perspective of the country of origin or destination (Table 3.2).

Analysing the migration theories, we may conclude that, so far, there hasn't been any theory that can fully explain the specifics of the migration phenomenon, but depending on the characteristics of migration in a particular country, and the theory that is considered to be at the basis of the decision to migrate, the authorities of those states may take decisions and implement measures aimed at reducing or increasing the migratory flow.

Table 3.2 Synthesis of migration theories and the role of remittances

Migration theories	*Authors*	*Period*	*Characteristics*	*The role of remittances in migration theories*
Push-Pull theory	Ravenstein	1885–1990	The main ideas of Ravenstein's migration laws: – Short migration – Migrants come from agricultural regions and move to industrial ones – Women migrate over short distances and men over long distances – The main factor generating migration is the economic one	Remittances play an important role in the beneficiary households, covering current consumption expenditures, in the situation where there are large gaps between the level of development of agricultural and industrial regions. Thus, the wages obtained by migrants in developed areas are a source of income for households in poor agricultural areas Rudimentary money transfer systems were used, and later official transfer channels were developed
Dual market theory	Piore	1970s	Migration is caused by: – Structural inflation – Motivation issues – Economic dualism – Demographic changes in the labour supply	The theory explains the migration process from the perspective of the specificity of the destination country and does not refer to the situation in the country of origin. However, if migrants from the host country are willing to accept jobs disregarded by the natives, it is clear that, in theory, they come from poor countries, and the money sent home is needed for the family's current expenses and possibly endowment with durable goods, and less towards entrepreneurial activities
Rational choice theory	Brown and Moore; de Jong; Opp	1970s	Migration is a rational decision that aims to maximize the benefits for individuals. The individual's intention to migrate is seen as a result of summing up the expected utilities in areas such as health, status, comfort, independence and morality	Individuals tend to migrate without necessarily having remittances as their main motivation. The theory analyses the destination country from the perspective of the migrant's personal utility, which is not only economic. Therefore, the idea of short-term migration that has remittances as a goal is not specific to this theory. Migrants analyse the state of destination, according to the theory, from the perspective of long-term establishment or permanent migration

World-systems theory	Wallerstein; Sassen; Massey	1974–End of the 1990s	According to the theory, the dominant powers in the centre of the world system exploit the poor nations – International migration is a natural consequence of the emergence and formation of the capitalist market in underdeveloped countries – The migration of the population takes place towards the former colonial powers, from the former colonies – International migration is due to the globalization of the market economy, and the solution of home state governments through which they could influence migration would be to regulate FDI and control financial and trade flows	The theory analyses the phenomenon only from the perspective of migration from poor to rich states, in order to increase the standard of living of households in the country of origin, which, exploited by the great powers, are becoming poorer. Thus, the money sent home is intended for the consumption of current or durable goods and services, making it impossible to set up new businesses as a result of monopolization and control of the market by transnational companies
The theory of neoclassical economics	Stark and Taylor; Harris and Todaro	1930–1970	Migration is determined by economic factors, in particular the wage differential between the country of origin and the country of destination	Due to the fact that neoclassical theory considers economic factors as determinants of migration, remittances are an important element. According to the theory, following the migration of the population and following remittances, wages in the country of origin increase, balancing the labour market, so remittances are no longer intended to cover current expenses, but can be directed to the acquisition of property or the establishment of new businesses

(*continued*)

Table 3.2 (continued)

Migration theories	*Authors*	*Period*	*Characteristics*	*The role of remittances in migration theories*
Neo-Marxist theory	Richmond 1994	Starting with 1970–1990	Migration has only negative consequences for the country of origin due to the fact that the country is being exploited, both in terms of its workforce and its resources	Remittances received by beneficiary families are aimed at covering current consumption expenditure, due to the very low standard of living
Migration network theory	Thomas, Znaniecki, and Zaretsky; Massey	Starting with 1918	Migration networks increase the likelihood of migration due to low costs and risks for migrants and high estimated incomes. The salary differential is not a significant selection criterion for the destination country	This theory analyses the phenomenon of migration from the perspective of networks that could help the migrant, especially due to the importance of family reunification. This means that the theory does not see migration as short-lived, with remittance as objective for raising living standards, but considers the decision to migrate as a definitive departure for the purpose of reuniting the family in the destination country. Thus, the motivation for remission decreases as the decision to migrate family members is made
The institutional theory	Massey	1980–1990	The theory focuses on the analysis of the institutions that appear as a result of the migration phenomenon, private institutions and voluntary organizations meant to satisfy the demand created by the imbalance between the number of people willing to migrate to a host country and the number of visas granted by the authorities	According to the theory, migrants tend to choose a destination state taking into account the institutions that can help them once they arrive. From a theoretical point of view, remittances are not considered the main purpose of migration, especially due to the importance of institutions in arranging false marriages between natives and migrants, which helps the latter to establish their residence in the destination country, thus no longer being motivated to remit at home

Cumulative causation	Myrdal; Taylor	Starting with 1957	According to the theory, the determinants of migration are: – Unequal distribution of income (increasing the standard of living of the household receiving remittances entails the migration process in the other households) – Ownership of land and property among migrants, as a source of income after retirement – Regional distribution of human capital (initially highly qualified people migrate, then migration becomes less selective)	According to the theory of causation, highly qualified people tend to migrate initially from the poorly developed country of origin, and they may become focused on professional and career development. The motivation to remit decreases with the achievement of goals and the low probability of return. When migration becomes less selective, low-skilled migrants do not behave in the same way, their migration is for a short term; they aim to obtain higher incomes for remittance

References

Brown, L. A., & Moore, E. G. (1970). The Intra-Urban Migration Process: A Perspective. *Geografiska Annaler Series B, Human Geography, 52*(1), 1. https://doi.org/10.2307/490436

de Haas, H. (2010). Migration and Development: A Theoretical Perspective. *International Migration Review, 44*(1), 227–264. https://doi.org/10.1111/J.1747-7379.2009.00804.X

de Jong, G. F., & Fawcett, J. T. (1981). Motivations for Migration: An Assessment and a Value-Expectancy Research Model. In G. F. de Jong & R. W. Gardner (Eds.), *Migration Decision Making:Multidisciplinary Approaches to Microlevel Studies in Developed and Developing Countries* (pp. 13–58). Pergamon Press.

Frank, A. (1966). *The Development of Underdevelopment.* New England Free Press.

Harris, J. R., & Todaro, M. P. (1970). Migration, Unemployment and Development: A Two-Sector Analysis. *The American Economic Review, 60*, 126–142.

Hicks, J. R. (1932). *The Theory of Wages.* Macmillan.

Massey, D. S. (1986). The social organization of Mexican migration to the United States. *The Annals of the American Academy of Political and Social Science, 487*(1), 102–113.

Massey, D. S. (1990). Social Structure, Household Strategies, and the Cumulative Causation of Migration. *Population Index, 56*(1), 3. https://doi.org/10.2307/3644186

Massey, D. S. (1999). International Migration at the dawn of the Twenty-First Century: The Role of the State. *Population and Development Review, 25*(2), 303–322.

Massey, D. S., Arango, J., Hugo, G., Kouaouci, A., Pellegrino, A., & Taylor, J. E. (1993). Theories of International Migration: A Review and Appraisal. *Population and Development Review, 19*(3), 431. https://doi.org/10.2307/2938462

Meyer, J. W., & Rowan, B. (1977). Institutionalized Organizations: Formal Structure as Myth and Ceremony. *American Journal of Sociology, 83*(2), 340–363.

Moyo, I., Nicolau, M. D., & Fairhurst, J. (2012). Migration Theories and Zimbabwean Migrant Teachers as Reflected in a South African Case Study. *Scientific Annals of "Alexandru Ioan Cuza" University of Iași, 58*(2), 123–146.

Myrdal, G. (1957). *Rich Lands and Poor: The Road to World Prosperity* (16th ed.). Harper & Row.

Opp, K.-D. (1999). Contending Conceptions of the Theory of Rational Action. *Journal of Theoretical Politics, 11*(2), 171–202. https://doi.org/10.1177/0951692899011002002

Piore, M. J. (1979). *Birds of Passage: Migrant Labor and Industrial Societies.* Cambridge University Press.

Ravenstein, E. G. (1885). The Laws of Migration. *Journal of the Statistical Society of London, 48*(2), 167. https://doi.org/10.2307/2979181

Ravenstein, E. G. (1889). The Laws of Migration. *Journal of the Royal Statistical Society, 52*(2), 241. https://doi.org/10.2307/2979333

Rhoades, R. E. (1978). Foreign Labor and German Industrial Capitalism 1871–1978: The Evolution of a Migratory System. *American Ethnologist, 5*(3), 553–573. https://doi.org/10.1525/AE.1978.5.3.02A00080

Samers, M. (2015). Migration Policies, Migration and Regional Integration in North America. In S. McMahon (Ed.), *Talani LS* (pp. 373–398). Edward Elgar Publishing Ltd..

Sassen, S. (1988). *The Mobility of Labor and Capital: A Study in International Investment and Labor Flow*. Cambridge University Press.

Sjaastad, L. A. (1962). The Costs and Returns of Human Migration. *Journal of Political Economy, 70*(5), 80–93.

Stark, O., & Taylor, J. E. (1989). Relative Deprivation and International Migration. *Demography, 26*(1), 1–14. https://doi.org/10.2307/2061490

Stark, O., & Taylor, J. E. (1991). Migration Incentives, Migration Types: The Role of Relative Deprivation. *The Economic Journal, 101*(408), 1163. https://doi.org/10.2307/2234433

Taylor, J. E. (1992). Remittances and Inequality Reconsidered: Direct, Indirect, and Intertemporal Effects. *Journal of Policy Modeling, 14*(2), 187–208. https://doi.org/10.1016/0161-8938(92)90008-Z

Thomas, W. I., & Znaniecki, F. (1918). *The Polish Peasant in Europe and America*. The Gorham Press.

Thomas, W. I., & Znaniecki, F. (1920). *The Polish Peasant in Europe and America*. The Gorham Press.

Wallerstein, I. (1974). The Rise and Future Demise of the World Capitalist System: Concepts for Comparative Analysis. *Comparative Studies in Society and History, 16*(4), 387–415. https://doi.org/10.1017/S0010417500007520

CHAPTER 4

Historical Evolution and Trends of the Migration Phenomenon and Remittances

Valentina Vasile and Elena Bunduchi

The Historical Evolution of Global Migration

The first evidence of massive human movement dates back over 200,000 years ago, when people began to migrate, initially from Africa to Southern Europe and then Northern Europe (Manning & Trimmer, 2013). Migratory movements across the European continent from South to North lasted until around 80,000 BC, some settling permanently, others only temporarily. Groups of people migrated across Europe due to their growing numbers and insufficient food. As a result of the glaciation that affected Europe between 70,000 and 20,000 BC (USGS, 2019), the migrant population changed direction from North to South again, due to extremely low temperatures.

With the end of the ice age, groups of people began to migrate again to North. At the same time, between 35,000 and 8000 BC, new migratory flows moved from East to West (Manning & Trimmer, 2013). There are no data on the specific causes of migration, or whether groups of migrants had a leader, but it is considered that the determinants of migration were climate change and food availability.

Around 8000–1000 BC the lifestyle of Europe's population had gradually begun to change, moving from hunting to cultivating the land and harvesting. The lack of fertile soil in the Middle East led to the migration

V. Vasile et al., *International Labour Mobility*,
https://doi.org/10.1007/978-3-031-18683-7_4

of farmers to the South-Eastern region of Europe, specifically to the Balkans and the Mediterranean (Mazzucco et al., 2020).

The years 800–400 BC are characterized by the largest migration flows that have taken place so far. The tribes of the Asian steppes migrated to Europe (McNeill, 1999), being one of the most significant migrant tribes for a long time; the Germans moved from the shores of the Baltic Sea to the South (Murphy et al., 2002), as a result of climate change, which in turn caused the Celts to migrate to Europe (Mikhailova, 2020). The Scythian tribes from northern Europe (Russian territory in the present days) moved to Greece, which led to the formation of the Thracian people.

At the same time, the development of the economy of Greek cities between 200 and 400 AD contributed to the increase in the number of migrants, due to the fact that the newly conquered territory required intermediate stations on trade routes, which had to be founded and populated by Greek citizens (Knight, 2019). Also, the population in the conquered areas was turned into slaves and brought to Greek cities. Another category of migrants consisted of political exiles, which usually led to the migration of a group of people outside Greece and their founding colonies. Migratory flows similar to those in Greek cities took place during the expansion of the Roman Empire, when soldiers and officials moved to the conquered areas to provide defence and administration services. Slaves were brought into the territory of the Empire, while Christians left as a result of religious persecution (Roselaar, 2016). Following all these migratory flows during that period, the first trade relations between Northern Europe and the Mediterranean countries emerged.

Between 300 and 1000 AD, three great waves of migration took place. The first wave (300–500 AD) was composed of tribes of Huns, Goths, Germans and Avars migrating to Europe (Drake, 2017), the second wave (500–700 AD) set in motion tribes of Slavs and Arabs (Kobyliński, 2005) and the third wave (700–900 AD) consisted of Norwegians and Hungarians (Moravcsik, 1946; Heen-Pettersen, 2019). The lack of information about that period makes it difficult to establish with certainty what reasons the tribes might had had to migrate; however, certain causes have been established. Some tribes were attracted by the wealth of the Western Roman Empire, such as the Huns and Germans, and their invasion eventually led to the fall of the Empire (Drake, 2017). The Northern tribes migrated South as a result of climate change, while Hungarians and Norwegians were attracted by the available land. In addition to these external factors, internal migration factors included population growth, changing living conditions and the development of social structures. As a result of the settlement of Germanic tribes in Europe, preliminary forms of state formation emerged.

Although in the medieval period there were no significant waves of migrants, they still had an important influence on the societies of that time, leading to the development of new states. The migration of the Vikings and their settlement in Normandy, Northern England, Scotland and Ireland led to the emergence of developed urban centres (Heen-Pettersen, 2019). Iberia was invaded by the Arabs (Fancy & García Sanjuán, 2021), who founded new kingdoms, such as Andalus, and brought with them a wave of North African colonists.

During the crusades of the eleventh and thirteenth centuries, European Christian armies conquered Palestine, founding four Christian kingdoms and settling there with their families (Bethencourt, 2015). Due to the relatively small number of those who settled permanently in that region, the Crusaders eventually lost their dominance.

In the fourteenth century, the Germanic peoples settled in the Baltic region turned into the dominant elite (Aguilera-Barchet, 2015). At the end of the Middle Ages, the Roma migrated to Europe (Iberia and the Balkans) from the Middle East, coming from the Indus River region (Mendizabal et al., 2011).

European internal migration intensified in the early modern era. During this period, major migration to Europe included the recruitment of landless workers by monarchs to populate demographically disadvantaged regions. A similar approach of labour recruitment is found between 1560 and 1690, the English Protestant settlers being moved to Ireland (Canny, 1985), and in the seventeenth century, Catherine the Great, Empress of Russia, recruited Germans to populate the Volga region (Pleve et al., 2001). Another form of migration was forced relocation due to religious persecution. Notable examples of forced migrations caused by religious oppression include the mass migration of Protestants from the Spanish Netherlands to the Dutch Republic after the 1580s (Dunthorne, 2016), the expulsion of Jews from Spain in the 1590s (Pérez, 2005) and the expulsion of the Huguenots from France in the 1680s (McCloy, 1951).

With the industrialization of the world's economies, the pace of migration increased. Manning and Trimmer (2013) distinguished three types of migration at that time: labour migration, refugee migration and internal migration to urban areas. Millions of farmers left the rural area and migrated to cities, generating an unprecedented phenomenon of urbanization, which began in Britain in the late eighteenth century. Industrialization encouraged migration, and improved infrastructure and means of transportation made migration even easier. In Europe, with the onset of World War I, labour migration and urbanization were replaced by refugee migration. In August 1914, the Russian invasion of East Prussia triggered the migration of about one million Germans (Gatrell, 2014). Austria's invasion of Serbia led to the migration of soldiers and civilians (Gatrell, 2014), who wanted to break away from the occupation regime. And in the Russian Empire, national minorities, such as Lithuanians, Latvians, Poles, Ukrainians, and Jews, were concentrated in the Western border areas. However, these minorities were deported to the centre of Russia, being wrongly accused of helping the enemy. Meanwhile, in the Ottoman Empire, Turkish troops forced the Armenian people to migrate from the occupied territory (Şeker & Nesim, Şeker & Nesim, 2013). Therefore, the major causes of the refugee crisis in Europe were the invasion and occupation by the enemy and the forced displacement of people, in other words organized deportation.

In the United States, World War I was the cause of the acceleration of the mass migration of agricultural workers from South to North and West, in search of higher wages and better living conditions. The increase in the number of African Americans led to the rapid growth of urban communities in cities such as New York, Chicago and Los Angeles. According to estimates (Gregory, 2005), about 500,000 African Americans migrated to Northern cities between 1915 and 1920, while between 1920 and 1930 nearly 1 million people migrated.

Between 1917 and 1922, more than 1.5 million Russians, Ukrainians and Belarusians left Russia's borders as a result of the Soviet regime (Kulischer, 1948). By the start of World War II, about 60 million people had migrated from Europe to America, and another 2.5 million from Asia to America; out of these, 65% went to the United States (Harris & Wulker, 1953) and the rest migrated to Argentina, Brazil, Cuba and Canada. Over six million people in Europe were migrants during the interwar period. Ethnic Greeks were displaced from western Turkey to Greece, and Turks and other Muslim peoples were forced to leave Romania, Yugoslavia and Czechoslovakia (Kulischer, 1948). During the same period, a similar number of people migrated long distances to Asia. More than 50 million migrants, mainly from India and South China, arrived in South Asia. North Asia-Manchuria, Siberia, Central Asia and Japan combined received another 50 million migrants (Gatrell, 2014). Data on the exact number of migrations from and to Africa at that time are not known with certainty.

World War II was also marked by an increase in the number of migrants, although signs of migration existed before the actual start of the war, as actions of Nazi aggression determined the German population and its neighbours, and in particular Jews, to seek safety in other states. Thus, during the war more than 5.2 million Jews and about 400,000 Roma migrated from countries such as Germany, Austria and Poland, as a result of the measures taken by the German leader at that time (Rosenhaft, 2021). Over the course of the war, more than 60 million Europeans became refugees (Harris & Wulker, 1953).

At the same time, between 1941 and 1970, a second wave of African Americans migrated from the South to the North on the American continent. More than 5 million African Americans migrated to Northern cities in search of jobs, better living conditions and reduced discrimination (Paige & Witty, 2010).

With the end of World War II, European countries began to be attractive destinations for potential migrants again, opening their doors to rebuilding their economies. Moreover, in the post-war period, technological improvements in land and air transportation reduced the cost of migration.

A significant flow was that of British migrants to Australia, and it was perceived as a permanent movement supported by the Australian government, which paid £10 for each migrant (Department of Immigration and Border Protection (DIBP), 2015). In the post-war period, Turkish migrants to Germany were one of the most visible groups of migrants. They were brought to Germany as workers for a short time, between 1950 and 1960, to supplement the country's post-war labour demand. However, the German government never intended for these migrants to remain permanently in Germany, so they were not granted citizenship and did not become fully integrated into German society, leading to social conflicts. Also, in the post-war period, the population of the former colonies of the European powers began to migrate as a result of the links between the colonial states and their colonies. The migrant groups consisted of Indians, Pakistanis who migrated to England (Messina, 2001), and Vietnamese, Algerians, Moroccans and other Africans who chose France (McCloud et al., 2013). Population migration from the former colonies led to important social and demographic changes in European countries, which were facing the effects of growing multicultural societies. In the United States, the largest number of migrants came from Latin America and Asia.

The Global Migration Phenomenon in 1990–2020

Since the 1990s, the migration phenomenon has increased significantly. In the last 30 years, the migrant population has almost doubled, from 150 million people to almost 280 million people (Fig. 4.1), and only in the last 5 years the number of migrants has increased by over 30 million people (United Nations, 2022). Although in absolute terms, the number of migrants worldwide has increased significantly, their share in relation to the world's population has grown relatively slow between 1990 and 2020, being around 2.8 to 3.6‰ of the world's total population.

In addition to traditional destination countries, such as those in Western Europe, the United States or Australia, several other states have begun to attract more and more migrants. These include countries which were previously the source of migrants, such as Portugal, Italy and Spain. In addition, the boom of oil prices and the resulting economic growth in the Gulf region led to a huge increase in migration in these countries in order to meet the demand for work, although migration was predominantly

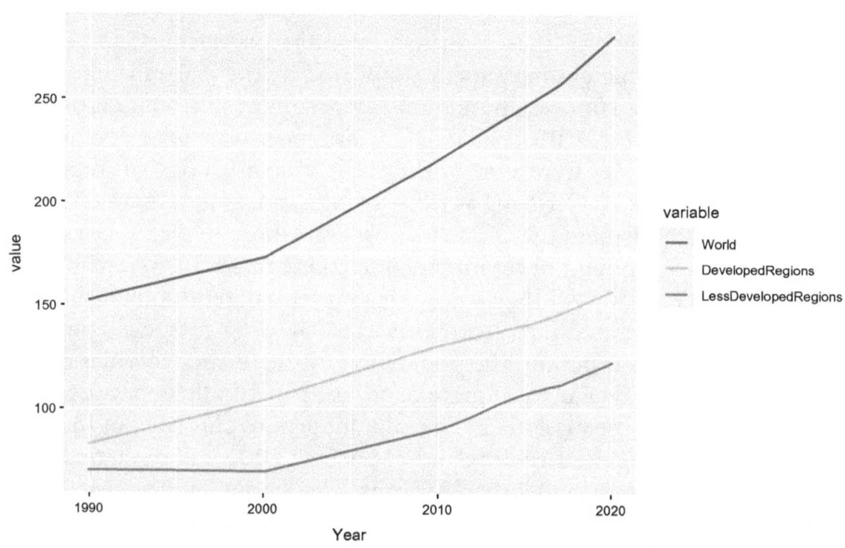

Fig. 4.1 Stock of international migrants by development level of the destination regions in 1990–2020, millions of people. (Source: Based on United Nations (2022) data)

temporary. There has also been an increase in labour migration in newly industrialised countries in Asia, such as Thailand, Malaysia, Hong Kong and Singapore.

The period 1990–2020 was characterized by a considerable increase in the number of the global migrants. According to United Nations (2022), between 1990 and 2000 the average annual number of migrants grew by 2 million people, between 2000 and 2010 by 4.8 million annually and from 2010 to 2020 there was an average annual increase of 5.9 million people. The number of migrants who preferred a developed state as a destination increased by 74 million people between 1990 and 2020, that is 56% of all migrants.

Between 1990 and 2020, Asia, Europe and Africa documented the largest increases in the number of migrants. According to the United Nations (2022), 68.5 million migrants from Asia are from the same continent, while the geographical distribution of migrants from Europe and America is much wider. Half of all European migrants come from countries on the European continent, and in North America 54% of migrants are from Latin America.

Analysing the main corridors of migration, it is found that the largest one is Asia-Asia, with over 68 million migrants, followed by the Europe-Europe corridor with 44 million people and Latin America-North America with 25 million migrants (Table 4.1).

Although the number of international migrants has been growing all these years, during the COVID-19 pandemic the migration phenomenon has been severely affected. With the measures introduced by the authorities of all states in order to reduce the spread of the virus, the COVID-19 pandemic has had an important impact on mobility and migration. Restricting the mobility of people in order to reduce the spread of the pandemic materialized in different measures, adapted to the particularities of each pandemic wave, from the total closure of borders at the beginning of the pandemic, to measures associated with the severity of cases, geographically and temporally differentiated. Labour mobility in most countries has been temporarily suspended, with few exceptions for critical workers, and assistance for asylum seekers has been slowed. All these restrictions lead to a drastic decrease in the number of migrants, with an estimated 46% reduction in the number of migrants at OECD level (Migration Data Portal, 2021).

Table 4.1 Migrants by development group and region of origin and destination in 2020, millions of people

Destination	*Origin*							
	Developed regions	*Less developed regions*	*Europa*	*Northern America*	*Asia*	*Africa*	*Latin America*	*Oceania*
Developed regions	58.4	92.9	54.1	2.5	46.8	14.9	31.4	2.5
Less developed regions	11.3	105.2	9.2	1.8	68.1	25.7	11.5	1.8
Europe	69.8	39.5	44.2	1.1	23.2	11.0	5.4	0.4
North America	8.5	46.2	6.9	1.1	17.6	3.3	25.5	0.3
Asia	7.9	73.5	7.2	0.5	68.5	4.7	0.4	0.1
Africa	0.7	22.2	0.6	0.1	1.2	20.9	0.03	0.01
Latin America	2.7	11.7	1.4	1.3	0.4	0.01	11.3	0.001
Oceania	4.0	5.2	2.9	0.3	4.1	0.6	0.2	1.1

Source: Based on (United Nations, 2021) data

Migration at European Union Level

Migration at European Union (EU) level can be analysed from two perspectives: on the one hand, it is the free movement of labour within the Member States, on the other hand, it can refer to the immigration of people from third countries. Labour mobility of people was a factor in reducing employment deficits on specific segments of the labour market: (a) mobility of low- and medium-skilled workers to occupy jobs unattractive to the indigenous population, including in activities defined as "essential", (b) covering the employment deficit resulting from the more pronounced demographic aging in the developed countries of the EU, (c) the mobility of highly qualified personnel, who pursued professional performance and career development.

The free movement of labour is one of the basic principles of the European Union's competitiveness (European Parliament, 2021), helping to reduce economic, social and geographic inequalities. However, in addition to the free movement of labour from the EU member states, there are also non-EU migrants who want to reach one of the Member States.

According to the latest available Eurostat data, the net migration balance has fluctuated over the last ten years, almost tripling from over 600,000 people to around 1.8 million in 2019 as compared to 2010. The highest value of net migration was registered in 2015, and the lowest in 2011 (Annex 4.1), because of the economic crisis, including on the labour market. Although there are still no data provided by Eurostat on the total number of migrants and immigrants for the years 2020 and 2021, a decrease is expected.

Analysing the total net balance of migration by country of origin, we note that migrants from outside the EU who chose a Member State as their destination country exceeded the migrants from EU member states throughout the analysed period (Fig. 4.2). The highest value of the third countries migrants was registered in 2019—2.3 million people, up from 1.08 million people in 2013.

Mobility within the EU did not register significant fluctuations, with the indicator hovering below one million people for the entire period, with a slightly decreasing trend in the last four years.

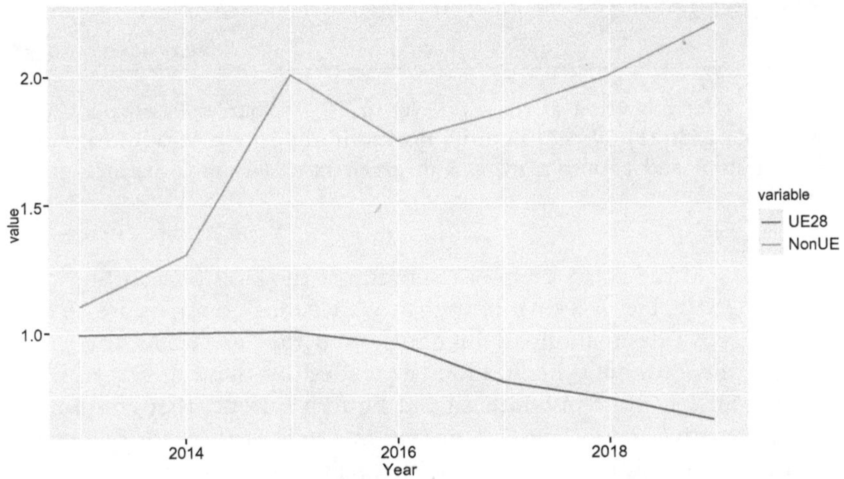

Fig. 4.2 Net migration (Net migration—the difference between immigration into and emigration from the area over the course of one year) at the level of the European Union by country of birth in 2013–2019, millions of people. (Source: Based on Eurostat (2021) data)

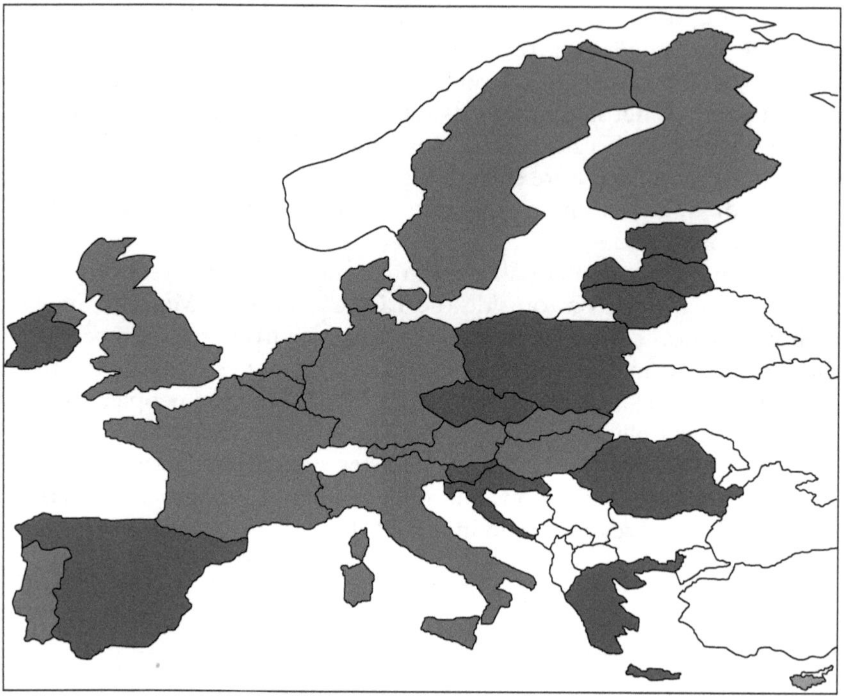

Fig. 4.3 Net migration at the EU level in 2010. Source: Based on United Nations data (2021). Note: Countries marked in red have a negative balance of net migration and countries marked in green have a positive balance of net migration

Looking at the balance of net migration at the level of each European states in 2010 (Fig. 4.3), we note that, while some countries are considered attractive destinations by migrants—and they are facing the social, political and economic implications generated by these flows—in other regions, such as those in Southern and Eastern Europe, they continue to have a negative net balance of migration, such as the case of Greece, Croatia, Latvia, Lithuania, Romania and Spain. This is also exacerbated by the fact that, between 2005 and 2010, almost two-thirds of the EU-13 population lived in regions with negative demographic growth, compared to only less than one-fourth of the EU-15 population (European Commission, 2017).

Of course, we note that the countries of Western Europe are preferred by migrants, being economically developed and with obvious comparative advantages, that is, higher earnings from work, and/or better working and living conditions, opportunities for professional development for the highly qualified.

Nevertheless the latest trend was accompanied by an increase in the socio-political opposition directed towards the free movement of labour, even if the net benefits of labour mobility for host countries are internationally recognized (OECD, 2014).

At the level of 2020, we note that the Western countries of the EU maintain their status as a country of immigration (Fig. 4.4), but in addition to these, some countries of emigration have also changed their status

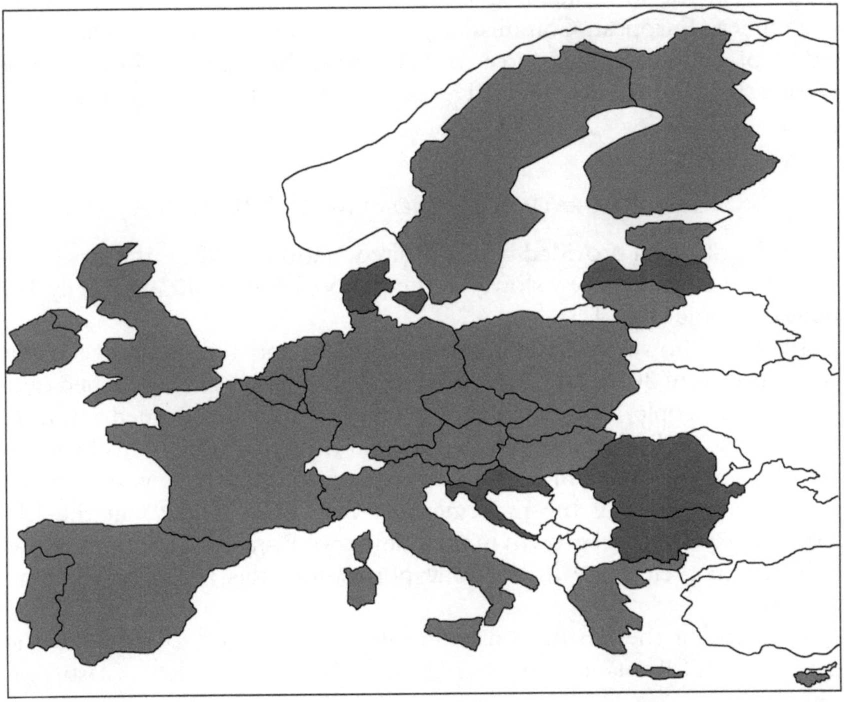

Fig. 4.4 Net migration at EU level in 2020. (Source: Based on United Nations (2021) data). Note: Countries marked in red have a negative balance of net migration and countries marked in green have a positive balance of net migration

compared to 2010, such as: Ireland, the Czech Republic, Greece, Spain, Poland, Slovenia and the Baltic countries with the exception of Latvia. The profile of the country of emigration (with a negative net migratory balance) is present in the countries of Southern and Eastern Europe, although they are the main beneficiaries of the financial funds of the European Union's cohesion policy. This means that these policies, based on compensatory measures and subsidy measures for the affected regions, do not adequately reduce territorial and economic disparities, and the comparative advantages of labour migration remain significant.

However, countries such as Latvia, Bulgaria, Romania and Croatia continue to have a negative net migration balance, which increases the demographic deficit and the ageing of the population. These trends have increased in the decade since the global financial crisis of 2008, which interrupted the long-standing trend towards convergence in European economies (European Commission, 2014). A hierarchy of the main providers of migrant labour force in 2019 ranks Romania on in 5th place among the countries from the EU space and in the 17th place in the world (IOM, 2021).

The Migration Phenomenon in Romania

According to data provided by the United Nations (2022), the stock [1] of Romanian migrants grew slowly in the period 1990–2000, with only 1.1 million people (Fig. 4.5).

In 2005, however, their number doubled, and the increasing trend continued until 2010, when the stock of Romanian migrants reached over 3.3 million people. The economic and financial crisis determined a modest trend of the indicator, and only in 2015 did the stock of migrants begin to grow again, reaching almost 4 million persons in 2020, one year after the total liberalization of the movement of Romanian workers in the EU space. The substantial growth in the number of Romanian migrants is also reflected in their share in the total population, this indicator reaching over 20%.

Concerning the destination countries, in the period 2010–2020 the preferences of Romanians registered some changes (Fig. 4.6). Classifying

[1] According to the World Bank methodology, the international stock of migrants refers to the mid-year estimate of the number of people living in a country or area other than the one in which they were born or, in the absence of these data, to the number of foreign citizens.

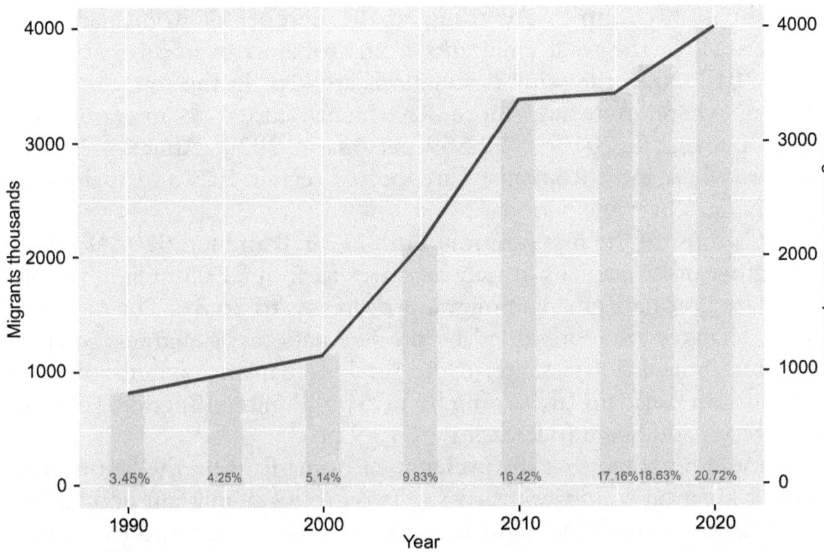

Fig. 4.5 Romanian migrants in the period 1990–2020 and their share in the total population. (Source: Based on United Nations (2022) data)

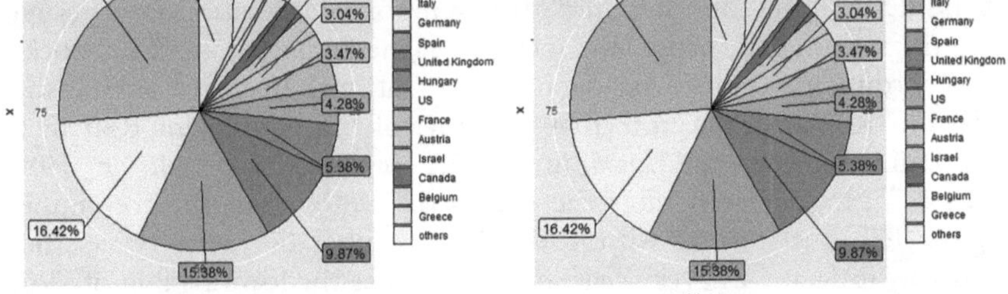

Fig. 4.6 Distribution of Romanian migrants by destination countries at the level of 2010 and 2020, %. (Source: Based on United Nations (2022) data)

the destination countries according to the number of Romanians who exceeded 1% of the total emigrants from Romania, we find that in the period 2010–2020 the same destinations are kept in the top, except for Belgium, where more and more Romanians started to migrate: from 21,634 persons in 2010 to 92,559 persons in 2020 (Annex 4.2). The countries where most Romanians are located remain Italy and Spain, with some changes over the period.

Italy is thus on the first position, both in 2010 and in 2020. Although the number of Romanians in Italy increases to about 1.05 million people, their share in total Romanian migrants decreases to 26.3%. The most significant changes are represented by the fluctuations of migrants in absolute value, but also as a share in the total Romanian migrants of those established in Germany (increasing by 11.6 pp), United Kingdom (increasing by 8 pp) and Spain (decreasing by 13.9 pp).

It should be noted that the presence of Romanians on the labour market of destination countries consists of two groups of migrant population, with different developments in the last three decades, respectively, final migration (more pronounced in the last decade of the twentieth century, with definitive residency change) and temporary multiannual migration for work (more pronounced in the first decade of the twenty-first century, with multiannual usual residence). After the crisis of 2008–2009, labour migration is repositioned between the destination countries, the mobility of Romanians who were already migrants happening between the developed countries of the EU space. Some migrants with several years of work in the destination countries turn their temporary migration into permanent migration, and, hence, the increase of the final net migration stock.

According to the official data of the National Institute of Statistics (NIS) in Romania, we note that the flow of the permanent Romanian emigrants registers the maximum value of 96,929 people in 1990 (Fig. 4.7), immediately after the events of 1989, when the communist regime fell, but starting with 1991 their number decreases twice, then gradually it decreases every year, until it reaches the lowest value of 7906 people in 2010. However, since 2014, the number of people has gradually increased to 21,031 people in 2020.

In the case of immigrants, the situation is different, their number increases from 1602 people in 1991 to 62,250 people in 2020, with some insignificant fluctuations over the period.

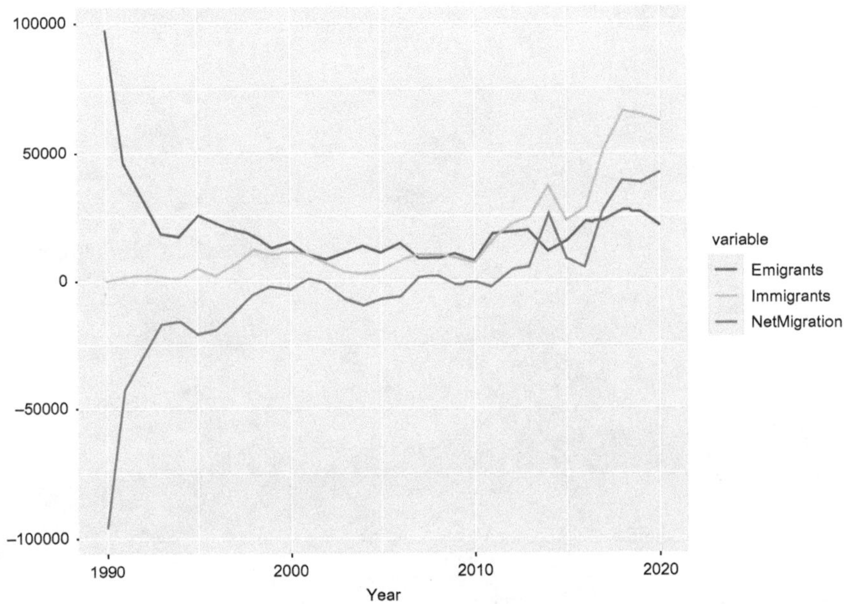

Fig. 4.7 Permanent migration flows, Romania, between 1990 and 2020, persons. (Source: Based on National Institute of Statistics (2021) data)

As for the net balance of the final migration, it is positive in the last six years, the highest values being in 2014 and 2018, when it is registered with 25,393 and 38,449, respectively; consequently, there are more permanent immigrants than emigrants.

Temporary migration is much higher than the permanent one. The latest data provided by NIS (National Institute of Statistics, 2021) on temporary migrants cover the period 2008–2020. According to the data, the flow of temporary emigrants does not fluctuate significantly over the period under review, reaching around 250,000 people, with slight declines in times of crisis, such as the economic crisis of 2011–2013, and the crisis caused by the COVID-19 pandemic (Fig. 4.8).

As for the flow of immigrants who chose Romania as the destination state, it registers a relatively constant evolution with flows oscillating around 150,000, with an upward trend in 2017, when over 177 thousand foreigners entered Romania, and, of course, a downward trend in 2020.

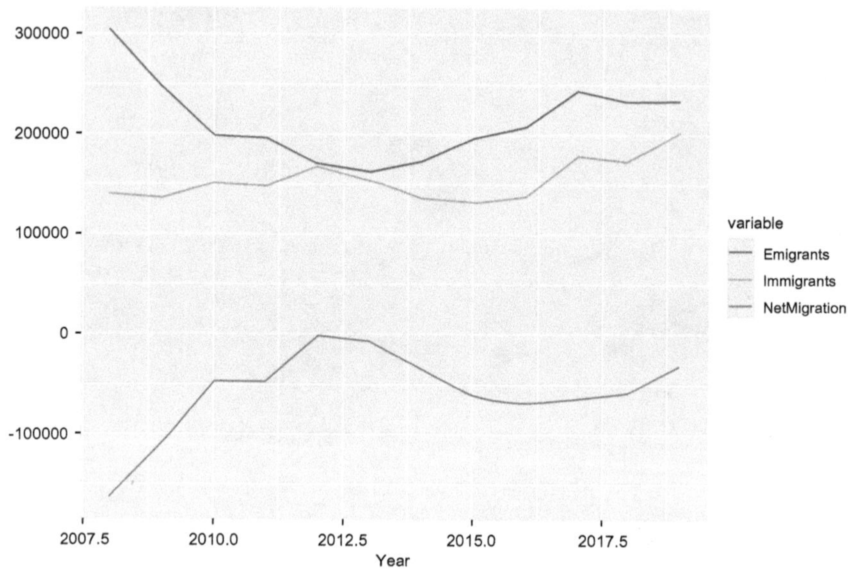

Fig. 4.8 Temporary migrants (According to the NIS, temporary emigrants are people who emigrate abroad for a period of at least 12 months, having another habitual residence, but keeping their domicile) in Romania between 1990 and 2020, persons. (Source: Based on National Institute of Statistics (2021) data)

Throughout the analysed period, the net balance of temporary migration recorded negative values, the Romanians who left each year abroad exceeding the number of foreigners who chose to come to Romania.

In the last three decades, Romania has been a country of emigration, the stock of migrant workers growing continuously, from about 812 thousand people in 1990 to almost 4 million people in 2020 (United Nations, 2022). The main reason for migration remained the comparatively higher earnings obtained on the labour market of the destination country compared to the Romanian labour market and the migrants' intention to remit money.

Consequently, the evolution of remittances flow in Romania has the same trend as that of migrants (Fig. 4.9), which confirms that the main motivation for population migration is remittances.

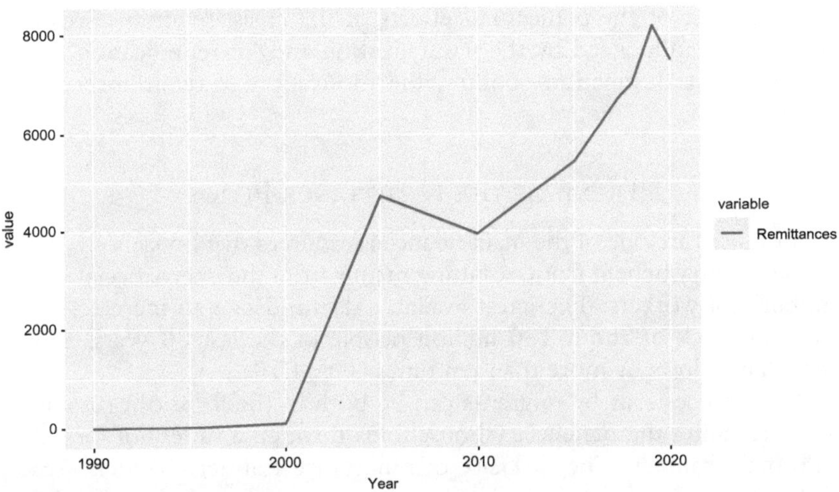

Fig. 4.9 Remittance inflow received by Romania in the period 1990–2020[e], $ million. (Source: Based on United Nations (2021) and World Bank (2022) data)

The growing number of migrant workers has led to a significant increase in remittance flows, from $2 million in 1990 and $96 million in 2000 to over $4.7 billion in the years before the economic and financial crisis (World Bank, 2022). Since the crisis, the amounts transferred decreased to $2.9 billion in 2015, followed by a period of increase to $5.5 billion in 2018. The reduction in the flow of remittances in Romania can be explained by:

1. The economic crisis, which has temporarily reduced the level of remittances in order to cope with lower income conditions or temporary availability.
2. Circular mobility in another EU country may temporarily reduce or stop remittance due to additional relocation costs or other causes inherent to a new job (lower-income probationary period, lower-performing income job than the previous one, etc.).
3. The COVID-19 pandemic seriously affected Romanian migrants, and according to some estimates more than a million people were forced to return home, while others did not have enough disposable income to cover the cost of living in the destination country and remit to their family members in Romania.

Regardless of the conjectural effects of the crisis, remittances can be significantly influenced by the naturalization and/or reunification of the family in the destination country, the motivation of remittances being reconsidered.

Trend of the Remittance Flows

Remittances are one of the main financial resources that households in the home country benefit from, resulting mainly from the international labour mobility of workers. The latest available data indicate an increase in the migrant stock of about 130 million people in the last 30 years, and of remittance flows by more than ten times (Fig. 4.10).

Remittances sent by migrants can be both in the form of cash and in kind, reaching the beneficiary households through a variety of formal or informal channels. The diversity of remittance transfer channels creates difficulties in accurately quantifying these flows. Although the official data of the World Bank (2022) shows an increase in remittance flows from $61 billion in 1990 to about $700 billion in 2020, studies conducted by Ratha

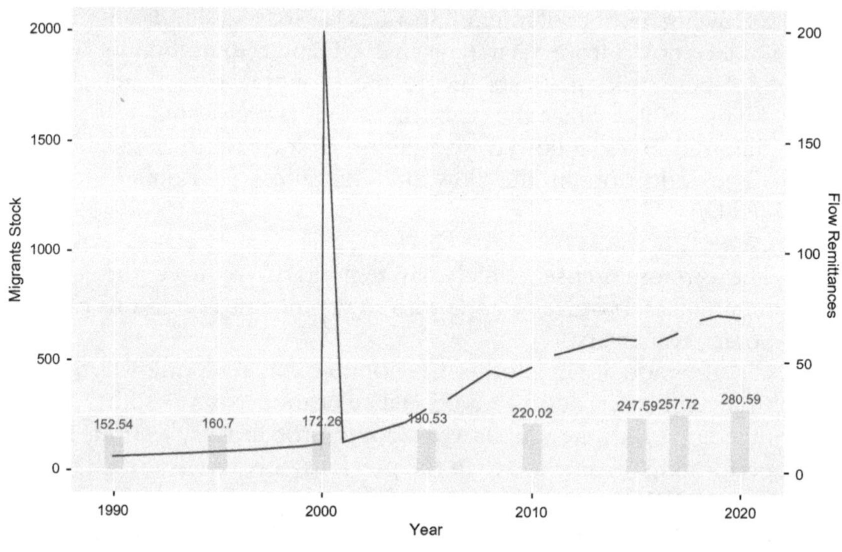

Fig. 4.10 Flow of remittances and the stock of international migrants globally in 1990–2020[e]. (Source: Based on United Nations (2021) and World Bank (2022) data)

Table 4.2 Top 10 countries by migration indicators in 2020[e]

Top 10 countries receiving remittances, $ billion		*Top 10 countries by share of remittances in GDP, %*		*Top 10 countries by the stock of migrants, millions of people*		*Top 10 countries by share of emigrants in the total population of the country of origin, %*	
India	83.1	Tonga	37.7	India	17.86	Dominica	108.61
China	59.5	Somalia	35.3	Mexico	11.18	Saint Kitts and Nevis	94.53
Mexico	42.9	Lebanon	32.9	Russian Federation	10.75	Polynesia	91.94
Philippines	34.9	South Sudan	29.5	China	10.461	Monaco	82.95
Egypt	29.6	Kyrgyz	29.4	Syrian Arab Republic	8.45	Tonga	70.53
Pakistan	26.1	Tajikistan	27.3	Bangladesh	7.40	Samoa	68.41
France	24.5	El Salvador	24.1	Pakistan	6.32	Antigua and Barbuda	67.97
Bangladesh	21.7	Honduras	23.5	Ukraine	6.13	Puerto Rico	57.94
Germany	17.9	Nepal	23.5	Philippines	6.09	Guyana	55.74
Nigeria	17.2	Haiti	21.8	Afghanistan	5.85	Grenada	55.28

Source: Based on United Nations (2021) and World Bank (2022) data

et al. (2016) estimate that the volume of these flows could be at least 50% higher than the official data.

The distribution of remittances by country of origin and the importance of their level is different from multiple perspectives. To mention just a few of the factors that adjust the economic and social significance of the money flows from migrants to the family left in the country, they are as follows: (a) the level of economic development, as reflected in the share of remittances in GDP; (b) the size of the country from a demographic perspective (population number); (c) the proportion of poverty, expressed in income, etc.; (d) the size of external labour mobility measured in the migrant stock.

According to Table 4.2, India ($83.1 billion) and China ($59.5 billion) are the countries with the largest remittance flows in the world, as a result of the significant stock of migrants in the destination states—over 18 million Indians and over 10 million Chinese, respectively. However, the situation is totally different for the other indicators of the migration phenomenon. They are no longer in the top 10; in China migrants represent only 0.75% of the total population; in India they represent 1.3%, and the share of remittances in GDP is insignificant (3.1% in India and 0.4% in China) (Annex 4.3).

In Mexico, we encounter a similar situation in terms of the level of the migrant stock: there are about 11 million Mexicans in different destination countries, who remit $42.9 billion back home, but their number is also significant in terms of share in the total population compared to that of India and China, which implies that migration has a greater impact on the labour market in Mexico.

The largest diaspora consists of Indians, Mexicans, Russians, Chinese, Syrians and Bangladeshis. As a result of the armed conflicts in Syria, over 48% [2] of the total population currently has the status of immigrant.

At the same time, we note that remittances are especially important in the less developed countries, accounting in some cases for over 1/3 of GDP, as in Tonga—37.7%, Somalia—35.3% or Lebanon—32.9%. In the case of these countries, the high values of remittances in GDP are due to the low level of economic development, but in absolute terms the remittances received are not significant.

In the case of Tonga, which ranks first in the hierarchy by the share of remittances in GDP in 2020, it is found that a modest volume of remittances of only $ 193 million is sent to the country by over 74,000 immigrants, who represent 70% of the country's population in the year of analysis.

Therefore, at the level of the country of origin, the magnitude of the volume of remittances and the stock of migrants is different, and the impact on economic and social development can vary considerably.

Analysing the data presented in Table 4.3 from the perspective of the former socialist states, we conclude the following:

1. No former socialist state appears in the top 10 countries according to the level of remittances received; Ukraine, with the highest remittance inflows from this pool of countries, is only on the 12th position worldwide, with over $ 15.1 billion.
2. Countries such as Kyrgyzstan (5th place) and Tajikistan (6th place) are registered in the world's top 10 by the share of remittances in GDP with a level of remittances more than 7 times lower than that of Ukraine (31st place).
3. Out of the countries already mentioned, only Ukraine is in the top 10 in the world by the stock of migrants (8th place), but it is surpassed by Russia, which has almost twice as many migrants (it ranks 3rd worldwide);
4. As a share of migrants in the total population of the country of origin, no former socialist state is in the rankings.

[2] According to World Bank data, the total population in Syria is 17.5 million people.

Table 4.3 Top former socialist states by migration indicators in 2020[e]

Top 10 countries receiving remittances, $ billion		*Top 10 countries by share of remittances in GDP, %*		*Top 10 countries by the stock of migrants, millions of people*		*Top 10 countries by share of emigrants in the total population of the country of origin, %*		*Top 10 countries according to combined migration indicators' ranks*	
Ukraine	15.05	Kyrgyz	29.4	Russia	10.75	Bosnia and Herzegovina	51.4	Ukraine	1
Russia	9.83	Tajikistan	27.3	Ukraine	6.13	Republic of Moldova	44.3	Republic of Moldova	2
Romania	7.44	Republic of Moldova	16.3	Poland	4.82	Albania	44.1	Bosnia and Herzegovina	3
Uzbekistan	6.98	Georgia	13.4	Kazakhstan	4.20	Kazakhstan	41.2	Romania	4
Poland	5.93	Montenegro	12.5	Romania	3.98	North Macedonia	33.3	Croatia	5
Czech Republic	4.18	Uzbekistan	12.1	Uzbekistan	2.02	Armenia	32.3	Albania	6
Croatia	3.97	Armenia	10.8	Bosnia and Herzegovina	1.68	Croatia	25.7	Uzbekistan	7
Serbia	3.86	Ukraine	9.9	Bulgaria	1.68	Bulgaria	24.3	Georgia	8
Hungary	3.65	Albania	9.7	Belarus	1.48	Lithuania	23.5	Kyrgyz	9
Kyrgyz	2.20	Bosnia and Herzegovina	9.3	Albania	1.25	Georgia	23.2	Armenia	10

Source: Based on United Nations (2021) and World Bank (2022) data

Conducting a similar analysis in the case of the former socialist states, the hierarchy of the first 10 countries is the following (Table 4.3):

Therefore, within the former socialist states, Ukraine is the most affected country by the migration phenomenon, holding the 1st place by volume of remittances received, the 2nd place by number of migrants, the 6th place by the share of remittances in GDP and the 17th position by the share of the migrant stock in the total population (Annex 4.4). In contrast, Turkmenistan is the least affected by the migration phenomenon and is on the last position in the ranking. In the top 10 former socialist states, the Republic of Moldova ranks third due to the low level of economic development. On the one hand, although the volume of remittances does not exceed $2 billion, the share of these amounts in GDP is over 16%. On the other hand, the low level of economic development triggers the population to migrate, so the 1.1 million migrants represent over 44% of the total population of the Republic of Moldova.

Romania holds the 4th place in the hierarchy after the analysis of the four indicators, registering a different situation compared to the Republic of Moldova, with a significant impact of absolute indicators, being on the

3rd place by the volume of remittances received ($7.44 billion) and on the 5th place considering the stock of migrants (3.98 million). Although remittances collected are higher compared to flows from the Republic of Moldova or Kyrgyz, their share in GDP does not exceed 3%, while in the Republic of Moldova they represent 16% of GDP, and in Kyrgyz 29%. Also, the share of migrants in the total population does not exceed 20%, compared to over 44% in the Republic of Moldova.

At the level of the former socialist states, we observe the following situations regarding the impact of the migration phenomenon:

1. The top 10 former socialist states by remittances are led by Ukraine with over $15.1 billion, followed by Russia with $9.8 billion, and Romania with $ 7.4 billion.
2. By relative figures, that is, the share of remittances in the GDP, Kyrgyzstan ranks first, with an absolute level of remittances more than five times lower than that of Ukraine, which is on the 6th place, followed by Tajikistan and the Republic of Moldova.
3. In terms of the stock of migrants, Russia is on the first position with more than 10.75 million people, almost two times more than the second position—Ukraine (6.13 million migrants).
4. Considering the share of migrants in the total population of the country of origin, we see states where the analysed indicator registers significant values, such as: Bosnia and Herzegovina (51.4%), the Republic of Moldova (44.3%) and Albania (44.1%).

Despite the economic reforms of the last decade, poverty remains a threat to most countries with a high level and/or share of remittances in GDP. Remittances are an important source of income for many households, which see these external flows as a way of securing the basic needs of their family members.

Within the EU Member States, according to Table 4.4, we note the following situations regarding the impact of the migration phenomenon:

1. In the top 10 EU member states by remittance level, France holds the 1st place with over $24 billion, followed by Germany with $17.8 billion and Belgium with $13 billion, whereas Romania holds only the 6th position, while in the ranking of the former socialist states it is on the fourth position.

Table 4.4 Top EU member states by migration indicators in 2020[c]

Top 10 countries receiving remittances, $ billion		*Top 10 countries by share of remittances in GDP, %*		*Top 10 countries by the stock of migrants, millions of people*		*Top 10 countries by share of emigrants in the total population of the country of origin, %*		*Top 10 countries according to combined migration indicators' ranks*	
France	24.44	Croatia	7.0	Poland	4.82	Croatia	25.7	Croatia	1
Germany	17.89	Latvia	3.3	United Kingdom	4.73	Bulgaria	24.3	Romania	1
Belgium	13.12	Romania	3	Romania	3.98	Lithuania	23.5	Portugal	2
Italy	9.71	Luxembourg	2.9	Germany	3.85	Romania	20.7	Bulgaria	3
Spain	8.50	Belgium	2.6	Italy	3.25	Portugal	20.1	Poland	4
Romania	7.44	Hungary	2.4	France	2.34	Latvia	20	Lithuania	5
Poland	5.93	Cyprus	2.4	Portugal	2.08	Malta	19.5	Hungary	6
Portugal	4.32	Portugal	1.9	Bulgaria	1.68	Estonia	15.5	Germany	7
Czech Rep	4.18	Malta	1.9	Spain	1.48	Ireland	14.7	Latvia	8
Croatia	3.97	Slovakia	1.8	Greece	1.08	Cyprus	14.3	United Kingdom	8

Source: Based on United Nations (2021) and World Bank (2022) data

2. After the share of remittances in GDP, Croatia holds the first place (7%), although it ranks 10th by the absolute value of remittance inflows, and Latvia is on the 2nd place (3.3%), whose remittance flow of $1.08 billion ensured it the 17th position (Annex 4.5). Only Romania, Portugal and Croatia are in the top 10 countries, both by relative and absolute indicator of remittances.
3. In terms of the stock of migrants, Poland occupies the first position with more than 4.8 million people, followed by UK (4.7 million), Romania and Germany (4.1 million).
4. After the share of migrants in the total population of the country of origin, Croatia holds the first position, representing a quarter of the country's total population, followed by Bulgaria (24.3%) and Lithuania (23.5%).

Aggregating the four indicators' ranks, we note that Romania and Croatia share the first position, but the impact is different. Croatia holds the first position in terms of the shares of remittances in GDP and migrants in the total population, and in absolute values, it is in the middle of the ranking. On the other hand, Romania is in the top 10 in terms of all four indicators. In contrast, Sweden, Finland and Denmark hold the last positions in each indicator, being the least affected by the migration phenomenon (Annex 4.5).

Thus, we note that the lower the level of economic development of the states, the higher migration and remittances are, respectively, compared to the developed countries where the migration phenomenon does not generate significant effects.

Conclusions

Migration is a phenomenon that has arisen since the first days of humanity, taking on more and more forms over time and encompassing more and more individuals, with an estimated 281 million migrants globally in 2020 (United Nations, 2022). Each of us is descended from migrants, no matter where we are now, and so will our descendants.

Analysing the evolution of the migration phenomenon and the globalisation, some researchers believe that the number of migrants will continue to increase. Pritchett (2006) considers that divergences in demographic trends and differences in the level of economic development are major causes of the increase in the number of international migrants in the future. The most significant factor remains the wage differential (Bunduchi et al., 2019). Surveys conducted among adults from underdeveloped countries show that more than 25% would like to migrate, and in some African states, the share of eager people exceeds even 50% (Torres & Pelham, 2008). Of course, only a fraction of the respondents will eventually migrate due to financial, political or family reasons, but the trends remain high (Kovacs, 2019).

As a result of the increase in the scale of the migration phenomenon, remittances, being its consequence, have become an important element of the analysis of the impact on the countries of origin. Although official data shows an increase in these financial flows, reaching the maximum value of about $719 billion in 2019 (Statista, 2021), the effects on the beneficiary countries can be even higher if we are to also take into account the amounts transferred through informal channels.

The global analysis carried out in dependence on the four indicators of the migration phenomenon shows us that the most affected states are those whose level of economic development is lower, or which register special political and military events, such as the case of Tajikistan, Ukraine or Syria, or recently Afghanistan. A similar analysis at the level of the EU states presents us with a relatively comparable situation, with Romania and Bulgaria in the top three most affected countries by migration, due to their lower level of economic development and unattractive labour markets.

Annexes

Annex 4.1 Net migration in EU member states, persons

Countries	*2010*	*2011*	*2012*	*2013*	*2014*	*2015*	*2016*	*2017*	*2018*	*2019*
Belgium	69,268	63,229	35,877	17,421	28,585	56,832	31,231	37,013	48,925	47,070
Bulgaria	–	–	-2512	-1108	-2112	-4247	-9329	-5989	-3666	-2012
Czech Republic	-12,752	-28,796	-11,769	4230	1429	3918	25,219	24,531	39,168	28,090
Denmark	10,780	11,240	10,746	17,002	23,962	33,867	21,729	12,176	4288	-5136
Germany	151,599	240,377	352,174	433,385	560,672	1,232,644	496,090	356,409	353,471	310,022
Estonia	-2484	-2505	-3682	-2631	-733	2410	1030	5258	7071	5458
Ireland	-25,760	-25,757	-20,473	-11,021	2412	13,632	23,129	14,431	43,977	23,626
Greece	-1579	-32,315	-66,494	-59,148	-47,791	-44,905	10,332	8920	16,440	34,439
Spain	-42,672	-37,703	-142,553	-251,531	-94,976	-1761	87,421	163,272	334,158	454,232
France	37,580	28,222	71,509	98,939	32,280	39,704	64,087	154,151	86,490	86,490
Croatia	-4171	-4165	-3918	-4884	-10,220	-17,945	-22,451	-31,799	-13,486	-2422
Italy	380,085	303,332	244,556	181,719	141,303	133,123	143,758	188,330	175,364	153,273
Cyprus	15,913	18,142	-629	-12,078	-14,826	-2000	2499	6201	8102	8797
Latvia	-35,640	-20,077	-11,860	-14,262	-8652	-10,640	-12,229	-7808	-4905	-3360
Lithuania	-77,944	-38,178	-21,257	-16,807	-12,327	-22,403	-30,171	-27,557	-3292	10,794
Luxembourg	7660	11,004	10,036	10,348	11,049	11,159	9446	10,548	10,659	11,075
Hungary	12,154	12,918	10,822	4277	12,368	15,119	13,729	28,241	34,759	38,786
Malta	74	1659	4251	6119	9346	9841	8748	14,656	17,102	20,343
Netherlands	30,806	25,917	14,135	16,803	32,423	54,542	77,755	81,415	84,671	107,850
Austria	19,327	31,033	39,745	47,795	62,771	109,634	65,081	45,657	38,421	40,887
Poland	-62,995	-108,739	-58,057	-56,135	-46,024	-40,690	-28,139	-9139	24,289	46,055
Portugal	3815	-24,331	-37,352	-36,232	-30,056	-10,481	-8348	4886	11,570	44,506
Romania	-48,100	-47,866	-2920	-8109	-36,836	-61,923	-70,123	-64,758	-59,083	-31,314
Slovenia	-521	2059	644	487	-490	507	1051	1253	14,928	16,213
Slovakia	3383	2966	3416	2379	1713	3127	3885	3722	3955	3632
Finland	13,731	16,821	17,433	18,048	16,021	12,441	16,823	14,824	11,965	15,495
Sweden	49,948	45,288	51,312	65,130	75,729	78,410	117,127	98,869	85,621	68,087
United Kingdom	251,644	215,341	176,823	209,112	312,905	332,269	248,553	284,544	259,606	312,521
Total	**673,881**	**595,887**	**626,638**	**642,935**	**993,452**	**1,873,599**	**1,266,031**	**1,381,233**	**1,585,309**	**1,798,439**

Source: Based on Eurostat (2021) data

Annex 4.2 Romanian migrants by destination countries in 2020 and 2010, persons

Countries	*2020*	*2010*
Italy	1,048,862	813,037
Germany	654,822	134,911
Spain	613,336	810,471
United Kingdom	393,569	53,081
Hungary	214,330	189,055
US	170,469	171,253
France	138,550	54,305
Austria	121,355	56,932
Israel	100,528	182,099
Canada	97,253	96,209
Belgium	92,559	21,634
Greece	47,120	45,289

Source: Based on United Nations (2022) data

Annex 4.3 Ranking of world countries according to migration indicators in 2020[c]

Top 10 countries receiving remittances, $ billion		*Top 10 countries by share of remittances in GDP, %*		*Top 10 countries by the stock of migrants, migrants*		*Top 10 countries by share of emigrants in the total population of the country of origin, %*	
India	83.1	Tonga	37.7	India	17,869,492	Dominica	108.6
China	59.5	Somalia	35.3	Mexico	11,185,737	Saint Kitts and Nevis	94.53
Mexico	42.9	Lebanon	32.9	Russia	10,756,697	Polynesia	91.94
Philippines	34.9	South Sudan	29.5	China	10,461,170	Monaco	82.95
Egypt	29.6	Kyrgyz	29.4	Syria	8,457,214	Tonga	70.53
Pakistan	26.1	Tajikistan	27.3	Bangladesh	7,401,763	Samoa	68.41
France	24.5	El Salvador	24.1	Pakistan	6,328,400	Antigua and Barbuda	67.97
Bangladesh	21.7	Honduras	23.5	Ukraine	6,139,144	Puerto Rico	57.94
Germany	17.9	Nepal	23.5	Philippines	6,094,307	Guyana	55.74
Nigeria	17.2	Haiti	21.8	Afghanistan	5,853,838	Grenada	55.28
Vietnam	17.2	Jamaica	21.2	Venezuela	5,415,337	Bosnia and Herzegovina	51.44
Ukraine	15.1	Lesotho	20.6	Poland	4,825,096	Saint Vincent and the Grenadines	50.05
Belgium	13.1	Samoa	18.7	United Kingdom	4,732,510	Syria	48.33
Guatemala	11.4	Kosovo	18.4	Indonesia	4,601,369	Suriname	46.57
Russian Federation	9.8	West Bank and Gaza	17.1	Kazakhstan	4,203,899	Micronesia	44.34
Italy	9.7	Republic of Moldova	16.3	Romania	3,987,093	Republic of Moldova	44.29
Indonesia	9.7	Gambia. The	15.6	Germany	3,855,268	Albania	44.06
Spain	8.5	Nicaragua	15.3	Myanmar	3,711,751	Kazakhstan	41.20
Dominican Republic	8.3	Guatemala	14.8	Egypt	3,610,461	Gibraltar	39.74
Nepal	8.1	Cabo Verde	13.9	Turkey	3,411,408	Saint Lucia	38.79
Thailand	8.1	Georgia	13.4	Viet Nam	3,392,025	Jamaica	37.79

(*continued*)

Annex 4.3 (continued)

Top 10 countries receiving remittances, $ billion		*Top 10 countries by share of remittances in GDP, %*		*Top 10 countries by the stock of migrants, migrants*		*Top 10 countries by share of emigrants in the total population of the country of origin, %*	
Romania	7.4	Marshall Islands	13.2	Morocco	3,262,222	Barbados	34.66
Morocco	7.4	Comoros	13.2	Italy	3,258,831	Cabo Verde	33.73
Korea Rep.	7.4	Montenegro	12.5	Colombia	3,024,273	Macedonia	33.31
Sri Lanka	7.1	Uzbekistan	12.1	United States of America	2,996,223	Bermuda	33.03
Uzbekistan	7.0	Liberia	11.0	Nepal	2,599,701	Armenia	32.34
Colombia	6.9	Armenia	10.8	South Sudan	2,575,870	Greenland	31.70
Lebanon	6.3	Dominican Republic	10.6	France	2,341,908	Tuvalu	31.12
United States	6.2	Senegal	10.5	Republic of Korea	2,204,554	Seychelles	29.72
Israel	6.1	Pakistan	9.9	Sudan	2,104,887	Faroe Islands	26.45
El Salvador	5.9	Ukraine	9.9	Portugal	2,081,419	Fiji	26.09
Poland	5.9	Albania	9.7	Iraq	2,077,976	Croatia	25.69
Honduras	5.6	Philippines	9.6	Somalia	2,034,221	El Salvador	24.65
Japan	4.9	Kiribati	9.5	Uzbekistan	2,027,823	Bulgaria	24.30
Portugal	4.3	Dominica	9.5	Algeria	2,022,337	Trinidad and Tobago	23.62
Czech Republic	4.2	Bosnia and Herzegovina	9.3	Sri Lanka	1,960,025	Lithuania	23.55
Croatia	4.0	Jordan	9.0	Brazil	1,897,128	Georgia	23.18
Jordan	3.9	Sri Lanka	8.8	Malaysia	1,860,037	South Sudan	23.01
Serbia	3.9	Vanuatu	8.8	Puerto Rico	1,850,529	Nauru	22.65
Hungary	3.6	Timor-Leste	8.7	Democratic Republic of the Congo	1,832,069	China. Macao SAR*	22.36
Brazil	3.6	Guinea-Bissau	8.6	Haiti	1,769,671	Micronesia	21.69

Ghana	3.6	Egypt	8.2	Cuba	1,757,300	Montenegro	21.39
Ecuador	3.3	Serbia	7.3	Bosnia and Herzegovina	1,687,639	Romania	20.67
United Kingdom	3.3	Fiji	7.2	Bulgaria	1,683,074	Portugal	20.20
Haiti	3.1	Croatia	7.0	Nigeria	1,670,455	Aruba	20.10
Kenya	3.1	Bangladesh	6.6	Dominican Republic	1,608,567	Latvia	19.98
Sweden	3.1	Morocco	6.5	Burkina Faso	1,599,347	Malta	19.57
Austria	3.1	Guyana	6.3	El Salvador	1,599,058	Venezuela (Bolivarian Republic of)	19.04
Jamaica	3.0	Togo	5.9	Peru	1,519,635	Marshall Islands	18.39
Peru	2.9	Zimbabwe	5.8	Spain	1,489,823	Sao Tome and Principe	18.07
West Bank and Gaza	2.7	Micronesia. Fed. Sts.	5.7	Belarus	1,483,626	Lao People's Democratic Republic	17.81
Senegal	2.6	Belize	5.6	Guatemala	1,368,431	British Virgin Islands	17.71
Switzerland	2.6	St. Vincent and the Grenadines	5.6	Iran (Islamic Republic of)	1,325,113	Comoros	17.34
Netherlands	2.5	Mali	5.6	Mali	1,303,511	Central African Republic	16.91
Myanmar	2.2	Tunisia	5.3	Yemen	1,301,166	New Zealand	15.86
Kyrgyz Republic	2.2	Ghana	5.2	Lao People's Democratic Republic	1,296,051	Belarus	15.79
Tajikistan	2.2	Vietnam	5.0	Canada	1,292,329	Estonia	15.52
Luxembourg	2.1	Cambodia	4.9	Albania	1,250,451	Haiti	15.52
Georgia	2.1	Grenada	4.7	Zimbabwe	1,243,314	Cuba	15.51
Tunisia	2.1	Mongolia	4.2	Azerbaijan	1,163,922	Afghanistan	15.04
Congo. Dem. Rep.	1.9	Afghanistan	4.1	Republic of Modova	1,159,443	Dominican Republic	14.83
Slovak Republic	1.9	Nigeria	4.0	Côte d'Ivoire	1,149,298	Ireland	14.70
Republic of Moldova	1.9	Mexico	4.0	Ecuador	1,127,891	Palau	14.68

(*continued*)

Annex 4.3 (continued)

Top 10 countries receiving remittances, $ billion		*Top 10 countries by share of remittances in GDP, %*		*Top 10 countries by the stock of migrants, migrants*		*Top 10 countries by share of emigrants in the total population of the country of origin, %*	
Nicaragua	1.9	Congo. Dem. Rep.	3.9	Jamaica	1,118,931	Serbia	14.53
Bosnia and Herzegovina	1.8	Ecuador	3.5	Cambodia	1,104,819	Mauritius	14.46
Somalia	1.7	Macedonia	3.4	Greece	1,088,507	Andorra	14.41
Algeria	1.7	Bhutan	3.3	Thailand	1,086,985	Cyprus	14.35
Bermuda	1.5	Azerbaijan	3.3	Argentina	1,076,148	Isle of Man	14.15
Denmark	1.5	Latvia	3.3	Croatia	1,039,526	Ukraine	13.91
Albania	1.5	Kenya	3.1	Czech Republic	1,026,108	Bahamas	13.68
Malaysia	1.5	India	3.1	China. Hong Kong SAR	1,007,788	China. Hong Kong SAR	13.47
Kosovo	1.4	St. Kitts and Nevis	3.0	Ghana	1,004,324	Belize	13.27
Azerbaijan	1.4	Romania	3.0	Serbia	1,003,962	Luxembourg	12.93
Iran. Islamic Rep.	1.3	Luxembourg	2.9	Honduras	985,077	Somalia	12.80
Armenia	1.3	Bolivia	2.8	Netherlands	970,403	Poland	12.71
Cambodia	1.3	Eswatini	2.8	Armenia	958,190	Paraguay	12.57
Zimbabwe	1.2	Madagascar	2.8	Ethiopia	946,129	Lebanon	12.55
South Sudan	1.2	Burkina Faso	2.8	Bolivia	927,244	Iceland	11.80
Australia	1.2	Uganda	2.8	South Africa	914,901	Kyrgyzstan	11.75
Bolivia	1.1	Myanmar	2.8	Tunisia	902,268	Azerbaijan	11.51
Latvia	1.1	Belgium	2.6	Paraguay	896,484	Nicaragua	10.84
Uganda	1.1	Colombia	2.5	Georgia	861,077	Uruguay	10.57
Belarus	1.0	Barbados	2.5	Lebanon	856,814	Brunei Darussalam	10.36
Mali	1.0	Mozambique	2.4	Central African Republic	816,668	Greece	10.16

Bulgaria	1.0	St. Lucia	2.4	Jordan	814,909	Honduras	9.95
Canada	0.9	Cyprus	2.4	Japan	808,825	Channel Islands	9.87
South Africa	0.8	Mauritius	2.4	New Zealand	806,159	Liechtenstein	9.72
Finland	0.8	Hungary	2.4	Uganda	781,440	Czech Republic	9.59
Turkey	0.8	Rwanda	2.3	Kyrgyzstan	774,377	Lesotho	9.44
Lithuania	0.8	Malawi	2.2	Ireland	734,317	Equatorial Guinea	9.18
Afghanistan	0.8	Niger	2.2	Nicaragua	718,154	Sri Lanka	8.94
Iraq	0.7	Malta	1.9	Hungary	714,420	Nepal	8.92
Qatar	0.7	Portugal	1.9	Switzerland	713,623	Morocco	8.84
Argentina	0.6	Slovakia	1.8	North Macedonia	693,896	Mexico	8.68
New Caledonia	0.6	Antigua and Barbuda	1.8	Senegal	693,765	Zimbabwe	8.37
Greece	0.6	Solomon Islands	1.8	Benin	681,827	Switzerland	8.26
Montenegro	0.6	Czech Republic	1.7	Angola	668,066	Guatemala	8.12
Paraguay	0.6	Belarus	1.7	Lithuania	658,057	Jordan	7.99
French Polynesia	0.6	Djibouti	1.6	Chile	643,800	Bolivia	7.94
Norway	0.6	Estonia	1.6	Mozambique	640,160	Slovakia	7.69
Cyprus	0.6	Paraguay	1.6	Austria	600,740	Burkina Faso	7.65
Slovenia	0.6	Thailand	1.6	Australia	598,765	Tunisia	7.63
Mongolia	0.5	Burundi	1.5	Tajikistan	586,851	Slovenia	7.63
Estonia	0.5	Israel	1.5	Belgium	577,463	Russia	7.46
Ethiopia	0.5	Sudan	1.4	Burundi	551,105	Hungary	7.33
Costa Rica	0.5	Peru	1.4	Guinea	550,790	San Marino	7.09
Sudan	0.5	Sao Tome and Principe	1.4	Togo	545,409	United Kingdom	7.04
Burkina Faso	0.5	Aruba	1.4	Kenya	535,348	Turks and Caicos Islands	6.95
Hong Kong SAR. China	0.5	Lithuania	1.4	Rwanda	492,489	Myanmar	6.82

(*continued*)

Annex 4.3 (continued)

Top 10 countries receiving remittances, $ billion		*Top 10 countries by share of remittances in GDP, %*		*Top 10 countries by the stock of migrants, migrants*		*Top 10 countries by share of emigrants in the total population of the country of origin, %*	
Panama	0.4	Sierra Leone	1.4	Cameroon	441,015	Bhutan	6.74
Togo	0.4	Bulgaria	1.4	Guyana	438,413	Austria	6.74
Lesotho	0.4	Lao PDR	1.4	Slovakia	419,651	Cambodia	6.61
Macedonia	0.4	Benin	1.4	Niger	399,707	Togo	6.59
Tanzania	0.4	Algeria	1.2	Latvia	380,010	Mali	6.44
New Zealand	0.4	Slovenia	1.1	Uruguay	367,060	Ecuador	6.39
Madagascar	0.4	Poland	1.0	Israel	358,691	Tajikistan	6.15
Kazakhstan	0.4	Guinea	1.0	Singapore	348,464	Singapore	6.13
Ireland	0.4	France	0.9	Trinidad and Tobago	330,519	Colombia	5.94
Guyana	0.4	Indonesia	0.9	United Republic of Tanzania	327,863	Uzbekistan	5.92
Mozambique	0.3	Seychelles	0.9	Sweden	327,581	Gambia	5.76
Cameroon	0.3	Cameroon	0.9	Finland	311,889	Guinea-Bissau	5.68
Liberia	0.3	Palau	0.9	Malawi	311,052	Finland	5.64
Cote d'Ivoire	0.3	Panama	0.8	Saudi Arabia	299,268	Benin	5.62
Fiji	0.3	Trinidad and Tobago	0.8	Suriname	273,209	Netherlands	5.56
Saudi Arabia	0.3	Costa Rica	0.8	Polynesia	258,262	Philippines	5.56
Niger	0.3	Iceland	0.8	Denmark	257,025	Italy	5.47
Gambia. The	0.3	Mauritania	0.7	Turkmenistan	242,554	Sint Maarten (Dutch part)	5.37
Malta	0.3	Austria	0.7	Fiji	233,856	Iraq	5.17
Venezuela. RB	0.3	Russia	0.7	Liberia	233,564	Belgium	5.00
Mauritius	0.3	Spain	0.7	Congo	223,767	Kuwait	4.97
Lao PDR	0.3	Tanzania	0.6	Chad	222,303	Curaçao	4.91

Cabo Verde	0.2	Venezuela. RB	0.6	Kuwait	212,271	Sudan	4.80
Rwanda	0.2	Sweden	0.6	Estonia	206,631	Northern Mariana Islands	4.76
Benin	0.2	Namibia	0.5	United Arab Emirates	203,214	Burundi	4.63
Tonga	0.2	Cote d'Ivoire	0.5	Lesotho	202,164	Germany	4.63
Malawi	0.2	Ethiopia	0.5	Zambia	200,700	Liberia	4.62
Trinidad and Tobago	0.2	Italy	0.5	Madagascar	193,526	Algeria	4.61
Iceland	0.2	Germany	0.5	Norway	191,392	Peru	4.61
Comoros	0.2	Korea. Rep.	0.5	Cabo Verde	187,558	Bangladesh	4.49
Timor-Leste	0.2	Qatar	0.4	Libya	185,518	Denmark	4.41
Guinea	0.2	Malaysia	0.4	Mauritius	182,973	Yemen	4.36
Samoa	0.2	Denmark	0.4	Cyprus	173,210	Côte d'Ivoire	4.36
Zambia	0.1	Iraq	0.4	Slovenia	160,197	Eswatini	4.31
Curacao	0.1	China	0.4	Sierra Leone	152,486	Kiribati	4.27
Guinea-Bissau	0.1	Switzerland	0.3	Comoros	150,823	Republic of Korea	4.26
Eswatini	0.1	Greece	0.3	Costa Rica	150,241	Guinea	4.19
Uruguay	0.1	Finland	0.3	China. Macao SAR*	145,192	Senegal	4.14
Barbados	0.1	Botswana	0.3	Panama	139,520	Congo	4.06
Belize	0.1	Netherlands	0.3	Gambia	139,210	Turkey	4.04
Bhutan	0.1	South Africa	0.3	Samoa	135,732	Turkmenistan	4.02
Vanuatu	0.1	Brazil	0.2	Montenegro	132,965	Israel	3.89
Chile	0.1	Kazakhstan	0.2	Mauritania	130,226	Rwanda	3.80
Mauritania	0.1	Iran	0.2	Equatorial Guinea	128,774	Norway	3.56
Sierra Leone	0.1	Uruguay	0.2	Guinea-Bissau	111,790	Egypt	3.53

(continued)

Annex 4.3 (continued)

Top 10 countries receiving remittances, $ billion		*Top 10 countries by share of remittances in GDP, %*		*Top 10 countries by the stock of migrants, migrants*		*Top 10 countries by share of emigrants in the total population of the country of origin, %*	
Namibia	0.1	New Zealand	0.2	Dem. People's Republic of Korea	110,377	Viet Nam	3.48
Djibouti	0.1	Argentina	0.2	Malta	102,793	France	3.48
Dominica	0.0	Norway	0.2	Barbados	99,611	Bahrain	3.42
Grenada	0.0	Hong Kong SAR. China	0.1	Mongolia	82,098	Canada	3.40
Botswana	0.0	United Kingdom	0.1	Luxembourg	81,757	American Samoa	3.32
Burundi	0.0	Gabon	0.1	Dominica	78,191	Panama	3.23
St. Vincent and the Grenadines	0.0	Maldives	0.1	Tonga	74,550	Ghana	3.23
St. Lucia	0.0	Turkey	0.1	Saint Lucia	71,227	Sweden	3.16
Oman	0.0	Japan	0.1	Antigua and Barbuda	66,561	Spain	3.15
Aruba	0.0	Macao SAR. China	0.1	Botswana	63,561	Timor-Leste	3.00
Sint Maarten (Dutch part)	0.0	Ireland	0.1	Grenada	62,204	Costa Rica	2.95
Marshall Islands	0.0	Australia	0.1	Bahrain	58,270	Cayman Islands	2.90
Solomon Islands	0.0	Oman	0.1	Saint Vincent and the Grenadines	55,525	Pakistan	2.86
St. Kitts and Nevis	0.0	Canada	0.1	Bahamas	53,793	Mauritania	2.80
Antigua and Barbuda	0.0	United States	0.03	Belize	52,756	Botswana	2.70
Micronesia. Fed. Sts.	0.0	Chile	0.03	Bhutan	51,998	Libya	2.70

Kuwait	0.0	Angola	0.01	Micronesia	50,998	Mongolia	2.50
Macao SAR. China	0.0	Papua New Guinea	0.0	Saint Kitts and Nevis	50,285	Argentina	2.37
Kiribati	0.0	Kuwait	0.0	Eswatini	50,039	Vanuatu	2.36
Gabon	0.0	Suriname	0.0	Gabon	48,392	Australia	2.33
Cayman Islands	0.0	Turkmenistan	0.0	Namibia	47,770	Gabon	2.17
Seychelles	0.0	Zambia	0.0	Brunei Darussalam	45,340	New Caledonia	2.15
Angola	0.0	Saudi Arabia	0.0	Iceland	43,251	United Arab Emirates	2.05
Turks and Caicos Islands	0.0			Sao Tome and Principe	39,608	Mozambique	2.05
Sao Tome and Principe	0.0			Timor-Leste	39,588	Democratic Republic of the Congo	2.05
Maldives	0.0			Monaco	32,552	Angola	2.03
Palau	0.0			Seychelles	29,258	Sierra Leone	1.91
Papua New Guinea	0.0			Qatar	25,705	Namibia	1.88
Turkmenistan	0.0			Oman	25,099	Djibouti	1.86
Suriname	0.0			Micronesia	24,945	Uganda	1.71
Central African Republic	0.0			Aruba	21,456	Indonesia	1.68
Chad	0.0			Bermuda	21,107	Cameroon	1.66
Tuvalu	0.0			Djibouti	18,365	Niger	1.65
				Greenland	17,866	Malawi	1.63
				Channel Islands	17,158	Iran	1.58
				Gibraltar	13,389	Thailand	1.56
				Faroe Islands	12,927	South Africa	1.54
				Isle of Man	12,032	Chad	1.35
				Andorra	11,132	Guam	1.31
				Marshall Islands	10,886	India	1.29
				Curaçao	7611	Zambia	1.09

(*continued*)

Annex 4.3 (continued)

Top 10 countries receiving remittances, $ billion		*Top 10 countries by share of remittances in GDP, %*		*Top 10 countries by the stock of migrants, migrants*		*Top 10 countries by share of emigrants in the total population of the country of origin, %*	
				Vanuatu	7246	Kenya	1.00
				New Caledonia	5839	United States of America	0.91
				British Virgin Islands	5355	Brazil	0.89
				Kiribati	5103	Qatar	0.89
				Papua New Guinea	4810	Saudi Arabia	0.86
				Solomon Islands	4270	Ethiopia	0.82
				Maldives	3715	Nigeria	0.81
				Liechtenstein	3706	French Polynesia	0.77
				Tuvalu	3670	China	0.75
				Northern Mariana Islands	2741	Madagascar	0.70
				Turks and Caicos Islands	2689	Maldives	0.69
				Palau	2656	Japan	0.64
				Nauru	2454	Solomon Islands	0.62
				San Marino	2407	United Republic of Tanzania	0.55
				Guam	2213	Malaysia	0.51
				Sint Maarten (Dutch part)	2191	Oman	0.49
				French Polynesia	2157	Dem. People's Republic of Korea	0.21
				Cayman Islands	1908	Papua New Guinea	0.05
				American Samoa	1832	Chile	0.05

Source: Based on United Nations (2022) and World Bank (2022) data

Annex 4.4 Ranking of the former socialist states according to migration indicators in 2020[c]

Top 10 countries receiving remittances, $ billion		*Top 10 countries by share of remittances in GDP, %*		*Top 10 countries by the stock of migrants, millions of people*		*Top 10 countries by share of emigrants in the total population of the country of origin, %*		*Combined migration indicators' ranks*	
Ukraine	15.05	Kyrgyz	29.4	Russia	10.7	Bosnia and Herzegovina	51.4	Ukraine	1
Russia	9.83	Tajikistan	27.3	Ukraine	6.13	Republic of Moldova	44.3	Republic of Moldova	2
Romania	7.44	Moldova	16.3	Poland	4.82	Albania	44.1	Bosnia and Herzegovina	3
Uzbekistan	6.98	Georgia	13.4	Kazakhstan	4.20	Kazakhstan	41.2	Romania	4
Poland	5.93	Montenegro	12.5	Romania	3.98	Macedonia	33.3	Croatia	5
Czech Republic	4.18	Uzbekistan	12.1	Uzbekistan	2.02	Armenia	32.3	Albania	6
Croatia	3.97	Armenia	10.8	Bosnia and Herzegovina	1.68	Croatia	25.7	Uzbekistan	7
Serbia	3.86	Ukraine	9.9	Bulgaria	1.68	Bulgaria	24.3	Georgia	8
Hungary	3.65	Albania	9.7	Belarus	1.48	Lithuania	23.5	Kyrgyz	9
Kyrgyz	2.20	Bosnia and Herzegovina	9.3	Albania	1.25	Georgia	23.2	Armenia	10
Tajikistan	2.18	Serbia	7.3	Azerbaijan	1.16	Montenegro	21.4	Serbia	11
Georgia	2.11	Croatia	7.0	Republic of Moldova	1.15	Romania	20.7	Poland	12
Slovakia	1.87	Macedonia	3.4	Croatia	1.03	Latvia	20.0	Russia	13
Republic of Moldova	1.87	Azerbaijan	3.3	Czech Republic	1.02	Belarus	15.8	Czech Republic	14
Bosnia and Herzegovina	1.81	Latvia	3.3	Serbia	1.00	Estonia	15.5	Tajikistan	15
Albania	1.46	Romania	3.0	Armenia	0.95	Serbia	14.5	Bulgaria	16
Azerbaijan	1.40	Hungary	2.4	Georgia	0.86	Ukraine	13.9	Azerbaijan	17

(*continued*)

Annex 4.4 (continued)

Top 10 countries receiving remittances, $ billion		*Top 10 countries by share of remittances in GDP, %*		*Top 10 countries by the stock of migrants, millions of people*		*Top 10 countries by share of emigrants in the total population of the country of origin, %*		*Combined migration indicators' ranks*	
Armenia	1.32	Slovakia	1.8	Kyrgyz	0.77	Poland	12.7	Belarus	18
Latvia	1.08	Belarus	1.7	Hungary	0.71	Kyrgyz	11.7	Kazakhstan	19
Belarus	1.00	Czech Republic	1.7	North Macedonia	0.69	Azerbaijan	11.5	North Macedonia	20
Bulgaria	0.95	Estonia	1.6	Lithuania	0.65	Czech Republic	9.6	Montenegro	21
Lithuania	0.79	Lithuania	1.4	Tajikistan	0.58	Slovakia	7.7	Hungary	22
Montenegro	0.60	Bulgaria	1.4	Slovakia	0.41	Slovenia	7.6	Latvia	23
Slovenia	0.55	Slovenia	1.1	Latvia	0.38	Russia	7.5	Lithuania	24
Estonia	0.50	Poland	1.0	Turkmenistan	0.24	Hungary	7.3	Slovakia	25
Macedonia	0.41	Russia	0.7	Estonia	0.20	Tajikistan	6.2	Estonia	26
Kazakhstan	0.37	Kazakhstan	0.2	Slovenia	0.16	Uzbekistan	5.9	Slovenia	27
Turkmenistan	0,000001	Turkmenistan		Montenegro	0.13	Turkmenistan	4.0	Turkmenistan	28

Source: Based on United Nations (2022) and World Bank (2022) data

Annex 4.5 Ranking of EU member states according to migration indicators in 2020[e]

Top 10 countries receiving remittances, $ billion		*Top 10 countries by share of remittances in GDP, %*		*Top 10 countries by the stock of migrants, millions of people*		*Top 10 countries by share of emigrants in the total population of the country of origin, %*		*Combined migration indicators' ranks*	
France	24.44	Croatia	7.0	Poland	4.82	Croatia	25.7	Croatia	1
Germany	17.89	Latvia	3.3	United Kingdom	4.73	Bulgaria	24.3	Romania	2
Belgium	13.12	Romania	3	Romania	3.98	Lithuania	23.5	Portugal	3
Italy	9.71	Luxembourg	2.9	Germany	3.85	Romania	20.7	Bulgaria	4
Spain	8.50	Belgium	2.6	Italy	3.25	Portugal	20.1	Poland	5
Romania	7.44	Hungary	2.4	France	2.34	Latvia	20	Lithuania	6
Poland	5.93	Cyprus	2.4	Portugal	2.08	Malta	19.5	Hungary	7
Portugal	4.32	Portugal	1.9	Bulgaria	1.68	Estonia	15.5	Germany	8
Czech Republic	4.18	Malta	1.9	Spain	1.48	Ireland	14.7	Latvia	9
Croatia	3.97	Slovakia	1.8	Greece	1.08	Cyprus	14.3	United Kingdom	10
Hungary	3.65	Czech Republic	1.7	Croatia	1.03	Luxembourg	12.9	France	11
United Kingdom	3.30	Estonia	1.6	Czech Republic	1.02	Poland	12.7	Italy	12
Sweden	3.09	Bulgaria	1.4	Netherlands	0.97	Greece	10.1	Belgium	13
Austria	3.08	Lithuania	1.4	Ireland	0.73	Czech Republic	9.6	Luxembourg	14
Netherlands	2.52	Slovenia	1.1	Hungary	0.71	Slovakia	7.7	Slovakia	15
Luxembourg	2.13	Poland	1.0	Lithuania	0.65	Slovenia	7.6	Spain	16
Slovakia	1.87	France	0.9	Austria	0.600	Hungary	7.3	Malta	17
Denmark	1.49	Spain	0.7	Belgium	0.57	United Kingdom	7	Czech Republic	18
Latvia	1.08	Austria	0.7	Slovakia	0.41	Austria	6.7	Austria	19
Bulgaria	0.95	Sweden	0.6	Latvia	0.38	Finland	5.6	Netherlands	20
Finland	0.80	Italy	0.5	Sweden	0.32	Netherlands	5.5	Estonia	21

(continued)

Annex 4.5 (continued)

Top 10 countries receiving remittances, $ billion		*Top 10 countries by share of remittances in GDP, %*		*Top 10 countries by the stock of migrants, millions of people*		*Top 10 countries by share of emigrants in the total population of the country of origin, %*		*Combined migration indicators' ranks*	
Lithuania	0.79	Germania	0.5	Finland	0.31	Italy	5.4	Ireland	22
Greece	0.61	Denmark	0.4	Denmark	0.25	Belgium	4.9	Cyprus	23
Cyprus	0.57	Finland	0.3	Estonia	0.20	Germania	4.6	Greece	24
Slovenia	0.55	Netherlands	0.3	Cyprus	0.17	Denmark	4.4	Slovenia	25
Estonia	0.50	Greece	0.3	Slovenia	0.16	France	3.4	Sweden	26
Ireland	0.36	United Kingdom	0.1	Malta	0.10	Spain	3.1	Finland	27
Malta	0.28	Ireland	0.1	Luxembourg	0.08	Sweden	3.1	Denmark	28

Source: Based on United Nations (2022) and World Bank (2022) data

References

Aguilera-Barchet, B. (2015). From the Germanic Tribes to Kingdoms. In: *A History of Western Public Law* (pp. 93–119). Springer.

Bethencourt, F. (2015). Christian Reconquest. In: *Racisms* (pp. 19–36). Princeton University Press.

Bunduchi, E., Vasile, V., Comes, C.-A., & Stefan, D. (2019). Macroeconomic Determinants of Remittances: Evidence from Romania. *Applied Economics, 51*(35), 3876. https://doi.org/10.1080/00036846.2019.1584386

Canny, N. (1985). Migration and Opportunity: Britain, Ireland and the New World on JSTOR. *Irish Economic and Social History, 12*, 7–32.

Department of Immigration and Border Protection (DIBP). (2015). *A History of the Department of Immigration Managing Migration to Australia.*

Drake, B. L. (2017). Changes in North Atlantic Oscillation drove Population Migrations and the Collapse of the Western Roman Empire. *Scientific Reports, 7*(1), 1–7. https://doi.org/10.1038/s41598-017-01289-z

Dunthorne, H. (2016). Migration to and from the Low Countries as a Factor in the Religious History of Early Modern Britain. *Journal of Low Countries Studies, 31*(2), 253–270. https://doi.org/10.1080/03096564.2007.11730902

European Commission. (2014). *Investment for Jobs and Growth: Promoting Development and Good Governance in EU Regions and Cities: Sixth Report on Economic, Social and Territorial Cohesion.* Publications Office of the European Union.

European Commission. (2017). *My Region, My Europe, Our Future: Seventh Report on Economic, Social and Territorial Cohesion.* Publications Office of the European Union. https://doi.org/10.2776/176864

European Parliament. (2021). Free Movement of Workers. In: *Fact Sheets on the European Union.* Accessed December 5, 2021, from https://www.europarl.europa.eu/factsheets/en/sheet/41/free-movement-of-workers.

Eurostat. (2021). Migration and migrant population statistics - Statistics Explained. In: *Statistics Explained.* Accessed October 17, 2021, form https://ec.europa.eu/eurostat/statistics-explained/index.php?title=Migration_and_migrant_population_statistics.

Fancy, H. A., & García Sanjuán, A. (2021). *What Was the Islamic Conquest of Iberia? Understanding the New Debate* (1st ed.). Routledge.

Gatrell, P. (2014). *Europe on the Move: Refugees and World War One.* British Library.

Gregory, J. N. (2005). *The Southern Diaspora: How the Great Migrations of Black and White Southerners Transformed America.* University of North Carolina Press.

Harris, C. D., & Wulker, G. (1953). The Refugee Problem of Germany. *Economic Geography, 29*(1), 10. https://doi.org/10.2307/142127

Heen-Pettersen, A. M. (2019). The Earliest Wave of Viking Activity? The Norwegian Evidence Revisited. *European Journal of Archaeology, 22*(4), 523–541. https://doi.org/10.1017/EAA.2019.19

IOM. (2021). World Migration Report 2022. In: *UN MIgration*. Accessed December 5, 2021, from https://publications.iom.int/books/world-migration-report-2022.

Knight, J. B. (2019). Migration Theory and 'Greek Colonisation'. Milesians at Naukratis and Abydos. *Revista do Museu de Arqueologia e Etnologia, 33*, 45–65. https://doi.org/10.11606/issn.2448-1750.revmae.2019.169246

Kobyliński, Z. (2005). The Slavs. In P. Fouracre (Ed.), *The New Cambridge Medieval History: Volume I C.500-C.700* (pp. 524–544). Cambridge University Press.

Kovacs, Z. (2019). *Migration Will Continue to Define Future Political Debates.* Accessed September 2, 2019, from http://abouthungary.hu/blog/pm-orban-migration-will-continue-to-define-future-political-debates/.

Kulischer, E. (1948). *Europe on the Move: War and Population Changes, 1917–1947.* Columbia University Press.

Manning, P., & Trimmer, T. (2013). *Migration in World History*. Routledge.

Mazzucco, N., Ibáñez, J. J., Capuzzo, G., Gassin, B., Mineo, M., & Gibaja, J. F. (2020). Migration, Adaptation, Innovation: The Spread of Neolithic Harvesting Technologies in the Mediterranean. *PLoS One, 15*(4), e0232455. https://doi.org/10.1371/JOURNAL.PONE.0232455

McCloud, A. B., Hibbard, S. W., & Saud, L. (2013). *An Introduction to Islam in the 21st Century*. Blackwell Publishing Ltd.

McCloy, S. T. (1951). Persecution of the Huguenots in the 18th Century. *Church History, 20*(3), 56–79. https://doi.org/10.2307/3161896

McNeill, W. H. (1999). The Steppe. In: *Britannica*. Accessed December 5, 2021, from https://www.britannica.com/place/the-Steppe/additional-info#history.

Mendizabal, I., Valente, C., Gusmão, A., Alves, C., & Gomes, V. (2011). Reconstructing the Indian Origin and Dispersal of the European Roma: A Maternal Genetic Perspective. *PLoS One, 6*(1), 15988. https://doi.org/10.1371/journal.pone.0015988

Messina, A. M. (2001). The Impacts of Post-WWII Migration to Britain: Policy Constraints, Political Opportunism and the Alteration of Representational Politics on JSTOR. *The Review of Politics, 63*(2), 259–285.

Migration Data Portal. (2021). Migration Data Relevant for the COVID-19 Pandemic. In: *Immigration & Emigration Statistics*. Accessed October 28, 2021, from https://www.migrationdataportal.org/themes/migration-data-relevant-covid-19-pandemic.

Mikhailova, T. A. (2020). Celtic Origin: Location in Time and Space? Reconsidering the "East-West Celtic" Debate. *Journal of Language Relationship, 13*(3–4), 257–280. https://doi.org/10.31826/jlr-2016-133-406

Moravcsik, G. (1946). Byzantine Christianity and the Magyars in the Period of Their Migration. *American Slavic and East European Review, 5*(3/4), 29. https://doi.org/10.2307/2492084

Murphy, A. B., Jordan-Bychkov, T. G., & Bella, B. J. (2002). *The European Culture Area: A Systematic Geography* (4th ed.). Rowman & Littlefield Publishers.

National Institute of Statistics. (2021). Internal and International Migration. In: *Tempo Online*. Social Statistics. Accessed October 22, 2021, from http://statistici.insse.ro:8077/tempo-online/#/pages/tables/insse-table.

OECD. (2014). *Is Migration Good for the Economy?* OECD.

Paige, R., & Witty, E. P. (2010). *The Black-White Achievement Gap: Why Closing It Is the Greatest Civil Rights Issue of Our Time*. AMACOM, American Management Association.

Pérez, J. (2005). *Los judíos en España. Castellano.*

Pleve, I. R., Rye, R. R., & American Historical Society of Germans from Russia. (2001). *The German Colonies on the Volga: The Second Half of the Eighteenth Century*. American Historical Society of Germans from Russia.

Pritchett, L. (2006). *Let Their People Come*. Center for Global Development.

Ratha, D., De, S., Plaza, S., Schuettler, K., Shaw, W., Wyss, H., & Yi, S. (2016). *Migration and Remittances*. World Bank. https://doi.org/10.1596/978-1-4648-0913-2

Roselaar, S. T. (2016). State-Organised Mobility in the Roman Empire: Legionaries and Auxiliaries. In: *Migration and Mobility in the Early Roman Empire* (pp. 138–157). Brill.

Rosenhaft, E. (2021). Strangers in Their Own Land: Romani Survivors in Europe 1945 | The National WWII Museum | New Orleans. In: *The National WWII Museum*. Accessed December 5, 2021, from https://www.nationalww2museum.org/war/articles/romani-holocaust-survivors-1945.

Şeker, N., & Nesim. (2013). *Forced Population Movements in the Ottoman Empire and the Early Turkish Republic: An Attempt at Reassessment through Demographic Engineering*. http://journals.openedition.org/ejts. https://doi.org/10.4000/EJTS.4396.

Statista. (2021). *Value of Remittance Flows Globally 2022*. Accessed December 5, 2021, from https://www.statista.com/statistics/962796/value-of-remittance-flows-globally/.

Torres, G., & Pelham, B. (2008). One-Quarter of World's Population May Wish to Migrate. In: *Gallup Poll*. Accessed October 2, 2019, from https://news.gallup.com/poll/108325/onequarter-worlds-population-may-wish-migrate.aspx.

United Nations. (2021). International Migrant Stock | Population Division. In: *Population Division*. https://www.un.org/development/desa/pd/content/international-migrant-stock.

United Nations. (2022). International Migrant Stock | Population Division. In: *Population Division*. Accessed October 17, 2021, from https://www.un.org/development/desa/pd/content/international-migrant-stock.

USGS. (2019). Glaciers Extended over Much of Europe during the Last Ice Age. In: *Science for a Changing World*. Accessed December 5, 2021, from https://www.usgs.gov/media/images/glaciers-extended-over-much-europe-during-last-ice-age.

World Bank. (2022). *Migration and Remittances Data. Annual Remittances Data*. Accessed August 13, 2021, from https://www.worldbank.org/en/topic/migrationremittancesdiasporaissues/brief/migration-remittances-data.

CHAPTER 5

Remittances vs. FDI: An Open Debate

Elena Bunduchi and Calin-Adrian Comes

In the process of economic growth, capital formation is extremely important, regardless of its origin. It is considered that foreign capital flows lead to increased availability, thus reducing the need for savings, while reducing, at the same time, trade constraints by expanding the import capacity of the beneficiary country (Prasad et al., 2007). Thus, the flow of foreign capital influences domestic economies and investments and stimulates economic development.

Along with the foreign direct investment, some countries benefit from remittances received from emigrants. Due to the fact that the volume of remittances exceeds \$700 billion globally in 2020 (World Bank, 2022a), and FDI—\$1.3 trillion (World Bank, 2022b), the role of these financial flows in economic development is of major interest for both researchers and policymakers alike. It is debatable, however, to what extent remittances can be considered as a financial flow for investments and to what extent they effectively and sustainably contribute to production-based growth in the migrants' country of origin.

There are a large number of studies on these determinants of economic growth, but only a few of these studies address the European Union and the less developed Member States with significant migration and/or remittances.

This research contributes to the debate on the influence of FDI level and of remittances on economic growth. The main objective is to assess the comparative impact of remittances and FDI on economic growth in

V. Vasile et al., *International Labour Mobility*,
https://doi.org/10.1007/978-3-031-18683-7_5

the recipient countries of remittances made by natives outside national borders.

With the increased emphasis of the international community on achieving the Sustainable Development Goals (United Nations, 2015), attention has been focused on the importance of various forms of capital flows and their effectiveness in achieving these goals.

Globally, remittances are the second largest source of foreign capital after FDI, surpassing the flows generated by official development assistance and portfolio investment (Ratha, 2019). For this reason, more and more researchers are conducting an associative analysis of the effects of both variables on the level of economic growth in beneficiary countries (Song et al., 2021; Driffield & Jones, 2013; Nwaogu & Ryan, 2015; Shafqat et al., 2017; Combes et al., 2019).

However, there are conflicting opinions concerning the impact of these capital flows on the growth of a state's economic level; some researchers argue that there is a positive impact on economic growth (Kashcheeva, 2013; Imai et al., 2014; Meyer & Shera, 2017; Bajra, 2021; Song et al., 2021; Kajtazi & Fetai, 2022); no link between the evolution of these variables and the economic growth of the beneficiary country (Beugelsdijk et al., 2008; Barajas et al., 2009; Gui-Diby et al., 2015; Lim & Simmons, 2015), while others have proved there is a contradictory impact on the level of economic development (Khaliq et al., 2007; Lartey et al., 2008; Song et al. 2021).

Therefore, the results of the experts show us:

- The limiting nature of the impact of remittances/FDI on economic growth, often with minimal, zero or even adverse effects.
- Limitation, with decreasing effects on the positive side and increasing effects for adverse effects, in particular on the sustainability of growth in time.
- Space limitation: In some geographical areas with poorly developed economies, economic growth is dependent on these sources and does not stimulate the multiplication of local growth engines. The reduction or cessation of these sources, through the major destructive intensive effects, annihilates/erodes the initial, previous positive effects.
- The dependence of the size of the impact on the nature of the activity for which financing is provided from these sources, respectively entrepreneurship vs. final consumption.

Data Analysis

The most important databases used were World Bank Indicators (for remittances and FDI), whereas data on total migrants are provided by the World Bank and the United Nations. The analysed time period is 2010–2019. Although data are also available for 2020, this year cannot be included in the analysis due to the COVID-19 pandemic, which generated atypical behaviours of migrants (mentioned in later chapters).

The present research is based on the comparative analysis of the impact of remittances/capita and of foreign direct investment/capita on GDP/capita in the Member States of the European Union and in the countries bordering the European Union, such as the Republic of Moldova, Serbia and Ukraine. These non-EU countries were included in the research due to the fact that they have a migration behaviour similar to the Eastern European states, and over 50% of the migrant population chose European Member States as their destination. Due to the differences between countries, in terms of both the magnitude of the migration phenomenon and its impact on the labour market, and in terms of the level of economic development, they were clustered into two stages. The first criterion was the rate of external labour mobility,[1] and the second was the value of GDP/capita. We consider it more relevant to classify states according to the rate of external labour mobility and not according to the emigration rate because people in labour mobility have a higher motivation in terms of remittances compared to those whose main residence is in another state. The number of the latter is much smaller, for example in Romania, according to National Institute of Statistics (2021) data, 21,031 people emigrated permanently in 2020. In comparison, the stock of the migrant population in Romania that is involved in the labour market of the destination states within the same period is 3.9 million people (United Nations, 2022).

Following the analysis of the external labour mobility rate, we note that it differs from one state to another, from about 44% in the Republic of Moldova to 3.15% in Spain, which also means that the impact of remittances on GDP/capita is different. At the same time, it is very important to take into account the size of GDP/capita, in order to analyse the effects of remittances in states with different levels of economic development. Thus, Fig. 5.1 shows that the higher the rate of external labour mobility,

[1] The rate of external labor mobility was calculated as the ratio between people in labour mobility and the total population in the country of origin.

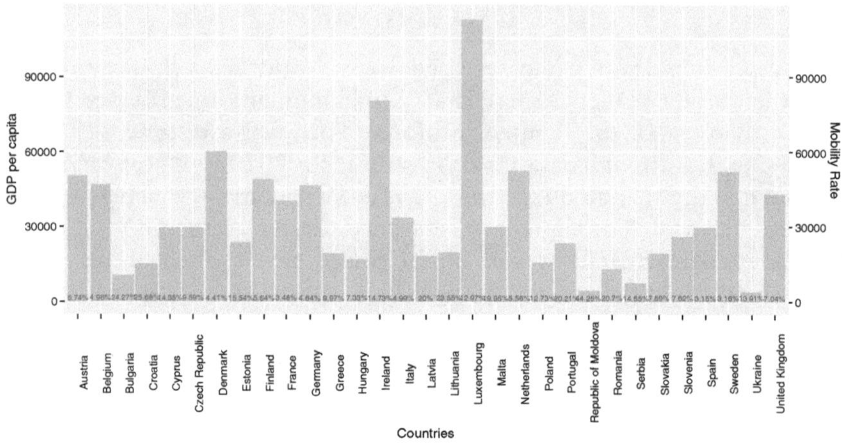

Fig. 5.1 External mobility rate for work and GDP/capita at the European level in 2019. (Source: Based on Eurostat (2021) and World Bank (2022c) data)

the lower the GDP/capita, with the exception of Ireland and Luxembourg. As a result, we decided on the following classification of the analysed states:

- Group no. 1—countries whose rate of external labour mobility exceeds 10%:

  (a) GDP/capita less than $15,000: Republic of Moldova, Romania, Bulgaria, Serbia and Ukraine
  (b) GDP/capita higher than $15,000: Malta, Portugal, Croatia, Lithuania, Latvia, Cyprus, Estonia and Poland, category from which we excluded Ireland and Luxembourg, due to the high value of GDP/capita and outlier behaviour

- Group no. 2—countries whose rate of external labour mobility is between 5 and 10%:

  (a) GDP/capita less than $30,000: Czech Republic, Greece, Slovakia, Slovenia and Hungary
  (b) GDP/capita higher than $30,000: United Kingdom, Austria, The Netherlands and Finland

- Group no. 3—countries whose rate of external labour mobility does not exceed 5%:

  (a) Germany, Italy, Belgium, Denmark, Sweden, France, Spain

Analysing Fig. 5.2 we can observe the classification of states depending on GDP/capita, with insignificant changes over the two years, except for Croatia and Cyprus. In the case of Croatia, there is an increase in remittances received in 2019 compared to 2010, due to the increase in remittance flows from 1.9 billion to 4.03 billion and the decreasing number of people with residence in the country of origin. Cyprus has a reverse evolution with a twice decrease in remittances/capita (from $774 to $365 per capita). The reduction of remittances/capita is registered due to the lack of motivation to remit to the country of origin, as the number of population and of migrants does not register significant changes, and only the flow of remittances is halved. This denotes the change of the motivation to migrate, from labour mobility to permanent or long-term migration.

In terms of GDP/capita there are no fluctuations which would require changes among the subgroups over the two years.

Within group no. 2, the tendency of subgrouping depending on the value of GDP/capita is also noticeable (Fig. 5.3). In the case of states whose GDP/capita does not exceed $30,000, there are changes in remittances/capita, even a tripling of these external financial resources per capita, except for Greece, where their value decreases. Thus, even in the case

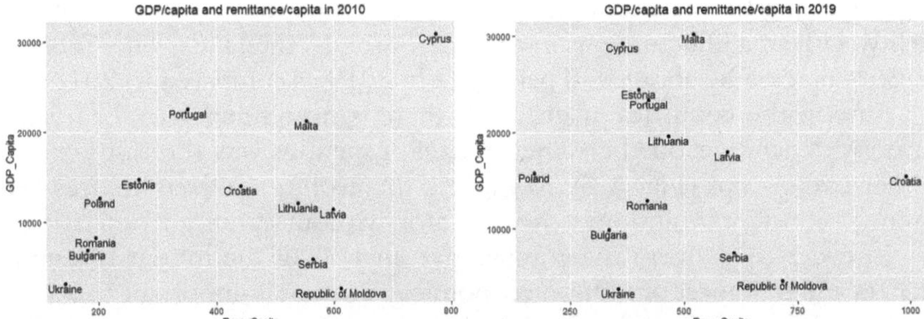

Fig. 5.2 GDP/capita and remittance/capita in 2010–2019, $ (group no.1). (Source: Based on World Bank (2022c) data)

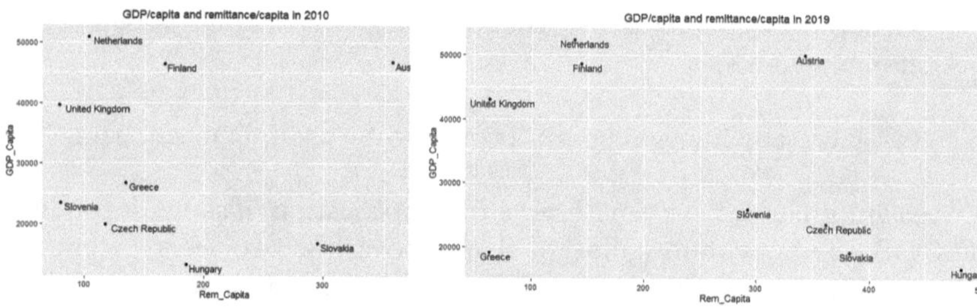

Fig. 5.3 GDP/capita and remittance/capita in 2010–2019, $ (group no.2). (Source: Based on World Bank (2022c) data)

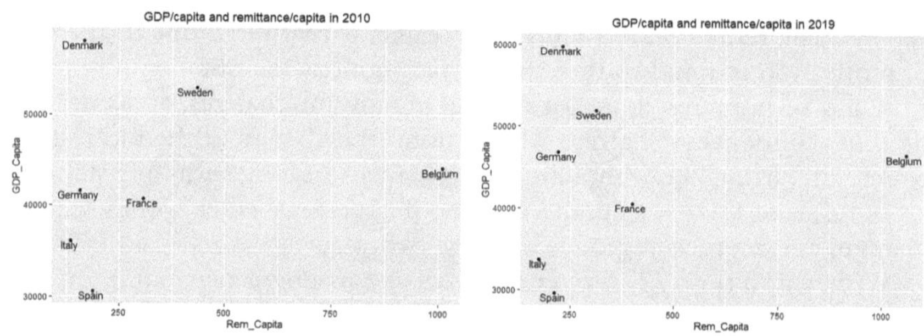

Fig. 5.4 GDP/capita and remittance/capita in 2010–2019, $ (group no.3). (Source: Based on World Bank (2022c) data)

of these countries, there is a noticeable tendency to increase interest in remittances.

Regarding the states with a higher GDP/capita, there is a trend of stability, with small fluctuations in the case of the Netherlands, where remittances increase by about $30 per capita in 2019 as compared to 2010.

Among the countries in group 3, there is no tendency to form subgroups depending on the value of GDP/capita, as was the case for the other two groups (Fig. 5.4). Regarding the evolution of remittances, we notice a constant evolution of this indicator, without significant oscillations.

In order to perform the comparative analysis of the impact of remittances and of impact of FDI on economic growth, it is important to follow the evolution of the FDI flow in the analysed states, in the previously established groups.

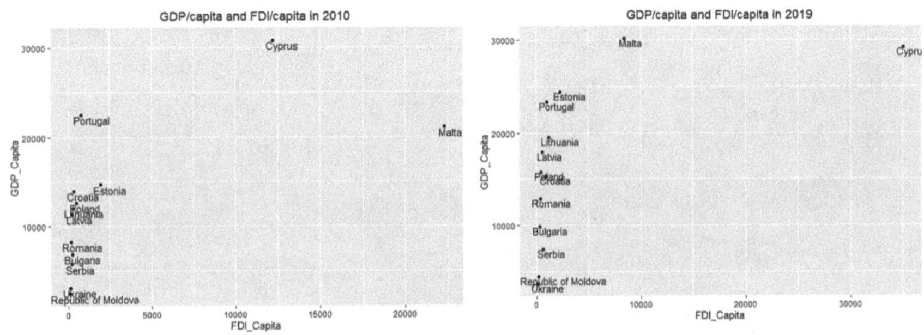

Fig. 5.5 GDP/capita and FDI/capita in 2010–2019, $ (group no.1). (Source: Based on World Bank (2022c) and (UNCTAD, 2022) data)

According to Fig. 5.5, at the level of 2019, all countries in group 1 are concentrated around the FDI level of $1000/capita, except for Malta and Cyprus. In comparison, in 2010 Malta registered over $20,000/capita, but as a result of the decisions taken by companies to withdraw FDI, decisions generated by the economic-financial crisis, it reached $8440/capita. Cyprus, on the other hand, has tripled its FDI/capita value to over $35,000. This increase is due to the significant improvement in the country's rating, attracting new investors in well-known fields, such as tourism, but also a significant investment of $500 million in casino space (Deloitte, 2019). In the case of the other states, there are no essential changes or high values of the indicator, due to the unattractiveness of the investment climate.

According to Fig. 5.6, we notice that the countries included in group 2 have a relatively constant evolution of FDI/capita in the period 2010–2019. Only the Netherlands and Hungary register significant changes from one period to another. As for Hungary, there is an increase in FDI/capita of over $12,000 in 2019 compared to 2010. From a totally unattractive country due to the excessive protection of local businesses, tax reforms and trade liberalization transformed Hungary into an interesting state for investors such as Germany, the United States or Austria. In opposition, the FDI/capita in the Netherlands decreased by almost $17,000. The reforms implemented in 2007–2008, during the financial crisis, strengthened the position of the Netherlands as one of the largest receipts and sources of FDI, but as a result of investor concern about higher trade costs with Europe following Brexit, FDI flows have fallen sharply.

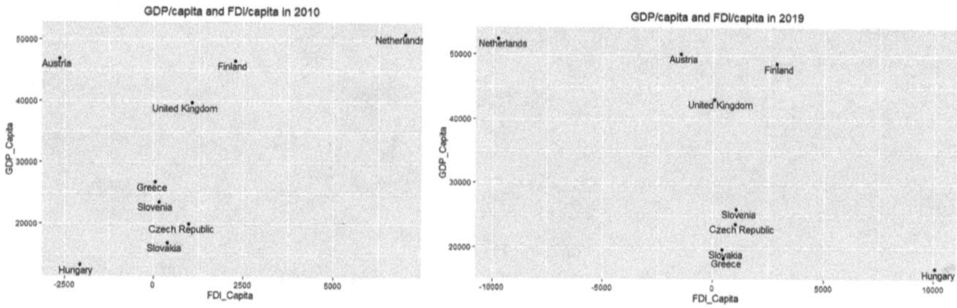

Fig. 5.6 GDP/capita and FDI/capita in 2010–2019, $ (group no.2). (Source: Based on World Bank (2022c) and (UNCTAD, 2022) data)

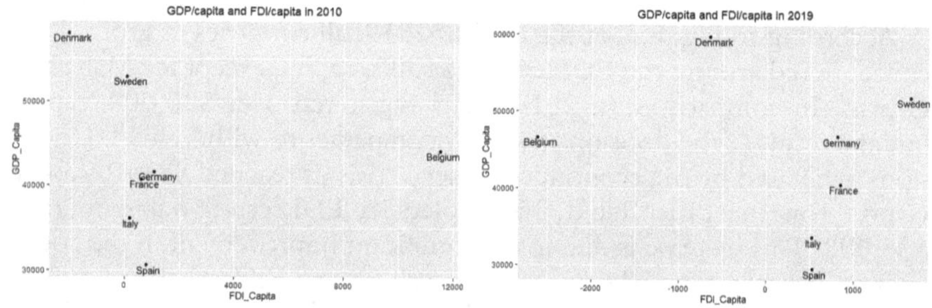

Fig. 5.7 GDP/capita and FDI/capita in 2010–2019, $ (group no.3). (Source: Based on World Bank (2022c) and (UNCTAD, 2022) data)

Within group 3, we can notice that flows fluctuate in both directions, in some states having a positive trend and in others—a negative one (Fig. 5.7). In France or Italy, for example, there have been increases in FDI/capita due to fiscal measures taken by the authorities to stimulate foreign investors. The countries with the largest reductions in FDI/capita are Belgium (from $11,500 to $2600), and Spain (from $1785 to $525). If in the case of Spain it is a matter of low labour productivity and its poor competitiveness, as well as the growing trade deficit, the decline in FDI in Belgium was driven by high energy prices and financial market instability.

Description of the Methodology and Econometric Model

In order to perform the empirical study, we used panel data to demonstrate the impact of the remittances on GDP on the one hand and of the foreign direct investment on GDP on the other hand.

In order to try to establish if there is a relationship between the analysed variables, we took into consideration the following economic hypotheses:

(a) H_1—the impact of remittance/capita and FDI/capita on GDP/capita is negative.
(b) H_2—the impact of remittance/capita and FDI/capita on GDP/capita is positive.
(c) H_3—remittance/capita and FDI/capita have no impact on GDP/capita.

To test the proposed hypotheses, we used the ordinary least squares method for the panel data model, in matrix form, which has the following econometric representation:

$$\text{GDP}_{it} = \beta_o + \text{Rem}_{it}^{'} \cdot \beta_1 + \text{FDI}_{it}^{'} \cdot \beta_2 + \epsilon_{it} \tag{5.1}$$

where

(i) represents the states on which the panel model was applied.
(t) represents the time coordinate, the period or the moment in time to which the terms of the time series refer, respectively 2010–2019, through annual variables.
(β_o) represents a scalar, which indicates the value of GDP when remittances are equal to zero.
(β_1) represents a dimensional vector $Kx1$, indicating the average value by which GDP/capita will change when remittances/capita change by one unit.
(β_2) represents a dimensional vector $Kx1$, indicating the average value by which FDI/capita will change when remittances/capita change by one unit.

(Rem_{it}) represents the observations of the explanatory variable remittances/capita.
(FDI_{it}) represents the observations of the explanatory variable FDI/capita.
(ϵ_{it}) represents the discrepancy or deviation variable.

The discrepancy or deviation variable is broken down into three components as follows (Baltagi, 2005):

$$\epsilon_{it} = \mu_{it} + \eta_{it} + \upsilon_{it} \tag{5.2}$$

where

(μ_{it}) represents the estimation of the individual specific effect of the analysed states, unobservable and not time dependent.
(η_{it}) estimates the specific temporal effect, which depends on time, invariable in the transversal structures, and on the analysed states respectively.
(υ_{it}) depends on the values recorded for remittance/capita, as well as on the analysed period, respectively the time interval 2010–2019.

We will perform the same analysis in the case of FDI, in order to demonstrate their impact on the GDP.

The selected econometric model ignores the other variables which could influence GDP/capita, using the Ceteris Paribus hypothesis.

Results and Discussions

In order to perform a comparative analysis of the impact generated by remittances and FDI on GDP/capita, we used a multifactorial model of econometric analysis, taking into account the Ceteris Paribus hypothesis (Table 5.1).

Applying the method of least squares on determining the impact of remittances and of foreign direct investments on economic growth for the period 2010–2019, we note that both the inflow of remittances and of FDI reported at the population level exert an influence, on average, in almost all countries in the analysis, except for the countries in group 3. Thus, without taking into account the country-specific elements of the analysed groups, the lower a country's level of development, the stronger the link between the level of economic development and the two external financial sources.

Table 5.1 Impact of remittances/capita and of FDI/capita on GDP/capita

	Estimated coeff	*Standard error*	*Test*	*Probability*	*First significance*	R^2	*F-stat*	*p-value*
Group 1 (GDP/capita <15,000$)								
Rem/cap	-6.6107	1.6457	-4.0171	0.000268	***	0.504	19.3319	1.6169e-06
FDI/cap	12.1004	2.3527	5.1433	8.48e-06	***			
Group 1 (GDP/capita > 15,000$)								
Rem/cap	-6.248524	3.2292	-1.9350	0.057279	.	0.218	9.20293	0.0002983
FDI/cap	0.370524	0.094322	3.9283	0.000207	***			
Group 2 (GDP/capita < 30,000$)								
Rem/cap	-14.81136	3.811140	-3.8863	0.000039	***	0.286	7.62709	0.00164
FDI/cap	0.046151	0.272614	0.1693	0.866465				
Group 2 (GDP/capita > 30,000$)								
Rem/cap	13.53795	4.901152	2.7622	0.01003	*	0.243	4.51774	0.01993
FDI/cap	0.166184	0.084193	1.9738	0.05834	.			
Group 3								
Rem/cap	5.95363	4.66237	1.2770	0.2067		0.028	0.84948	0.43289
FDI/cap	-0.26219	0.56215	-0.4664	0.6427				

Note: Significance threshold: 0 '***' 0.001 '**' 0.01 '*' 0.05 '.' 0.1 ' ' 1

For a more accurate analysis which takes into account the characteristics of each country, we included fixed and random effects, taking into account the results obtained after applying the Hausman test.

The results obtained in Table 5.2 allow us to apply the method of least squares with fixed effects for the states in group 1 and those with a GDP/capita lower than \$30,000 from group 2, as a result of the p-value value lower than 0.05, whereas for the states in group 2 (GDP/capita> \$30,000) and group 3 the application of the method of least squares with random effects is required.

The results obtained following the application of the least squares method differ when the random effects are introduced (Table 5.3); thus, we consider it necessary to apply the Breusch-Pagan test with the Lagrange multiplier (Table 5.4).

Following the application of the Breusch-Pagan test with the Lagrange multiplier, we find that the null hypothesis is rejected, the variations between the panel type data being obvious; thus, for the states in groups 2.1 and 3, the results obtained after the introduction of random effects are justified.

In order to draw economic conclusions, the results of the econometric tests taken into account will be those obtained from the application of the method of least squares with fixed or random effects, which are more conclusive compared to the application of a simple regression, except when the Breusch-Pagan Lagrange or Hausman test results prove otherwise.

Table 5.2 The Hausman test

		Chi sq	*Degrees of freedom*	*p-value*
Group 1 (external labour mobility rate > 10%)	GDP/capita < 15,000\$	9.2653	2	0.009729
	GDP/capita > 15,000\$	241.98	2	<2.2e-16
Group 2 (external labour mobility rate 5–10%)	GDP/capita < 30,000\$	60.842	2	6.142e-14
	GDP/capita > 30,000\$	3.3158	2	0.1905
Group 3 (external labour mobility rate <5%)		4.1314	2	0.1267

Table 5.3 The impact of per capita remittances and FDI on GDP per capita using fixed and random effects OLS

	Coeff	*Standard error*	*t test*	*probability*	*Pr sem.*	R^2	*F-stat*	*p-value*
Fixed effects								
Group 1 (GDP/capita < 15,000$)								
Rem/cap	6.0771	1.3106	4.6369	3.29e-05	***	0.5410	25.3421	5.354e-08
FDI/cap	2.8961	1.1974	2.4186	0.01989	*			
Group 1 (GDP/capita > 15,000$)								
Rem/cap	6.89319	3.437657	2.0052	0.04892	*	0.0589	2.1288	0.12684
FDI/cap	-0.046654	0.067442	-0.6918	0.49144				
Group 2 (GDP/capita < 30,000$)								
Rem/cap	10.1279	3.77176	2.6852	0.01026	*	0.1439	3.61534	0.035378
FDI/cap	-0.0462	0.13307	-0.3477	0.72978				
Random effects								
Group 2 (GDP/capita > 30,000$)								
Rem/cap	10.367	9.1641	1.1313	0.2579		0.0565	2.21811	0.32987
FDI/cap	-5.23e-02	7.05e-02	-0.7419	0.4582				
Group 3								
Rem/cap	3.28510	6.6832	4.9155	8.85e-07	***	0.2656	24.2308	5.474e-06
FDI/cap	8.850e-03	1.13e-01	0.0750	0.9402				

Note: Significance threshold: 0 '***' 0.001 '**' 0.01 '*' 0.05 '.' 0.1 ' ' 1

Table 5.4 The Breusch-Pagan test with the Lagrange multiplier

	Chi sq	*Degrees of freedom*	*p-value*
Group 2 (GDP/capita> 30,000$)	23.852	1	1.041e-06
Group 3—FDI	273.27	1	<2.2e-16

With the introduction of specific fixed effects, we note that, in the period 2010–2019, the remittances/capita generate positive effects among developing countries in group 1 and those in group 2.2 (GDP/capita> 30,000$), and in the case of the other countries, the lack of influence on the level of economic growth is confirmed (Table 5.5). Thus, on

Table 5.5 Synthesis of the fixed and random effects OLS

		Least squares method	*Least squares method fixed effects*	*Least squares method random effects*	*Hausman Test*	*Breusch-Pagan Lagrange test*
Group 1						
1.1 GDP/cap > $15,000	Rem/cap	Insignificant impact	Insignificant impact		Fixed effect	
	FDI/cap	Significant positive impact	Insignificant impact			
1.2 GDP/cap < $15,000	Rem/cap	Significant negative impact	Significant positive impact	–	Fixed effect	
	FDI/cap	Significant positive impact	Significant positive impact	–		
Group 2						
2.1 GDP/cap > 30,000$	Rem/cap	Significant positive impact	–	Significant positive impact		Random effect
	FDI/cap	Insignificant impact	–	Insignificant impact		
2.2 GDP/cap < 30,000$	Rem/cap	Significant negative impact	Insignificant impact	–	Fixed effect	
	FDI/cap	Insignificant impact	Insignificant impact	–		
Group 3						
	Rem/cap	Insignificant impact	–	Significant positive impact		Random effect
	FDI/cap	Insignificant impact	–	Insignificant impact		

average, developing countries in group 1 register an increase of $6.89 in GDP/capita when remittances/capita increase by $1, but FDI does not generate on average an influence on the level of economic development. The obtained results further confirm the theory according to which poor countries are dependent on remittances, and their entire economy is based on remittances, the active population being very involved in labour migration. In these countries, the population migrates mainly for economic reasons, especially for a higher wage differential in the country of destination, so that those flows ensure an increase in the standard of living of the family left at home. Regardless of the direction in which these external financial resources are used, to improve living standards, for current consumption or for investment, they generate economic growth, results supported as well by researchers such as (Adams & Page, 2005; Benmamoun & Lehnert, 2013; Meyer & Shera, 2017), the latter even analysing states such as Romania and the Republic of Moldova, by using the least squares method with fixed effects.

At the same time, countries in group 1 are less attractive to investors, due to economic, political or social instability, bureaucracy and the exodus of highly skilled labour.

As for the other group of states (GDP/capita > $15,000), both external financial flows are found as promoters of economic growth, having on average a positive impact on GDP per capita. This category includes the states that have recently joined the European Union and which are also more attractive to foreign investors. Although the citizens of these states enjoy the principle of free movement, with a rate of external labour mobility below 10% of the total population, which generates remittances, these states remain an opportunity for foreign investors.

The same positive impact of remittances can be found in group 2.1 and group 3, where the increase of $1 in remittances/capita leads to the increase of GDP/capita by $10.12 and 3.28 $, respectively. At the other extreme are the countries in group 2.2, where remittances do not significantly influence the value of GDP/capita. This phenomenon can be explained by the low value of remittances/capita within group 2.2 (Fig. 5.3).

The fact that remittances do not generate the expected effects in the economy can be explained by several factors. Firstly, in these states, the value of remittances/capita is the lowest (about $100/capita). Secondly, even if remittance increases over time were measured correctly, there would be too little power in the panel data to detect even the substantial growth effects of remittance developments. Thirdly, the volume of remittances and their impact in the beneficiary countries depend on the nature of the migration registered in the countries of origin.

Even if remittances positively influence almost all analysed groups of states, what is most important is the motivation behind the remittance decision. In less developed countries, the reason for labour migration is obvious: generating remittances to ensure a decent standard of living for family members left at home, migrants being mainly involved in seasonal, short- or medium-term migration. In the category of developed countries, the motivation for migration is not the increase of household income, but rather professional development and career opportunities. Thus, those people remit little to nothing, having no economic motivation for migration and remission.

Partial Conclusions

In order to draw a conclusion on the impact of remittances and foreign direct investment on the level of GDP/capita, we must take into account the nature of these explanatory variables and their behaviour in the economy. Although both remittances and FDI are considered to be promoters of economic growth, depending on their direction, they can generate short-term or long-term effects in the beneficiary economies. Remittances received by family members in the migrants' countries of origin are mainly directed towards consumption and/or the purchase of durable goods or small family businesses. Flows, which ensure the consumption level of the family left in the country of origin, may thus have an immediate impact on the level of economic growth, or a delayed impact and cannot be found in the value of GDP of the current year. Regarding the impact of FDI on the level of economic growth, it can only be felt in GDP in the long run. FDI, unlike remittances, does not aim to meet the needs of current consumption or purchases of goods, but mainly those of the real sector. Thus, the process required to set up FDI enterprises and their economic results will not have an immediate effect on GDP. Although the effects of FDI are felt in the long run, which could explain the lack of influence on the level of economic growth in the analysed countries, in the group of states with a GDP/capita below $15,000 the impact is positive in 2010–2019. Although FDI inflows are much lower compared to countries in the other groups, their share in GDP is much higher, thus explaining the significant impact of these external flows on the level of economic growth.

As a result of the delayed effects of these external flows, there is a need to use a dynamic econometric model, in order to ascertain the impact generated in the economy of the beneficiary states. But the application of a dynamic model, with lag variables, implies the reduction of the analysed period. Such a model would demonstrate the impact of the flow of remittances for the current year or for the next year following their inflow, if they were directed towards consumption. Their impact could otherwise be demonstrated after 2–3 years if we are talking about remittances and FDI flows investment-oriented on the level of economic growth. Therefore, the dynamic model arises by introducing a lag-dependent variable, but since the analysed period is short (2010–2019), the problem of endogeneity arises, and the results thus obtained will be insignificant.

References

Adams, R. H., & Page, J. (2005). Do International Migration and Remittances Reduce Poverty in Developing Countries? *World Development, 33*(10), 1645–1669. https://doi.org/10.1016/J.WORLDDEV.2005.05.004

Bajra, U. Q. (2021). The Interactive Effects of Remittances on Economic Growth and Inequality in Western Balkan Countries. *Journal of Business Economics and Management, 22*(3), 757–775. https://doi.org/10.3846/JBEM.2021.14587

Baltagi, B. H. (2005). *Econometric Analysis of Panel Data* (3rd ed.). John Wiley & Sons Ltd.

Barajas, A., Chami, R., Fullenkamp, C., Gapen, M., & Montiel, P. (2009). *Do Workers' Remittances Promote Economic Growth?*

Benmamoun, M., & Lehnert, K. (2013). Financing Growth: Comparing the Effects of Fdi, Oda, and International Remittances. *Journal of Economic Development, 38*(2), 43–65.

Beugelsdijk, S., Smeets, R., Zwinkels, R., Beugelsdijk, S., Smeets, R., & Zwinkels, R. (2008). *International Business Review*. Pergamon Press.

Combes, J.-L., Kinda, T., Ouedraogo, R., & Plane, P. (2019). Financial Flows and Economic Growth in Developing Countries. *Economic Modelling, 83*, 195. https://doi.org/10.1016/J.ECONMOD.2019.02.010

Deloitte. (2019). Foreign Direct Investment in Cyprus and the Real Economy. In: *A middle East Pint of View*. https://www2.deloitte.com/content/dam/Deloitte/xe/Documents/About-Deloitte/mepovdocuments/mepov30/cyprus-foreign-direct-investment_mepov30.pdf.

Driffield, N., & Jones, C. (2013). Impact of FDI, ODA and Migrant Remittances on Economic Growth in Developing Countries: A Systems Approach. *The European Journal of Development Research, 25*(2), 173–196. https://doi.org/10.1057/ejdr.2013.1

Eurostat. (2021). Migration and Migrant Population Statistics - Statistics Explained. In: *Statistics Explained*. https://ec.europa.eu/eurostat/statistics-explained/index.php?title=Migration_and_migrant_population_statistics.

Gui-Diby, S. L., Renard, M.-F., Gui-Diby, S., & Renard, M.-F. (2015). *Foreign Direct Investment Inflows and the Industrialization of African Countries.*

Imai, K. S., Gaiha, R., Ali, A., & Kaicker, N. (2014). Remittances, Growth and Poverty: NEW Evidence from Asian Countries. *Journal of Policy Modeling, 36*(3), 524–538. https://doi.org/10.1016/j.jpolmod.2014.01.009

Kajtazi, K., & Fetai, B. T. (2022). Does the Remittance Generate Economic Growth in the South East European Countries? *Scientific Annals of Economics and Business, 69*(1), 57–67.

Kashcheeva, M. (2013). The Role of Foreign Direct Investment in the Relation between Intellectual Property Rights and Growth. *Oxford Economic Papers, 65*(3), 699–720. https://doi.org/10.1093/oep/gpt015

Khaliq, A., Noy, I., Khaliq, A., & Noy, I. (2007). *Foreign Direct Investment and Economic Growth: Empirical Evidence from Sectoral Data in Indonesia.*

Lartey, E. K. K., Mandelman, F., & Acosta, P. A. (2008). Remittances, Exchange Rate Regimes, and the Dutch Disease: A Panel Data Analysis. *SSRN Electronic Journal.* https://doi.org/10.2139/ssrn.1109206

Lim, S., & Simmons, W. O. (2015). Do remittances Promote Economic Growth in the Caribbean Community and Common Market? *Journal of Economics and Business, 77*, 42–59. https://doi.org/10.1016/j.jeconbus.2014.09.001

Meyer, D., & Shera, A. (2017). The Impact of Remittances on Economic Growth: An Econometric Model. *Economia, 18*(2), 147–155. https://doi.org/10.1016/J.ECON.2016.06.001

National Institute of Statistics. (2021). Internal and International Migration. In: *Tempo Online. Social Statistics.* http://statistici.insse.ro:8077/tempo-online/#/pages/tables/insse-table.

Nwaogu, U. G., & Ryan, M. J. (2015). FDI, Foreign Aid, Remittance and Economic Growth in Developing Countries. *Review of Development Economics, 19*(1), 100–115. https://doi.org/10.1111/rode.12130

Prasad, E. S., Rajan, R. G., & Subramanian, A. (2007). *Foreign capital and economic growth.*

Ratha, D. (2019). Remittances on Track to Become the Largest Source of External Financing in Developing Countries. In: *World Bank.* https://blogs.worldbank.org/peoplemove/remittances-track-become-largest-source-external-financing-developing-countries.

Shafqat, M. M., Xia, E., Bari, M. W., & Baloch, M. A. (2017). Linkage between Remittances and FDI: Evidence from Low-Income Countries. In: *2017 4th International Conference on Industrial Economics System and Industrial Security Engineering (IEIS)* (pp. 1–5). IEEE.

Song, Y., Paramati, S. R., Ummalla, M., Zakari, A., & Kummitha, H. R. (2021). The Effect of Remittances and FDI Inflows on Income Distribution in Developing Economies. *Economic Analysis and Policy, 72*, 255–267. https://doi.org/10.1016/J.EAP.2021.08.011

UNCTAD. (2022). Foreign Direct Investment: Inward and Outward Flows and Stock Per Capita, Annual. In: *UNCTAD Statistics*. https://unctadstat.unctad.org/wds/TableViewer/tableView.aspx.

United Nations. (2015). Transforming our World: The 2030 Agenda for Sustainable Development A/RES/70/1.

United Nations. (2022). International Migrant Stock | Population Division. In: *Population Division*. https://www.un.org/development/desa/pd/content/international-migrant-stock.

World Bank. (2022a). *Migration and Remittances Data*. Annual Remittances Data. https://www.worldbank.org/en/topic/migrationremittancesdiasporaissues/brief/migration-remittances-data

World Bank. (2022b). *Foreign Direct Investment, Net Inflows (BoP, Current US$)*. In *The World Bank Indicators*. https://data.worldbank.org/indicator/BX.KLT.DINV.CD.WD

World Bank. (2022c). *GDP per Capita (Current US$)*. In *The World Bank*. https://data.worldbank.org/indicator/NY.GDP.PCAP.CD

CHAPTER 6

Are Remittances a Real Promoter of Economic Growth in Origin Countries? Case Study: Romania vs. Republic of Moldova

Elena Bunduchi

Remittances are considered as a determinant of economic growth in the specialized literature (through their use for consumption or investment), but we are interested to see if this impact is sustainable, respectively, if the amount of remittances is significant in volume, so as to generate sustainable economic growth in the medium and long term. Therefore, we consider that it is necessary to identify: (a) to what extent the use of remittances mainly for consumption stimulates the domestic/national production of goods and services (or only stimulates imports); (b) the level at which remittances used for development investment and entrepreneurship can be a sustainable source for economic growth (investment in fixed assets—durable goods, housing, holiday homes—vs. investment in business—new business or financing existing businesses). The available database includes the period 1995–2019.

The challenge and limitation of the research is that broken time series are available for some indicators, and the last two years cannot be included in the analysis due to the impact of the COVID-19 pandemic, which requires a completely different approach to the impact on migration and remittances and vice versa.

This chapter represents a continuation of the research, which was materialized through the publication of an article (Vasile et al., 2019), and

V. Vasile et al., *International Labour Mobility*,
https://doi.org/10.1007/978-3-031-18683-7_6

following the new virus, we considered it necessary to continue the research including data up to the year 2019, in order to capture the extent of the phenomenon before the COVID-19 pandemic.

Literature Review

The theory and especially economic practice have shown that any change in the components of development or in the functioning of an economic and social ecosystem produces externalities, both positive and negative, which are activated and act upon:

(a) In the short, medium and/or long term.
(b) With constant or variable intensity, often difficult to predict.
(c) Direct externalities are often associated with indirect ones, following different propagation models.
(d) The resilience of the primary economic and social ecosystem redefines the functioning parameters through adjustments of primary variables (long-term remittances adjust the size of labour supply in the home country for the present generation and especially for the future).

If the predominant externalities can be defined relatively clearly as positive or negative from the perspective of the components of the economic-social ecosystem, globally, it is cumulatively estimated that remittances produce favourable cumulative effects, the pillar of the win-win principle, but unbalanced as sustainable net benefits. The analysis of the effects of migration and remittances, regardless of the approach and level of detail, showed that the benefits are clearly to the advantage of the destination country, while at the level of the individual—the temporary migrant, they are differentiated in the long term depending on the mobility period and the cumulative benefits of migration adjusted for negative direct and indirect externalities, such as type of unemployment opportunities in the country of origin, and the option for migration of more educated children.

There is rich literature on the impact of remittances in the origin country, which addresses each area of influence of remittances separately. In the following we have made a synthesis of the latest research in the literature in the field (Table 6.1).

We can conclude that remittances are an essential source of income, particularly in poor households, and their primary destinations are towards the improvement of living and housing conditions, consumption, education and health expenditure and small investments in housing.

Table 6.1 Literature review regarding the impact of remittances on the country of origin

Authors	*Database*	*Empirical approach*	*Research conclusions*
Economic development			
(Eggoh et al., 2019)	49 developing states	Panel Smooth Transition Regression	Remittances have a positive impact on the economic growth
(Fromentin, 2017)	102 developing and transition states	Pooled Mean Group	In the short term, households that receive remittances are more prone to use official financial services and instruments for their transactions and payments
(Meyer & Shera, 2017)	Albania, Bulgaria, North Macedonia, Republic of Moldova, Romania, Bosnia and Herzegovina	Ordinary least squares (OLS) with fixed effects	The presence of the positive link between remittances and GDP growth in the research states
(Imai et al., 2014)	24 Asia Pacific states	Panel vector autoregressive model	Remittances contribute to economic growth in the analysed states
(Giuliano & Ruiz-Arranz, 2009)	100 developing states	Generalized method of moments	Remittances generate to GDP growth in the analysed states
Poverty and inequality			
(Vacaflores, 2018)	18 Latin American states	GMM estimator for dynamic panel data	Increasing remittances in countries of origin contributes to reducing poverty and inequality
(Girsberger et al., 2018)	Economic Community of West African States	Gini Index, IQ-Ratio, log-deviation and Theil T	Remittances help reduce inequality, but the impact is much stronger in countries with lower levels of development
(Imai et al., 2014)	24 Asia Pacific states	Panel vector autoregressive model	Remittances contributes to poverty reduction in analysed countries
(Giannetti et al., 2009)	Slovenia, Poland, Czech Republic and Hungary	OLS with fixed effects	Remittances contribute to economic growth and reduction of poverty in the countries analysed

(*continued*)

Table 6.1 (continued)

Authors	*Database*	*Empirical approach*	*Research conclusions*
Labour market			
(Vadean et al., 2019)	Tajikistan	3SL	Remittances reduce the employed population in favour of the self-employed, especially in agriculture. Also, they generate small family investments, with no macroeconomic effects and limited positive effects at household level
(Azizi, 2018)	122 developing states	OLS with fixed effects in dynamic panel data	Remittance inflows generate a decline in the number of employed women, but do not influence men
(Boboc et al., 2012)	Romania		Migration and remittance inflows have positive effects on reducing the unemployment rate and balance the labour market
Consumption			
(Basnet et al., 2022)	Central America	Fully modified ordinary least squares method (FMOLS)	Due to the fact that remittances are seen as elements of permanent income, they are directed to current consumption
(Mishra et al., 2022)	Nepal	2SLS Regression	Remittances have a major impact on the increase in spending on food and clothing among beneficiary families
(Beaton et al., 2017)	Latin America and the Caribbean	Dynamic panel model	Remittances increase consumption, mainly as a result of enabling access to sources of financing
(Medina & Cardona, 2010)	Columbia	Panel model	No effects of remittances on household current consumption, but they improve the living standards of the beneficiary households
Health			

(*continued*)

Table 6.1 (continued)

Authors	*Database*	*Empirical approach*	*Research conclusions*
(Azizi, 2018)	122 developing states	OLS with fixed effects in dynamic panel data	There is an increase in households' health care expenditure. In addition, the mortality rate decreases with the increase of remittances
(Adams et al., 2013)	Ghana	Two-stage multinomial logit model	Remittances lead to an increase in health care expenditure
(Zhunio et al., 2012)	69 developed and developing countries	GLS with side effects	Households receiving remittances experience an increase in life expectancy and an improvement in living standards
Education			
(Mishra et al., 2022)	Nepal	2SLS Regression	Remittances contribute to increased expenditures for education
(Ambler et al., 2015)	El Salvador	Panel model with fixed effects	For every $1 remittance received by migrants' households, education-related expenditures grew by $3.72
(Adams et al., 2013)	Ghana	Two-stage multinomial logit model	Remittances determine an increase in education-related expenditure
(Zhunio et al., 2012)	69 developed and developing countries	GLS with side effects	Remittance inflows to households increase the schooling rate

Data and Methods

The used databases in this chapter have the following sources: the Romanian National Institute of Statistics (NIS), the National Bureau of Statistics of the Republic of Moldova (NBS), the National Bank of Romania (NBR), the National Bank of Moldova (NBM) and the World Bank. The analysed period is 1995–2019, with some exceptions: for household savings we have data series only for Romania; for the Republic of Moldova, the share of households with internet access is available for the period 1996–2019, labour market indicators cover the period 2000–2019 and the types of household expenditures are available only starting from 2006.

Our comparative analysis includes Romania and the Republic of Moldova because of the importance these external financial flows have for their economy as we have previously demonstrated by the literature review. Even though the share of remittances in the GDP of the two states differs due to their economic level, and due to the predominant remittance model, the ever-increasing number of people leaving for work is a common feature for both.

The present research uses the OLS regression model, in order to analyse the impact of remittances from the perspective of the country of origin—Romania and the Republic of Moldova.

At the level of econometric research, we consider it important to analyse the following aspects which can be influenced by remittances (the variables used for the econometric analysis are found in Annex 6.1):

- The labour market and its balances
- Final consumption at macroeconomic level, respectively the consumption reflected in the variation in imports
- Potential disparities on the balance of payments
- Current consumption expenditures of households and expenditures for durable goods
- Quality of life, reflected in the evolution of expenditure on health and education
- Human capital, expressed through expenditures in education and pupils and students' propensity for education
- The degree of implementation of ICT technologies and services in households.

The econometric analysis in the present research is based on the simple linear regression model. Through the simple linear regression model, we will identify whether there is a direct and statistically significant link between remittance flows, acting as an independent variable, and dependent variables (Annex 6.1), by developing several equations.

The general model is presented in the following form:

$$Y_i = \beta_0 + \beta_1 X_i + \varepsilon_i \tag{6.1}$$

where:

Y_i represents the dependent variable,
X_i represents the independent variable—remittances,
β_0 is the intercept, it shows the mean value of the variable Y when the size of the independent variable X is equal to 0,
β_1 represents the slope, it shows the mean variation of the dependent variable Y, at an absolute variation by one unit of the variable X,
ε_i represents the residual variable.

Estimation of the parameters of the OLS regression model will be performed by the least squares method, using the *R* programming language.

In order to normalize the data series for some absolute value variables, their log transformation was used, so that the interpretation of the obtained results will take into account this aspect. The remittances independent variable was log-transformed, so that when the independent variable is not log-transformed, the coefficients will be interpreted by being divided by 100.

Part I. Macroeconomic Impact of Remittances in Countries of Origin

In order to underline the impact of remittances on the country of origin, we consider it important to perform a multidimensional analysis:

(a) *The effects of remittances on the labour market in the country of origin*

The trend of the key labour market indicators in the two countries shows similarities since 2002, when there is a reduction of both the active and the employed population (Fig. 6.1). The employment-to-population ratio has also been decreasing, which is a negative phenomenon for the labour market in the two states, and for the economy in general. The reduction in the number of the active population and the employment rate is caused both by the migration of the population and the discouragement of work for remittances' beneficiaries. Remittance recipients are no longer motivated to work long hours or even to work at all. Nguyen and Purnamasari (2011) and Acosta et al. (2008) demonstrated that the flow of remittances reduces the number of hours worked by family members left at home, and Guha (2013) shows that as the flow of remittances

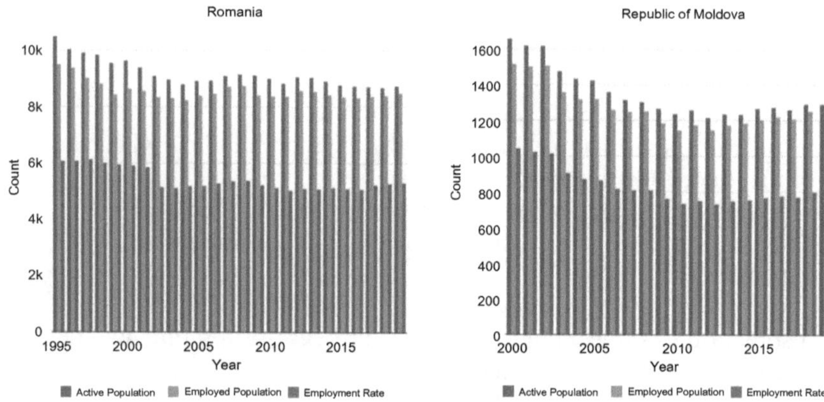

Fig. 6.1 Active and employed population and the employment rate. (Source: Based on data from NIS and NBS)

increases, the members of the beneficiary households are no longer motivated to work as much, or even to have a job in their home country.

If, in the case of the employed population and of the employment rate, the phenomenon of international migration has negative effects, but the same trend of the unemployment rate generated by migration is perceived as a positive impact. Balancing the labour market by reducing the number of people without a job has positive effects both at the macroeconomic level and at the level of households.

From Fig. 6.2 we notice that, both in Romania and in the Republic of Moldova, the unemployment rate is decreasing in the years after the crisis, compared to the period prior to the accession to the European Union. Since 2007, when Romanians obtained the right to free movement in some of the EU states, the number of unemployed decreased by over 200,000 people, but not all those who left the country were among the unemployed. Most of the new international migrants were employed at home. The reduction in the unemployment rate registered in the Republic of Moldova is closely correlated with Romania's accession to the EU, given the fact that many Moldovans hold Romanian citizenship (Necsutu, 2021) and choose one of Western Europe as a work destination. The obvious increase during the economic crisis is justified, both in terms of the economic context in the origin and in the destination countries. But after the economic and financial crisis, the unemployment rate in the two

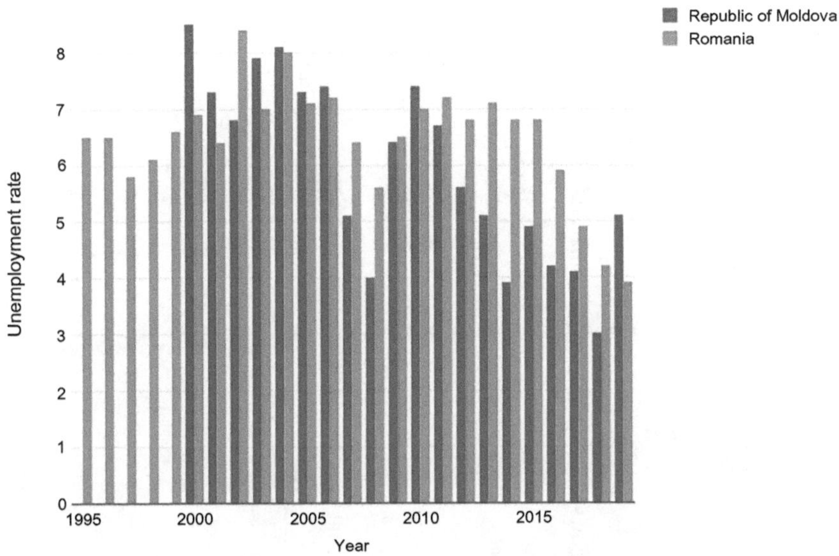

Fig. 6.2 Unemployment rate in Romania and the Republic of Moldova in 1995–2019, %. (Source: Based on NIS (National Institute of Statistics, 2022a) and NBS (National Bureaus of Statistics, 2022) data)

countries has unpredictable fluctuations, which cannot be associated with the trend of the flow of migrants to other destination states.

The analysis of the unemployment rate and of the other indicators of the labour market from the two countries in the period included in the research allowed us to emphasize the following findings:

- There is no strong dependence between the dynamics of the unemployment rate and the flows of external migration for work, because significant numbers of people who left were employed or graduates (without registration as unemployed or looking for a job in the country) (Table 6.2).
- The crisis has not generated long-term return migration or permanent return (International Organization for Migration (IOM), 2013), even if the unemployment rate has increased in immigration countries (Vasile, 2013).

Although there are numerous studies according to which, at the level of the country of origin, remittances have a positive impact on the labour

Table 6.2 Dynamics of the number of unemployed and the flows of migrants in Romania and the Republic of Moldova, persons

	Δ 2000/1995	Δ 2005/2000	Δ 2010/2005	Δ 2015/2010	Δ 2017/2015	Δ 2019/2017
Romania						
Unemployed	26,706	-74,901	-48,869	-27,785	-174,579	-95,961
Migrants flow	162,367	1,005,824	1,215,073	51,364	254,731	408,589
R. Moldova						
Unemployed	–	-36,400	-11,700	-29,900	-10,500	-4700
Migrants flow	-19,220	114,986	117,283	91,122	49,285	185,825

Source: Based on NIS (National Institute of Statistics, 2022a), NBS (National Bureaus of Statistics, 2022) and United Nations (2021) data

market imbalances (Boboc et al., 2012), the results obtained after applying the regression are different in the case of Romania and the Republic of Moldova.

Remittances exert a stronger impact on the labour market indicators in the Republic of Moldova than in Romania. It is expected, because remittances in the Republic of Moldova are much more important for households: in 2019 the share of remittances in GDP is 5 times higher in the Republic of Moldova than in Romania (15.95% compared to 3.25%) (World Bank, 2022a), and the share of labour migration in the total population in the Republic of Moldova is 44% compared to about 20% in Romania.

According to Tables 6.3, remittances have no effect on the unemployment rate in Romania and a moderate reduction of 0.0047% of the rate in the Republic of Moldova at each 1% increase in external flows. The results suggest that job mobility does not come mainly from the unemployed, but rather from the inactive or even from the employed population. The results also support the data of a European Commission (2010) report according to which Romanians are not willing to migrate in search of a job from the status of unemployed (only 34% of all respondents would migrate if they did not have a job in Romania). Likewise, the results can be more significant if we analyse the remittances considering the informal economy, which involves more than 1.2 million persons (European Commission, 2017) and represent over 21% of Romania's GDP, in the year 2020 (European Commission, 2020) and over 23.2% of the GDP of the Republic of Moldova (Medina & Schneider, 2018).

Regarding the employment market indicators, we notice the same effect of remittances, both in Romania and in the Republic of Moldova. Therefore, the growth of remittance inflows in Romania by 1% determines in average a decline of the active population by 0.021%, of the employed population by 0.0112%, as well as of the employment rate of Romanians by 0.0144%. In the Republic of Moldova, the influence of remittances is more pronounced, and as a result, on average, their increase by 1% determines the reduction of the active population by 0.125%, of the employed population by 0.108% and of the employment rate by 0.0658%.

Therefore, employed people leave their jobs, especially in the case of those in the Republic of Moldova, since the income gap is large and migration answers to the need for supplementary income in the household.

Table 6.3 Impact of remittance on the labour market indicators

Impact indicators		*Coefficients*	*Standard error*	*t-test*	*Sign threshold*
ROMANIA					
	Intercept	9.5552	0.0538	177.35	***
Active population	**Remittances**	-0.0216	0.002	-8.0577	***
p-value 3.79e-08					
	Intercept	9.2797	0.0596	155.63	***
Employed population	**Remittances**	-0.0112	0.0029	-3.7900	***
p-value 0.000946					
	Intercept	82.7441	5.8889	14.0506	***
Employment rate	**Remittances**	-1.4407	0.2912	-4.9463	***
p-value 6e-05					
	Intercept	14.8604	0.3178	46.7560	***
Unemployed	**Remittances**	-0.0750	0.0158	*-4.7385*	***
p-value 8.93e-05					
	Intercept	10.9704	2.2158	4.9509	***
Unemployment rate	**Remittances**	-0.2238	0.1096	-2.0427	
p-value 0.0532					
MOLDOVA					
	Intercept	8.0815	0.0487	165.84	***
Active population	**Remittances**	-0.1253	0.0069	-18.12	***
p-value 5.25e-13					
	Intercept	7.9034	0.0639	123.67	***
Employed population	**Remittances**	-0.1084	0.0090	-11.96	***
p-value 5.31e-10					
	Intercept	89.4984	2.7312	32.76	***
Employment rate	**Remittances**	-6.5839	0.3875	-16.98	***
p-value 1.58e-12					
	Intercept	7.0776	0.5093	13.89	***
Unemployed	**Remittances**	-0.3932	0.0722	-5.44	***
p-value 3.61e-05					
	Intercept	9.4743	1.4572	6.50	***
Unemployment rate	**Remittances**	-0.4770	0.2216	-2.15	.
p-value 0.042					

Note: Significance threshold: 0 '***' 0.001 '**' 0.01 '*' 0.05 '.' 0.1 ' ' 1

Simultaneously, the determinants of remittances as a consequence of labour mobility impacts the acceleration of the aging process of the active population and the increase of the average age in the country of origin, due to the fact that labour migrants are mostly young, of working age.

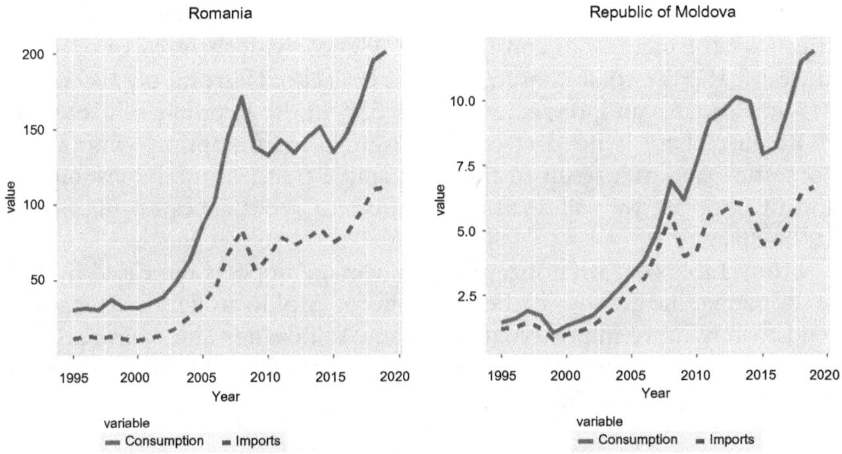

Fig. 6.3 Total household consumption and imports in 1995–2019, $ billion. (Source: Based on (World Bank, 2022b; World Bank, 2022c) data)

(b) *The effects of remittances on stimulating the consumption of households from domestic and imported sources*

In addition to the effects generated in the labour market, remittance inflows also affect the balance of payments at the macroeconomic level, due to the consumption of the population, especially of imported products.

Although the increase in consumption is considered to be an incentive for the economic environment and for the level of development, Fig. 6.3 shows that the trend of household consumption is similar to that of imports in the two countries. Therefore, we find that the members of the families left at home tend to consume more, especially immediately after joining the EU, when a large number of inhabitants of the Republic of Moldova, holders of Romanian citizenship, had the right to free movement. The incomes complemented by remittance flows do not generate positive effects by increasing the consumption of indigenous products, but contribute to imported consumption, which generates imbalances in the balance of payments. Thus, the increase in total household consumption is based on the increase in imports, negatively affecting domestic producers who cannot cope with the low prices of the scale economy. This can have negative effects on the money supply and stability of the national currency (Ito, 2019; Polat & Rodríguez Andrés, 2019).

According to Table 6.4, we notice that remittances generate significant effects on the increase in consumption. Hence, with the growth of remittance by 1%, the total consumption of households grows on average by 21% in Romania and, respectively, by 4.55% in the Republic of Moldova.

Because there is no data on the origin of consumption—imports or domestic—and as a result of the comparable trend of total consumption and of imports, we will analyse the effect of remittances on imports in 1995–2019.

From Table 6.4, we notice that, on average imports increased by 13% in Romania and 2.57% in the Republic of Moldova. Thus, Romanians tend to buy more imported goods than Moldovans. The main reason is the shortage of supermarket chains in the Republic of Moldova comparable to those in Romania.

Table 6.4 The impact of the remittance on the total consumption of households and imports

Impact indicators		*Coefficients*	*Standard error*	*t-test*	*Sign threshold*
ROMANIA					
	Intercept	67.5641	9.3100	7.25	***
Household consumption *p*-value 2.52e-06	**Remittances**	21.0011	3.3875	6.19	***
	Intercept	29.3001	5.0036	5.85	***
Imports *p*-value 2.85e-07	**Remittances**	13.0000	1.8206	7.14	***
	Intercept	-6.8263	1.7953	-3.80	***
Balance of payments *p*-value 0.8405	**Remittances**	-0.1329	0.6532	-0.20	
MOLDOVA					
	Intercept	0.5282	0.4605	1.14	
Household consumption *p*-value 3.34e-12	**Remittances**	4.5506	0.3453	13.17	***
	Intercept	0.6783	0.1609	4.21	***
Imports *p*-value 1.2e-16	**Remittances**	2.5729	0.1206	21.61	***
	Intercept	-0.0611	0.0693	-0.88	***
Balance of payments *p*-value 5.56e-19	**Remittances**	-1.1412	0.0520	-27.17	***

Note: Significance threshold: 0 '***' 0.001 '**' 0.01 '*' 0.05 '.' 0.1 ' ' 1

However, consumption based largely on imports has negative effects, both on the balance of payments and on the economy as a whole. Simultaneously, the increase in substitution imports has the effect of reducing the demand for domestic products, which implicitly affects in the negative direction the level of employment (Castles, 2010).

Regarding the balance of payments, remittances generate a negative impact by its imbalance in the case of the Republic of Moldova, and no impact in Romania.

Part II. Microeconomic Impact of Remittances in Countries of Origin

Regarding the impact that remittances have on microeconomic level, this mostly depends on the destination of these financial flows, such as households' current consumption, health, education, ICT implementation, investment and entrepreneurship.

Analysing the monthly current consumption expenditures of a Romanian household, we notice that they are constantly growing for the entire analysed period (Fig. 6.4), with a fast-tracked evolution between 1997 and 2008, a slight flattening in times of crisis and a more pronounced growth starting with 2015, reaching over $525/household. And in the case of endowment with durable goods, we notice that their number doubled in the period 1997–2007, reaching about 800 such goods per 100 households, but since 2008 their number has decreased to 600 goods.

Due to the limited availability of data, the analysed period does not correspond to that of Romania, data being public starting only with 2006. In that period, we observe a relatively constant evolution of consumer spending without significant changes during the crisis, their value being almost double in 2019 as compared to 2006. The insignificant influence of the crisis on consumption can also be a consequence of the fact that remittances are more important in Moldovan households, and their flow continued during the crisis period, so that in 2010 remittances accounted for more than 25% of GDP (World Bank, 2022d), a value similar to the pre-crisis period.

The same increasing evolution is registered in the case of endowment with durable goods, every 100 households owned over 500 such goods in 2019, an increase by 170 goods compared to 2006 (Table 6.5).

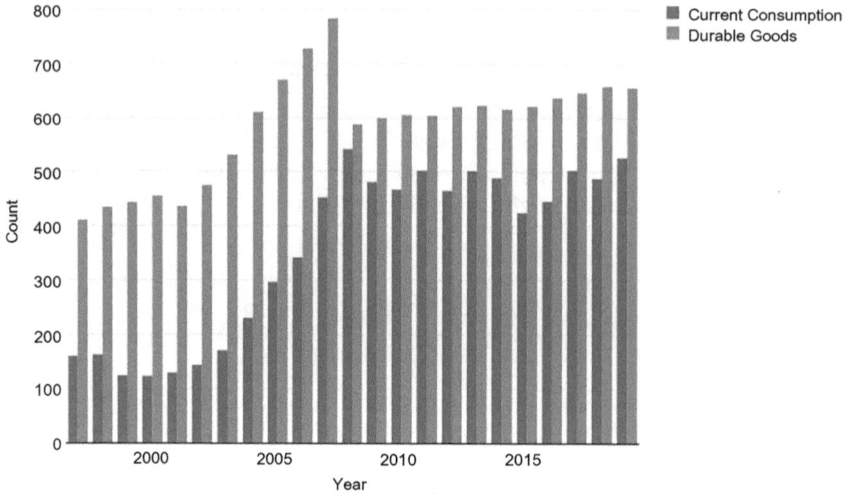

Fig. 6.4 Average monthly consumption per household and the endowment with durable goods of households in 1997–2019. (Source: Based on National Institute of Statistics (2022b) data)

Table 6.5 The impact of the remittances on current consumption expenditures

	Coefficients	*Standard error*	*t-test*	*Sign threshold*
ROMANIA				
Intercept	-3.2496	0.9105	-3.56	***
Remittances	0.4936	0.0447	11.03	***
p-value 3.36e-10				
MOLDOVA				
Intercept	1.2314	3.4349	0.35	
Remittances	0.8307	0.4617	1.79	.
p-value 0.097157				

Note: Significance threshold: 0 '***' 0.001 '**' 0.01 '*' 0.05 '.' 0.1 ' ' 1

Evaluating the impact of remittances on the level of households' current consumption, we find that the increase by 1% in remittances generates on average a growth of current consumption expenditures by 0.493% in Romania and by 0.830% in the Republic of Moldova (Table 6.6).

Table 6.6 Impact of remittances on endowment of households with durable goods

	Coefficients	*Standard error*	*t-test*	*Sign threshold*
ROMANIA				
Intercept	4.5629	0.2043	22.33	***
Remittances	0.088	0.0101	8.67	***
p-value 1.04e-08				
MOLDOVA				
Intercept	4.2458	1.1955	3.55	**
Remittances	0.2456	0.1606	1.52	
p-value 0.152273				

Note: Significance threshold: 0 '***' 0.001 '**' 0.01 '*' 0.05 '.' 0.1 ' ' 1

We also see increases in endowment with durable goods, but the effect is not as significant. The average increase of remittances by 1% determines a growth by only 0.088% of the endowment with such goods in Romania, and in the Republic of Moldova we find no link between the two variables. The explanation can be found in the fact that a category of those who remit are people who no longer take into consideration the option of returning home, and the remittances' direction of use changes, the parents left at home spend them either on health, education or current consumption. We also can observe a flattening trend of the endowment with durable goods (Fig. 6.5) specific for a household that receives remittances from multiannual migration. Another reason is the fact that remittances are being mostly targeted to the consumption of current goods and services, to increase the standard of living (Table 6.7).

In addition to durable goods, which include appliances and equipment using advanced technology, remittance inflows have contributed to the modernization of households and the use of ICT products and services (internet access, computer use, etc.). Thus, the share of households in Romania with internet access increased on average by 0.113% and of those with access to or equipped with a computer by 0.124%, as a result of received remittances. In the case of households with internet access from the Republic of Moldova, remittance growth by 1% leads to an increase of 0.097%, on average. Technological progress is inevitable, and therefore remittances have generated a significant impact on the digitalization of the households. The evolution of the share of Romanian households with

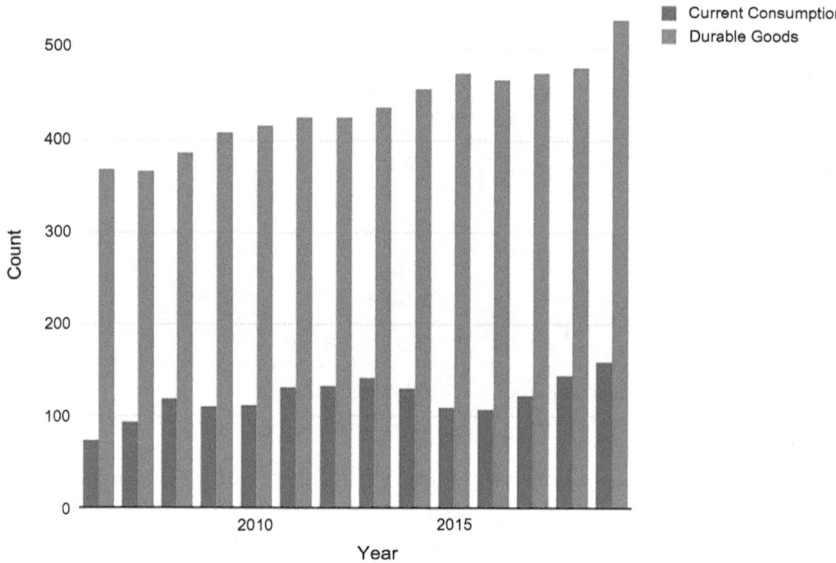

Fig. 6.5 Average monthly consumption per household (In order to compare the indicator of average monthly current consumption per household in Romania and the Republic of Moldova, we decided to express it in US dollars, thus taking into account the inflationary phenomenon recorded during the period) and the endowment with durable goods of households in 2006–2019 in the Republic of Moldova. (Source: Based on National Bureau of Statistics (2022a) data)

internet access being explained by the remittances in proportion of 84.69% (that of households with access to a computer of 36.35%) and in the Republic of Moldova in proportion of 41.17%.

(c) *The effects of remittances on the school/university population and of household expenditures on education*

The migration and the decision to remit have several implications on the educational field, both positive and negative. On the one hand, the effect is related to the sum of money that the family is ready to spend on the children education, and on the other hand, it is shaped by the number of pupils/students who choose to go to educational institutions in their country. In the case of a family receiving remittances, the level of net disposable income increases, having a positive effect on the children's

Table 6.7 Impact of remittances on internet access and use of ICT products/services

Impact indicators		*Coefficient*	*Standard error*	*t-test*	*Sign threshold*
ROMANIA					
	Intercept	-197.066	20.1896	-9.76	
Household internet access *p*-value 7.49e-11	**Remittances**	11.3516	1.0061	11.28	***
	Intercept	-211.122	110.718	-1.907	.
Household access to computers *p*-value 0.03796	**Remittances**	12.462	5.214	2.390	**
MOLDOVA					
	Intercept	-35.1657	16.4268	-2.14	*
Household internet access *p*-value 0.000966	**Remittances**	9.709	2.5326	3.83	***

Note: 1. We do not have available data un computer use in households in the Republic of Moldova. 2. Significance threshold: 0 '***' 0.001 '**' 0.01 '*' 0.05 '.' 0.1 ' ' 1

education. There may be two circumstances of increased expenditures on education:

- Studies conducted at home, with positive impact on human capital, funding of educational institutions in the country and a higher probability of young graduates being integrated in the origin country labour market
- Studies conducted abroad, which have a negative effect on the development of the origin country' education system by decreasing the demand for initial schooling, but also on the economic and social development, if they engage in migration

High school pupils or students studying abroad will be attracted by the opportunity of assimilation into the labour market in the destination country, reducing human capital in Romania and the Republic of Moldova. In this situation the authorities will not be able to retrieve the amounts invested for those pupils/students related to primary or secondary education, if applicable. A similar impact is registered following the decision to migrate taken by a member of the household, followed by the reunification of the family in the destination country, due to the migration of children who have finished state-funded compulsory education—full or partial studies.

The statistics of the school population is discouraging; in Romania the number of those enrolled in education is decreasing from 4.7 million in 1995 to 3.5 million in 2019. The reduction of the number of pupils/students is as well stated in the Republic of Moldova, but the situation is even worse, their number being approximately 2 times lower in 2019 compared to 1995, reaching 433 thousand people (Table 6.8).

Table 6.8 Number of pupils/students and the average monthly expenditure with household education

Year	*Pupils and students, persons*		*Education expenditure, $*	
	Romania	*Republic of Moldova*	*Romania*	*Republic of Moldova*
1995	4,703,277	766,500	1.90	
1996	4,688,311	778,000	2.10	
1997	4,643,351	786,500	2.50	
1998	4,631,164	788,100	2.70	
1999	4,578,383	770,900	1.76	
2000	4,565,279	753,000	1.34	
2001	4,554,466	746,700	1.05	
2002	4,496,786	738,000	1.02	
2003	4,472,493	726,000	1.31	
2004	4,403,880	709,400	2.08	
2005	4,360,831	697,200	2.52	
2006	4,345,581	675,300	2.90	0.32
2007	4,404,581	641,500	3.50	0.35
2008	4,324,992	607,900	4.49	0.49
2009	4,176,866	579,800	4.57	0.55
2010	4,029,226	557,900	3.40	1.40
2011	3,823,515	537,100	3.13	1.44
2012	3,734,326	520,000	2.82	1.30
2013	3,650,933	498,000	2.33	1.20
2014	3,735,552	477,800	2.63	0.94
2015	3,642,632	462,700	1.86	0.70
2016	3,597,280	457,200	1.70	0.73
2017	3,578,561	447,700	1.71	0.64
2018	3,547,301	439,100	2.09	0.70
2019	3,526,189	433,500	2.28	1.79

Source: Based on National Bureau of Statistics (2022a, 2022b) and National Institute of Statistics (2022c; 2022b) data

The determinants of this reduction can be found in:

- The demographic decline of the population
- The increased number of migrants who reunite their family in the destination country, taking their children from the Romanian/ Moldovan education systems
- The orientation towards studies abroad, as a result of the increase of the available incomes following the remittances
- Children born in the families of multi-year migrants become second-generation migrants, and the long-term parental mobility determines their school enrolment in the country of destination.

Simultaneously, the expenditures on education made by households are declining. Therefore, remittances stimulate investment in education for migrant children, but the possibility of their mobility causes them to move to the education system in the destination country or yet another destination where the education system is considered more efficient, while the additional cost is covered by remittance.

However, not all migrant children continue their studies abroad. For the children left at home, the remittances received increase the chances for better education and further studies, especially for the children of rural migrants, who need additional sources for education by moving to urban areas, for high school and university studies.

In poor households, the chance for education for migrants' children left in the country depends mainly on the volume of remittances. Education, even primary and secondary education, and although the public system is free, also involves increasing additional costs for parents. Moreover, the number of Moldovans enrolled in private institutions in primary and secondary education has increased, according to a report by the Ministry of Education, Culture and Research, and some of these students come from families with parents who work abroad (Table 6.9).

The results obtained from the application of the statistical method support the presented theory and confirm, in the cases of Romania and the Republic of Moldova, the research conducted by Ambler et al. (2015) and Adams and Cuecuecha (2010) according to whom remittances contribute to growing household education related expenditure. Therefore, following the increase of remittances by 1%, the education expenditures of households in Romania boosted on average by 0.26%, whereas in the

Table 6.9 Impact of remittances on school population and education expenditures

Impact indicators		*Coefficients*	*Standard error*	*t-test*	*Sign threshold*
ROMANIA					
	Intercept	16.1416	0.1124	143.52	***
Number of pupils/ students *p*-value 3.66e-08	**Remittances**	-0.0452	0.0056	-8.07	***
	Intercept	-3.4383	0.8553	-4.01	***
Education expenditures *p*-value 3.81e-06	**Remittances**	0.2602	0.0420	6.19	***
MOLDOVA					
	Intercept	6.9672	0.1259	55.33	***
Number of pupils/ students *p*-value 0.000144	**Remittances**	-0.0870	0.0191	-4.54	***
	Intercept	-12.6419	5.8750	-2.15	
Education expenditures *p*-value 0.024909	**Remittances**	2.0232	0.7896	2.56	*

Note: Significance threshold: 0 '***' 0.001 '**' 0.01 '*' 0.05 '.' 0.1 ' ' 1

Republic of Moldova the influence is higher, these expenditures increasing on average by 2.02%.

Additionally, the higher prevalence of remittances used to stimulate the participation in education of children from the households of migrant workers in the Republic of Moldova versus Romania can be explained by the following:

- Remittances are moreover used in the Republic of Moldova for efforts to finance compulsory secondary education rather than tertiary education. Also, the rate of passage to tertiary education is lower in the Republic of Moldova than in Romania also due to the linguistic component. Certain potential students thus choose to continue their university studies in Romania, having different qualitative advantages and opportunities, for employment abroad.

Table 6.10 The impact of the remittances on health expenditures

	Coefficients	*Standard error*	*t-test*	*Sign threshold*
ROMANIA				
Intercept	-9.6504	1.1690	-8.25	***
Remittances	0.6468	0.0574	11.26	***
p-value 2.32e-10				
MOLDOVA				
Intercept	-1.4029	3.7338	-0.37	
Remittances	0.8046	0.5018	1.60	
p-value 0.134842				

Note: Significance threshold: 0 '***' 0.001 '**' 0.01 '*' 0.05 '.' 0.1 ' ' 1

- The pressure of the costs borne by the households from the Republic of Moldova is higher than in Romania.
- The propensity to migrate after completing compulsory education is higher for young people in the Republic of Moldova compared to Romanians, the potential wage differential being higher for unqualified jobs, which are accessed by migrant workers/graduates in immigration countries.

Also, the increase in remittances generates a decrease in the school population by 0.045% in Romania and 0.087% in the Republic of Moldova, being in opposition to the results obtained by Azizi (2018), who examined the impact of remittances in poor countries, but it supports the results obtained by Amuedo-Dorantes and Pozo (2010), which analysed the Dominican Republic and Mexico. The discrepancies between the obtained results and those of other researchers can be clarified by the different economic levels of the analysed countries and the conditions of integration in the EU, with the facilities on free movement between Romania and the Republic of Moldova, but also other benefits in the development assistance offered by Romania to the Republic of Moldova (scholarships, aids etc.) (Table 6.10).

Another category of expenditures made by households receiving remittances, agreeing with Azizi (2018) and Ratha (2013), is that related to health. During the analysed period, in Romania and the Republic of Moldova, there is a growth in expenditures on health services, which can also be attributed to remittance inflows within the beneficiary households.

From an economic perspective, the explanation for the increase in health expenditures is positively correlated with the migrants' aim to remit. Equally in the case of households where only one member left, usually for short or medium-term mobility with the possibility of return, and in the case of multiannual and/or permanent migrants who left their members of their extended family at home, one of the purposes of remission is the financing of expenses meant to increase their quality of life, including expenditure on health services. The increase of received remittances by 1% facilitates the average growth of the amounts spent by Romanian households in the field of health by over 0.646%. Therefore, increasing the net disposable income of households based on remittances contributes to life quality improvement. In Moldovan households, on the other hand, there is no influence of remittances on health expenditures, a result that can be interpreted as being subject to the use of a shorter available data (2006–2019).

One more destination of remittances, as previously mentioned, is saving. The fact that Romanian households have higher incomes compared to the total value of their expenses led to the average increase of the savings in the analysed period, by 2248% at each increase of remittances by 1% (Tables 6.11 and 6.12).

As a result of the statistical data provided by the NBS of the Republic of Moldova, we notice that, on average, the disposable income does not cover the expenses incurred by households. However, analysing the incomes and expenditures on quantiles, we notice that the households located in the first two quantiles have higher incomes compared with their expenses. With regard to households in quantile III, there are fluctuations of income, expenditure and savings, whereas households in quantiles IV

Table 6.11 The impact of remittances on savings in Romania

	Coefficients	*Standard error*	*t-test*	*Sign threshold*
Intercept	-42.7884	6.8344	-6.26	***
Remittances	2.2489	0.3357	6.69	***
p-value 1.25e-06				

Note: Significance threshold: 0 '***' 0.001 '**' 0.01 '*' 0.05 '.' 0.1 ' ' 1

Table 6.12 Monthly incomes, expenditures and savings of households in the Republic of Moldova, $

Year	*Income*	*Expenditure*	Δ *V/Ch*
2006	63.93	72.59	-8.66
2007	83.96	92.23	-8.27
2008	114.43	118.18	-3.75
2009	104.91	109.52	-4.62
2010	103.00	110.92	-7.92
2011	123.10	130.72	-7.62
2012	124.56	131.97	-7.41
2013	133.53	141.02	-7.50
2014	125.82	129.32	-3.50
2015	103.94	108.82	-4.88
2016	103.40	106.24	-2.84
2017	121.44	121.73	-0.29
2018	141.83	143.31	-1.48
2019	163.92	158.56	5.35

Source: Based on the National Bureau of Statistics (2022a) data

and V have higher expenditures than the income obtained (Annex 6.2), according to the last available data.

This phenomenon can be explained by the following:

(a) Dependence on remittances of households with higher incomes, which demonstrates that migrants come from middle- and high-income families and not from poor families.
(b) the value of remittances received by households is much higher than officially measured. Although the National Bureau of Statistics includes the value of official remittances in determining household incomes, the expenses incurred by them have as a source of funding the unofficial remittances received in the country.
(c) The impact of the underground economy on households.
(d) The level of poverty of the population.

Another destination for the use of remittances, in fact the most significant from the perspective of economic sustainability and the increase of expected household income, are the investments made by households,

Table 6.13 Impact of remittances on the number of private enterprises

	Coefficients	*Standard error*	*t-test*	*Sign threshold*
Intercept	12.8234	0.3459	37.06	
Remitențe	-0.0083	0.0172	-0.48	
p-value 0.6327				

Note: Significance threshold: 0 '***' 0.001 '**' 0.01 '*' 0.05 '.' 0.1 ' ' 1

both in setting up business and in purchasing durable goods or housing construction.

The effects of directing remittances in setting up businesses are felt both at the macroeconomic level, by generating new added value and increasing tax revenues, and at the level of households, by increasing their disposable income (Table 6.13).

Although the literature presents remittances as a factor of increasing the employment rate and of stimulating entrepreneurship, factor resulted from the increase in the number of jobs, according to the results obtained in Romania, the situation is different. Thus, remittance inflows do not generate any significant effect on the number of small private enterprises (sole proprietor/self-employed and family enterprises), the statistical results showing the lack of any link between the two variables. This conclusion is also supported by the negative impact of remittances on the number of employed and active people and on the employment rate of the Romanian population.

Due to the lack of any link between remittance inflows and the number of private businesses, we can conclude that the flows received by the family members left at home are not directed towards investments, but rather predominantly towards consumption and to a lesser extent towards savings.

In the Republic of Moldova, the official database of the National Bureau of Statistics does not present a sufficiently long series of data on private enterprises in order to be able to apply linear regression.

Partial Conclusions

Remittances are the result of labour mobility and appear mainly as a motivation for migration for low- and middle-skilled groups in less economically developed and emerging countries with medium levels of development.

Remittances have an impact both at the macroeconomic and microeconomic level (households, respectively the individual), through the effects they produce and through their spending destination. In the present research stage, we tested the impact of remittances in the case of two former socialist countries—Romania and the Republic of Moldova.

Following the results obtained, we can conclude that the impact generated by the remitters has a similar impact in the two countries, even if Romania is part of the category of developed countries, and the Republic of Moldavia—under development.

Therefore, in the case of these savings, remittances do not have the expected effect and the impact is not only positive:

Labour market indicators—strong influence with negative impact on the employment indicators and weak (Republic of Moldova) and insignificant (Romania) impact on unemployment rate.

Consumption and imports—strong negative impact of remittances, as a result of the increase in consumption from imports and the modelling of the trend of total consumption after the evolution of imports, discouraging domestic production.

Household level—increasing the standard of living at household and individual level by directing remittances to current consumption, internet access, education and health expenses. However, external flows do not contribute to the creation of new businesses, import consumption being preferred.

Regarding the number of those who are enrolled in educational institutions in the country of origin, there is a decrease in their number, so that new potential migrants are taking shape, either from the perspective of migration for studies or from the perspective of the actual migrant status.

Annexes

Annex 6.1 Variables used in research

Indicators	*Definition*	*Database*
	Macroeconomic level	
Active population	Labour supply that includes the civilian employed population + legally registered unemployed.	NIS/NBS
Civilian employed population	Persons who, on the basis of an employment contract, carry out an income-generating activity in the form of wages or payment in kind. This category includes employees, employers, unpaid family workers and self-employed workers.	NIS/NBS
Employment rate	The employed population of a certain age relative to the total population of the same age.	NIS/NBS
Unemployed population	Able-bodied persons who are at least 16 years old and are looking for a job, being registered with the National Agency for Employment and have immediate availability of employment.	NIS/NBS
Unemployment rate	Ratio between the number of unemployed and the active population.	NIS/NBS
Final consumption expenditure of the population	The market value of all goods and services, including durable goods purchased by households (cars, appliances, rents, payments and fees for authorizations and licenses).	World Bank
Imports of goods and services	All transactions between residents and the rest of the world, involving a change of ownership from non-residents to residents of goods and services.	World Bank
Trade balance of payment	The difference between the value of imported and exported goods and services	World Bank
Savings	The difference between the net disposable income of households and the monthly expenditures	Author's calculation based on NIS data
Private entrepreneurs	Authorized natural persons or legal persons, who have the right to set up and manage a business, in which they participate with their capital and/or with attracted capital.	NIS
	Microeconomic level	
Households' total current consumption expenditures	Expenditures made by the population on current consumption needs (food and non-food products, services) and entered into consumption, the value of human consumption of agri-food products from the household's own resources.	NIS/NBS

(*continued*)

Annex 6.1 (continued)

Indicators	*Definition*	*Database*
Providing households with durable goods	The endowment of households with durable goods is expressed by the number of durable goods (large appliances, small appliances, automobiles, IT sector, etc.) in working order, which average 100 households.	NIS/NBS
Households' health expenditures	Expenditures made by the households on health products and services.	NIS/NBS
Households' education expenditures	Expenditures made by the households on education.	NIS/
School population	Children in kindergartens, pupils and students included in the training process in a school/ university year within the formal education, regardless of the forms of education, the study program and age.	NBS
The share of individuals with internet access	the share of individuals who have access to the internet	World Bank

Annex 6.2 Household incomes, expenditures and savings on quintiles in the period 2006–2017, $

	Quintile I	*Quintile II*	*Quintile III*	*Quintile IV*	*Quintile V*
2006					
Disposable income	29.89	44.64	56.96	73.47	114.67
Expenditures	27.18	43.33	59.23	81.13	152.04
Savings	2.72	1.31	-2.27	-7.66	-37.37
2007					
Disposable income	40.50	59.98	74.17	94.24	150.88
Expenditures	36.21	56.66	76.44	102.57	189.22
Savings	4.29	3.32	-2.27	-8.32	-38.34
2008					
Disposable income	58.54	78.42	101.66	131.60	201.97
Expenditures	47.64	74.08	96.85	129.33	243.02
Savings	10.90	4.33	4.80	2.27	-41.05
2009					
Disposable income	49.02	74.89	94.96	123.72	181.84
Expenditures	45.01	69.65	92.73	125.05	215.03
Savings	4.01	5.24	2.23	-1.33	-33.20

(*continued*)

Annex 6.2 (continued)

	Quintile I	*Quintile II*	*Quintile III*	*Quintile IV*	*Quintile V*
2010					
Disposable income	50.49	76.25	94.99	117.50	175.74
Expenditures	47.50	71.78	93.86	123.98	217.45
Savings	2.99	4.46	1.13	-6.48	-41.71
2011					
Disposable income	64.27	89.26	110.16	139.61	212.23
Expenditures	58.79	85.79	110.99	146.33	251.68
Savings	5.49	3.47	-0.84	-6.72	-39.45
2012					
Disposable income	67.08	88.42	113.22	137.86	216.60
Expenditures	61.28	88.79	113.62	147.01	249.63
Savings	5.80	-0.36	-0.40	-9.16	-33.04
2013					
Disposable income	72.89	96.74	117.46	148.69	231.86
Expenditures	66.40	95.90	122.76	158.85	261.23
Savings	6.50	0.84	-5.30	-10.17	-29.37
2014					
Disposable income	69.33	94.83	114.30	139.81	210.78
Expenditures	64.85	90.49	113.77	146.17	231.30
Savings	4.48	4.34	0.53	-6.36	-20.52
2015					
Disposable income	57.31	75.17	92.47	120.53	174.18
Expenditures	53.99	76.23	96.11	121.83	195.89
Savings	3.32	-1.06	-3.64	-1.31	-21.71
2016					
Disposable income	56.82	77.94	94.85	113.65	173.54
Expenditures	53.83	75.71	93.65	116.73	191.03
Savings	2.99	2.23	1.19	-3.08	-17.49
2017					
Disposable income	68.39	90.91	109.70	135.76	202.49
Expenditures	61.73	86.97	108.87	136.44	214.71
Savings	6.66	3.94	0.83	-0.68	-12.22

Source: Based on National Bureau of Statistics (2022a) data

References

Acosta, P., Fajnzylber, P., & Lopez, H. J. (2008). *Remittances and Household Behavior: Evidence for Latin America*. World Bank.

Adams, R. H., & Cuecuecha, A. (2010). Remittances, Household Expenditure and Investment in Guatemala. *World Development, 38*(11), 1626–1641. https://doi.org/10.1016/J.WORLDDEV.2010.03.003

Adams, R. H., Jr., Cuecuecha, A., & De Tlaxcala, E. C. (2013). The Impact of Remittances on Investment and Poverty in Ghana. *World Development, 50*, 24–40. https://doi.org/10.1016/j.worlddev.2013.04.009

Ambler, K., Aycinena, D., & Yang, D. (2015). Channeling Remittances to Education: A Field Experiment among Migrants from El Salvador. *American Economic Journal: Applied Economics, 7*(2), 207–232. https://doi.org/10.1257/app.20140010

Amuedo-Dorantes, C., & Pozo, S. (2010). Accounting for Remittance and Migration Effects on Children's Schooling. *World Development, 38*(12), 1747–1759. https://doi.org/10.1016/J.WORLDDEV.2010.05.008

Azizi, S. (2018). The Impacts of Workers' Remittances on Human Capital and Labor Supply in Developing Countries. *Economic Modelling, 75*, 377–396. https://doi.org/10.1016/J.ECONMOD.2018.07.011

Basnet, H. C., Baker, J., & Donou-Adonsou, F. (2022). Workers' Remittances in Central America: Where Does the Money Go? *International Journal of Social Economics, 49*(5), 765–779. https://doi.org/10.1108/IJSE-05-2021-0282/FULL/XML

Beaton, K., Cerovic, S., Galdamez, M., Hadzi-Vaskov, M., Loyola, F., Koczan, Z., Lissovolik, B., Martijn, J., Ustyugova, Y., & Wong, J. (2017). *Migration and Remittances in Latin America and the Caribbean: Engines of Growth and Macroeconomic Stabilizers?*

Boboc, C., Vasile, V., & Todose, D. (2012). Vulnerabilities Associated to Migration Trajectories from Romania to EU Countries. *Procedia - Social and Behavioral Sciences, 62*, 352–359. https://doi.org/10.1016/J.SBSPRO.2012.09.056

Castles, S. (2010). Understanding Global Migration: A Social Transformation Perspective. *Journal of Ethnic and Migration Studies, 36*(10), 1565–1586. https://doi.org/10.1080/1369183X.2010.489381

Eggoh, J., Bangake, C., & Semedo, G. (2019). Do Remittances Spur Economic Growth? Evidence from Developing Countries. *The Journal of International Trade & Economic Development, 28*, 391. https://doi.org/10.1080/09638199.2019.1568522

European Commission. (2010). *Geographical and Labour Market Mobility*.

European Commission. (2017). *Country Report Romania 2017*.

European Commission. (2020). *Country Report Romania*. European Commission.

Fromentin, V. (2017). The Long-run and Short-run Impacts of Remittances on Financial Development in Developing Countries. *Quarterly Review of Economics and Finance, 66*, 192–201. https://doi.org/10.1016/j.qref.2017.02.006

Giannetti, M., Federici, D., & Raitano, M. (2009). Migrant Remittances and Inequality in Central-Eastern Europe. *International Review of Applied Economics, 23*(3), 289–307. https://doi.org/10.1080/02692170902811710

Girsberger, E. M., Méango, R., & Rapoport, H. (2018). Discussion Paper Series Regional Migration and Wage Inequality in the West African Economic and Monetary Union Regional Migration and Wage Inequality in the West African Economic and Monetary Union. IZA Discussion Paper Series IZA DP No. 12048.

Giuliano, P., & Ruiz-Arranz, M. (2009). Remittances, Financial Development, and Growth. *Journal of Development Economics, 90*(1), 144–152. https://doi.org/10.1016/j.jdeveco.2008.10.005

Guha, P. (2013). Macroeconomic Effects of International Remittances: The Case of Developing Economies. *Economic Modelling, 33*, 292–305. https://doi.org/10.1016/j.econmod.2013.04.016

Imai, K. S., Gaiha, R., Ali, A., & Kaicker, N. (2014). Remittances, Growth and Poverty: NEW Evidence from Asian Countries. *Journal of Policy Modeling, 36*(3), 524–538. https://doi.org/10.1016/j.jpolmod.2014.01.009

International Organization for Migration (IOM). (2013). *The Extended Migration Profile of the Republic of Moldova*. International Organization for Migration (IOM).

Ito, K. (2019). Remittances and the Dutch Disease: Evidence from Panel Data for 18 Developing Countries. *International Economic Journal, 33*, 1. https://doi.org/10.1080/10168737.2019.1569709

Medina, C., & Cardona, L. (2010). The Effects of Remittances on Household Consumption, Education Attendance and Living Standards: The Case of Colombia. *Lecturas de Economia, 72*, 11–43.

Medina, L., & Schneider, F. (2018). *Shadow Economies Around the World: What Did We Learn Over the Last 20 Years?*

Meyer, D., & Shera, A. (2017). The Impact of Remittances on Economic Growth: An Econometric Model. *Economia, 18*(2), 147–155. https://doi.org/10.1016/J.ECON.2016.06.001

Mishra, K., Kondratjeva, O., & Shively, G. E. (2022). Do Remittances Reshape Household Expenditures? Evidence from Nepal. *World Development, 157*, 105926. https://doi.org/10.1016/J.WORLDDEV.2022.105926

National Bureau of Statistics. (2022a). *Population Living Standards*. National Bureau of Statistics. Accessed July 28, 2022, from http://statbank.statistica.md/PxWeb/pxweb/ro/30%20Statistica%20sociala/?rxid=b2ff27d7-0b96-43c9-934b-42e1a2a9a774.

National Bureau of Statistics. (2022b). *Education Indicators.* National Bureau of Statistics. Accessed July 28, 2022, from http://statbank.statistica.md/PxWeb/pxweb/ro/30%20Statistica%20sociala/?rxid=b2ff27d7-0b96-43c9-934b-42e1a2a9a774.

National Bureaus of Statistics. (2022). *Unemployment rate by Sexes, Averages, Years and Quarters.* National Bureaus of Statistics of the Republic of Moldova. Accessed July 27, 2022, from http://statbank.statistica.md/PxWeb/pxweb/ro/30%20Statistica%20sociala/30%20Statistica%20sociala__03%20FM__03%20MUN__MUN060/MUN160100.px/table/tableViewLayout1/?rxid=b2ff27d7-0b96-43c9-934b-42e1a2a9a774.

National Institute of Statistics. (2022a). *Populatia ocupata pe activitati, grupe de varsta si sexe.* AMIGO. Accessed February 5, 2022, from https://insse.ro/cms/files/publicatii/Statistica%20teritoriala/Forta%20de%20munca_ind_JudLoc.htm.

National Institute of Statistics. (2022b). *Living Standard Statistics.* National Institute of Statistics. Accessed July 28, 2022, from http://statistici.insse.ro:8077/tempo-online/#/pages/tables/insse-table.

National Institute of Statistics. (2022c). *Education Indicators.* National Institute of Statistics. Accessed July 28, 2022, from http://statistici.insse.ro:8077/tempo-online/#/pages/tables/insse-table.

Necsutu, M. (2021). Quarter of Moldovans Now Have Romanian Passports | Balkan Insight. In: *BalkanInsight.* Accessed July 10, 2022, from https://balkaninsight.com/2021/05/27/quarter-of-moldovans-now-have-romanian-passports/.

Nguyen, T., & Purnamasari, R. (2011). *Impacts of International Migration and Remittances on Child Outcomes and Labor Supply in Indonesia: How Does Gender Matter?* The World Bank.

Polat, B., & Rodríguez Andrés, A. (2019). Do Emigrants' Remittances Cause Dutch Disease? A Developing Countries Case Study. *The Economic and Labour Relations Review, 30*(1), 59–76. https://doi.org/10.1177/1035304619828560

Ratha, D. (2013). *The Impact of Remittances on Economic Growth and Poverty Reduction.*

United Nations. (2021). *International Migrant Stock.*

Vacaflores, D. E. (2018). Are Remittances Helping Lower Poverty and Inequality levels in Latin America? *Quarterly Review of Economics and Finance, 68,* 254–265. https://doi.org/10.1016/j.qref.2017.09.001

Vadean, F., Randazzo, T., & Piracha, M. (2019). Remittances, Labour Supply and Activity of Household Members Left-Behind. *Journal of Development Studies, 55*(2), 278–293. https://doi.org/10.1080/00220388.2017.1404031

Vasile, V. (2013). Studii Post-Doctorale în Economie Disertații Post-Doctorale.

Vasile, V., Bunduchi, E., & Ştefan, D. (2019). *Impact of Remittances on the Country of Origin. Multidimensional Analysis at Macro and Microeconomic Level. Case Study Romania and Moldova.*

World Bank. (2022a). *Migration and Remittances Data. Annual Remittances Data.* Accessed August 13, 2021, from https://www.worldbank.org/en/topic/migrationremittancesdiasporaissues/brief/migration-remittances-data.

World Bank. (2022b). *Final consumption expenditure (current US$).* The World Bank. Accessed July 27, 2022, from https://data.worldbank.org/indicator/NE.CON.TOTL.CD.

World Bank. (2022c). *Imports of goods and services (current US$).* The World Bank. Accessed July 27, 2022, from https://data.worldbank.org/indicator/NE.IMP.GNFS.CD.

World Bank. (2022d). *Personal Remittances, Received (% of GDP).* The World Bank. Accessed July 28, 2022, from https://data.worldbank.org/indicator/BX.TRF.PWKR.DT.GD.ZS?locations=MD.

Zhunio, M. C., Vishwasrao, S., & Chiang, E. P. (2012). The Influence of Remittances on Education and Health Outcomes: A Cross Country Study. *Applied Economics, 44*(35), 4605–4616. https://doi.org/10.1080/00036846.2011.593499

CHAPTER 7

Social Effects of Migration and of Remittances from the Perspective of the Home Country and of the Host Country

Elena Bunduchi

Social Basis of Migration

Migration has always been a phenomenon that has raised the interest of researchers in various fields, from historians, geographers, sociologists, to demographers or economists, each proposing theories, hypotheses, paradigms and different types of analysis, in an attempt to explain the causes, the specific, the characteristics and the impact of migration.

Over time, the analysis of migration has been done in a chaotic manner, and in the absence of a common idea of theoretical approaches, conceptualization has been based on various ideologies.

Therefore, the theorization of migration goes through a fragmented filter of theories that have evolved separately, being elaborated by various authors from interdisciplinary perspectives (King, 2012).

Arango (2017) emphasizes, however, the fact that while there are many theories and approaches to migration, none of them express or present a true theory that encompasses all aspects of this phenomenon, regardless of their empirical and heuristic significance. At the same time, Rotariu (2009) emphasizes that the diversity and lack of substance of theories are determined by the variety of forms of migration, which makes it difficult to choose a unique explanatory model.

V. Vasile et al., *International Labour Mobility*,
https://doi.org/10.1007/978-3-031-18683-7_7

From the perspective of the current research, the most important approaches are those that see migration as a phenomenon that can be explained from an economic and social point of view. Although the analysis of migration is frequently approached in the literature from a socio-economic perspective, it is important to clarify the two concepts.

Although international migration is now commonly accepted as an economic process, the idea that the foundations of migration are based solely on economic reasons is wrong. Even if a large income gap is obviously a motivation for migration, it is neither a necessary nor a sufficient condition.

We consider the main social causes of migration, implicitly of remittances, to be (Fig. 7.1):

- Age is a very important social element of the decision regarding migration and remittances. Young people, especially single people, will have no moral restrictions regarding migration and will have no reasons for saving money and sending remittances to their home country, except for their parents, compared to a middle-aged, married person who has children. The migration model for middle-aged people is most often mobility for work, with the purpose of remitting to family members in the origin country. At the same time, the elderly population does not have the same motivation, and for them migration can be, rather, a decision to change their home, rather than labour mobility.

Fig. 7.1 Social determinants of migration

- The level of education of potential migrants is another extremely important social criterion. The higher the level of education of the migrant, the lower the level of remittances. Thus, highly qualified people make the decision to migrate usually for professional and career development, they do not migrate for short periods of time, but for medium term at least. Instead, migrants with a medium and low level of education migrate mainly for remittances.
- Living conditions in the country of origin influence the type of migration chosen by individuals or families. People whose standard of living is above average migrate for reasons other than economic. Their motivation to migrate is influenced by career development/ opportunities, study scholarships, etc. Poor migrants are thus motivated either to migrate for short or medium periods of time for remittances, or they may decide to migrate permanently, in search of better alternatives.
- The size of the family in the country of origin also plays a significant role in the decision to migrate and remit. People with several minor children tend to migrate for short term for remittances, as there are too many risks in terms of permanent migration, such as the difficult social integration of children in a new environment.
- The type of residence (rural or urban) has an impact on the migration decision; thus, people living in cities tend to migrate more than those in rural areas.

Therefore, the migration decision does not appear only for strictly economic reasons, such as the low level of wages, but is a mix of economic and social reasons, which contribute to the decision to migrate of the potential migrant.

The Social Impact of Migration and Remittances at the Level of the Country of Origin and Destination

The migration decision is a long process, which requires a careful analysis of the factors in the origin and destination countries. In most cases, migration, especially job mobility, becomes a choice for individuals if their country of origin cannot provide them with sufficient opportunities to ensure a decent standard of living.

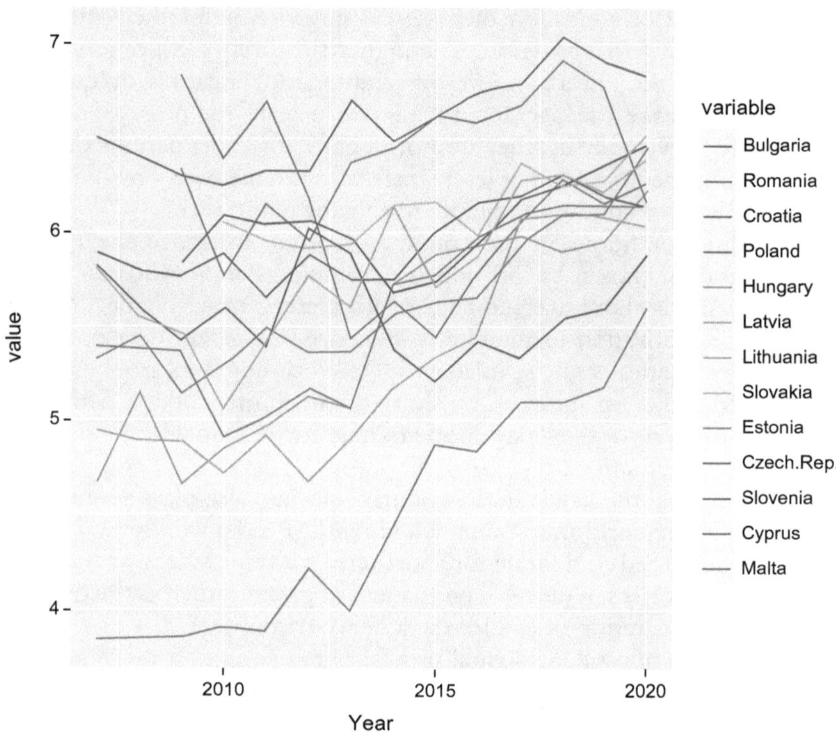

Fig. 7.2 Level of life satisfaction in the country of origin at EU-13 level between 2007 and 2020. (Source: Based on data in the World Happiness Report 2021)

According to the data presented in the "World Happiness Report" on a Cantril scale with values from 1 to 10 (Helliwell et al., 2021), in 2020 Romanians appreciated the level of life satisfaction[1] they feel at home as being around value of 6.15, the highest level in the entire analysed period, being in the middle of the ranking within the EU-13 states. Countries whose populations feel a lower level of life satisfaction are Hungary, Estonia, Latvia, Croatia and Bulgaria (Fig. 7.2).

[1] Life satisfaction assessment was measured by individual answers to the question: "Please imagine a scale, with steps numbered from 0 at the bottom to 10 at the top. The top of the ladder is the best possible life for you, and the bottom of the ladder is the worst life for you. At what level of the stairs would you say that you personally feel you are sitting at the moment?"

In these 13 EU Member States, we note that the Czech population is the most satisfied with the standard of living, so that even during the crisis they appreciated their level of satisfaction to be around 6.3, increasing until 2020, when they graded it at 6.83. At the other end of the spectrum is Bulgaria, whose population values life satisfaction as the lowest in the EU-13, throughout the period under review.

Although in the most recent years, Romanians are more satisfied with the life they have at home, they tend to migrate in increasing numbers to other destination states, which could provide them with additional income if the reason for migration is remittances. This would increase the satisfaction of the remaining members at home. When the reason for migration involves a change of residence and family reunification, Romanians choose countries that can provide them with better opportunities, both from an economic and social perspective.

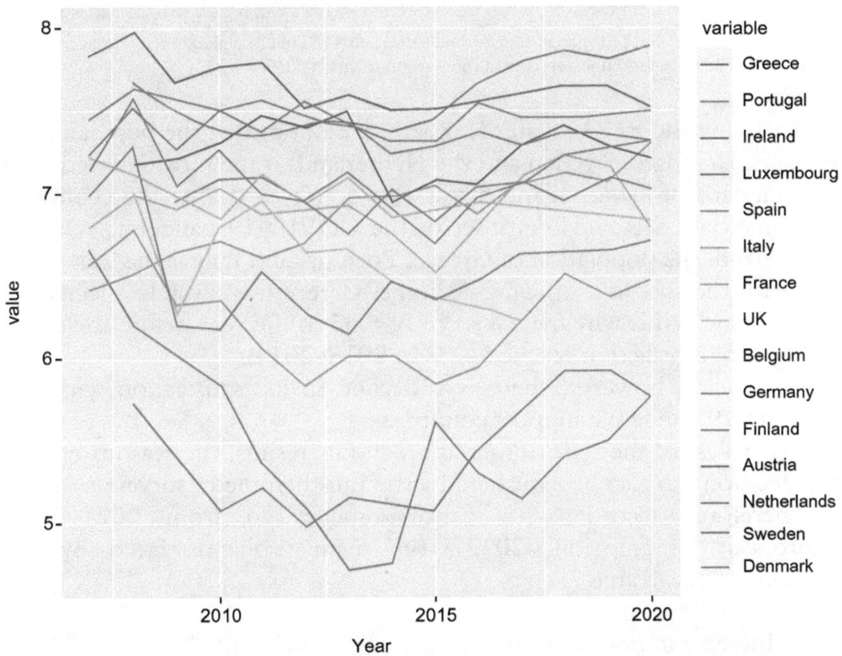

Fig. 7.3 Level of life satisfaction in the country of origin at EU-15 level between 2007 and 2020. (Source: Based on data in the World Happiness Report 2021)

Table 7.1 The results of Eurobarometer 96 and 91 on the opinion of the natives to the question "What are the problems your country is facing?"

Answers received in the order of importance	*2019, %*	*Winter 2021/2022, %*	*Δ22/19, pp*
Rising prices and cost of living	35	43	+8
Quality of health and social security services	30	30	–
Economic situation	25	27	+2
The pension system	18	11	-7
The education system	13	11	-2
The level of public debt	11	10	-1
Environmental problems	9	9	–
Crime level	9	8	-1
Unemployment	11	7	-4
Fiscal pressure	10	6	-4
Lack of housing	7	5	-2
Migration	7	3	-4
Terrorism	4	3	-1

Source: Based on the data provided in Eurobarometer 96 and 91 "Public opinion in the European Union Winter 2021/2022" and "Public opinion in the European Union 2019"

Analysing the EU-15 states (Fig. 7.3) we notice that the population in Finland, Denmark, Sweden and the Netherlands is the most satisfied with the standard of living, giving marks above 7, even during the economic and financial crisis and the onset of the COVID-19 pandemic. On the other hand, the population of Greece, Portugal and Italy is the least satisfied with the standard of living at home. Greece was severely affected by the crisis, which is why from a score of 6.65 in the year before the crisis, the level of satisfaction reached 4.72 in 2013–2014.

In general, however, there is a decline in life satisfaction with the COVID-19 pandemic in most countries.

Regardless of the type of migration and its results, the reasons behind the decision can also be explained by the Eurobarometer surveys.

Therefore, according to Eurobarometer 96 from 2021/2022 (European Commission, 2022), the main problems faced by the Romanians are (Table 7.1):

- Increase in prices and thus in the cost of living (43%)
- Quality and access to health and social security services (30%)
- Economic situation in the country (27%)

Similar results were obtained in the case of Eurobarometer 91 (European Commission, 2019), but increasing in weight, by 8 pp. and 2 pp., respectively. These results actually show the population's dissatisfaction with very important issues. If the net disposable income of households does not allow them to cover the expenses necessary for a decent standard of living, and the quality of health and social security services does not meet the expectations of the population, the solution to increasing the quality of life is migration.

However, migration in turn generates positive and/or negative effects not only at household or individual level, but also at macroeconomic level, both in the origin and in the destination country.

Effects at the Level of the Country of Destination

Positive Macroeconomic Effects

Balancing the Labour Market

Labour migration can have positive effects on the country of origin as a result of reducing imbalances and tensions in the labour market by reducing the unemployment rate (Boboc et al., 2012). Low wages, which lead to a low standard of living, associated with a large level of unemployment can be the cause of migration, and with it, the labour market balances with the new free jobs.

Reduction of State Expenditures on Social Assistance and Unemployment Benefits

In addition to balancing the labour market, migration can lead to a reduction in budget spending on allowances and benefits if the persons who migrate for remittance purposes are registered as unemployed in their origin country.

Investing Remittances in Education

The formation of highly qualified human capital must become a target of every country. Migrants can help achieve this goal by directing remittances to investments in the education and training of children left at home. Studies (Ambler et al., 2015; Askarov & Doucouliagos, 2020) have shown that remittance households have changed their budget, allocating more money to the education of children compared to households whose members have not migrated. Medina and Cardona (2010) found that beneficiary households spend 10% more out of the total budget for education than non-beneficiaries.

Investing Remittances in Raising Living Standards
Remittance flows to recipient households in the country of origin can help increase living standards by providing households with water, sanitation and hygiene, thus ensuring a reduction in disease and epidemics (Taylor, 1999).

Positive Effects at Household and Individual Level

Knowledge and Technology Transfer
Migration to a usually more developed destination country involves, in addition to remittances, a transfer of knowledge, skills and technologies that help reduce poverty, raise living standards and make life easier (Valette, 2018).

Increasing the Enrolment of Children in the Education System
Remittances are additional income for beneficiary households, which are mainly used for consumption, but some of these flows provide access to education. Matano and Ramos (2018) emphasize the importance of remittances in increasing the number of high school students of the local population. In addition to access to education for pupils/students in households with migrant family members, remittances can influence the enrolment in education for those who do not have family members involved in migration, through the ease of credit constraints (Dustmann & Mestres, 2010).

Poverty Reduction
Studies show that remittance households tend to improve their living standards as a result of the positive impact of these financial flows on poverty reduction. Yoshino et al. (2017) proved that a 1% increase in the share of remittances in GDP can lead to a 22.6% decrease in the poverty rate and a 16.0% decrease in the severe poverty rate in the sample of 10 developing Asian countries. Similar results have been obtained by Adams and Page (2005), who suggest that, on average, a 10% increase in the share of international migrants in a country's population will lead to a 2.1% decrease in

the share of people living with less than $1 per person per day, and a 10% increase in official remittances per capita will lead to a 3.5% decrease in the share of people living in poverty.

Negative Effects at the Macroeconomic Level

The Aging of the Population and the Registration of the Demographic Deficit

At the level of 2019, the average age of migrants globally was 39, increasing compared to 2010, when it was 38 (United Nations, 2020). In underdeveloped countries, however, the age is even lower, which results in an aging population. Short-term or temporary migration, which aims to remit, does not pose an immediate danger to the aging population of the country of origin, but if migrants tend to engage in long-term circular migration or permanent migration, the impact on the demographic situation is a negative one. At the same time, an aging population cannot influence the demographic deficit, and in the long run, if there is no return migration, there can be a drastic reduction in the population left at home.

The Impossibility of Ensuring a High Level of Pensions

Due to the fact that the number of taxpayers in the pension budget is decreasing as a result of the migration of able-bodied persons, 74.2% being aged between 20 and 64 (United Nations, 2020), the state cannot ensure an adequate level of pensions. Increasing the tax burden on taxes, fees and social security contributions is necessary to ensure a decent pension, but this could lead to an increase in migration, resulting in a vicious circle.

Negative Effects at Household and Individual Level

Encouraging Unemployment

The impact of remittances on recipient households may be negative if these financial flows become the sole source of income. Due to the fact that household members can cover their current expenses from remittances, they are no longer motivated to find a job (Stănculescu et al., 2011).

Changing the Composition and Roles within the Family

Lu et al. (2021) pointed out that increasing the separation time between children and parents leads to the loss of the relationship between them and of the authority over household management. Parents are gradually replaced by other family members or their children take over their own care. Feelings of loss, abandonment and rejection follow children and cannot be offset by gifts and goods sent from abroad, which could have negative effects on the success and results in education.

Increasing the Dropout Rate Among Children from Migrant Families

Remittances resulting from migration are a benefit meant to cover household expenses, but the stress felt by children and caused by the absence of one or both parents has important consequences in terms of the school situation of the children. Studies (Smita, 2008; Adunts & Afunts, 2019) show that the probability of school dropout is significant among children whose parent(s) are away as a result of the stress they experience.

Another consequence of migration and remittances is the change in the career orientation of teenagers, as children may consider migration and remittances as their ultimate goal (Katseli et al., 2006), to the detriment of participation in the education system.

Abandonment of Children and of the Elderly

Abandonment of children and of elderly parents is common, especially in situations where the purpose of migration is remittances. Migrants tend to leave their children in the care of their elderly parents (Cheianu-Andrei et al., 2011), being motivated by the economic reward in the form of remittances, without realizing that this event has a negative effect on the psychological well-being of children and parents (Lam & Yeoh, 2019).

The Loss of Values and Traditions Among the Second Generation of Migrants

Migration to the destination country involves a long process of integration. If migrants decide to reunite their family or form a new family with other migrants from the same country of origin, the children, who are considered the second generation of migrants, will gradually lose some of the values and traditions from the home country or they will never be able to share them as their own (Harder et al., 2018).

Effects at the Level of the Country of Destination

The impact of migrants on the country of destination can be viewed from several points of view: on the one hand migrants exert macroeconomic influence, and on the other hand, they have an impact on households and native individuals, be it positive or negative, through their presence, actions and way of life.

Positive Macroeconomic Effects

Reducing the Demographic Deficit and Balancing the Age Pyramid

According to United Nations statistics (United Nations, 2019), the total fertility rate in the world has dropped by almost half, from 5.0 to 2.5 births per woman in the last 50 years, and is expected to fall to the replacement level of 2.2 births per woman by 2050 and to 1.9 by 2100. In consequences the number of older people has tripled in the last 50 years. And it is expected to triple again in the next 50 years, raising serious concerns about the sustainability of social security systems. The total fertility rate is currently below the replacement level in all developed countries. The consequences of this phenomenon can be reduced by migrants, who usually come from less developed countries whose fertility rate is higher.

Contributes to Stimulating Innovation and Technological Progress

Joint research conducted by the OECD, the ILO and the World Bank (2015) highlights that the share of skilled migrants compared to all other migrant groups has been steadily increasing. Thus, migrants arrive with skills and knowledge and complete the highly qualified human capital stock of the host country. Studies (OECD, 2010; Gelb & Krishnan, 2018; Fassio et al., 2019) show that skilled migrants contribute to the stimulation of research and innovation, as well as to technological progress through the novelties brought in the companies in which they operate, but also as a result of the business developed by them.

The Emergence of New Services, Adapted to the Requirements of Migrants

Markets that offer culture-specific products or services to various categories of migrants are proving to be important opportunities for industries such as financial services, telecommunications, media and entertainment, travel and tourism, consumer goods and hotels, restaurants and catering. More and more companies targeting migrant markets are developing innovative relationships with their migrant customer base. An example might be Univision Communications, which is a US television company that distributes only Spanish-language stations to Latin American migrants (World Economic Forum, 2013).

Positive Effects at Household and Individual Level

Contributes to the Increase of the Country's Cultural Diversity (Music, Theatre, Cinema, Sports, Literature, Cuisine)
According to the results of the special Eurobarometer 469 (European Commission, 2017), the natives of most developed countries receiving the most migrants consider that they contribute to the enrichment of their cultural life (Table 7.2).

Although, at media level, the attitude of destination countries towards migrants is described as negative (Vasile et al., 2019), we note that natives recognize the merits of migrants in terms of diversity and cultural enrichment of the states in which they migrate. Sweden is at the top of the list, with 93% of the population believing that migrants bring a boost to the social life of the host countries; on the other hand, only 27% of Bulgarians share the same opinion. The population in countries such as the United

Table 7.2 The results of Eurobarometer 469 on the answer of the natives to the question "Do you consider that migrants contribute to the enrichment of the cultural life in your country?"

Share of natives who answered "YES"	*Country*	*Impact*
<25%	–	Modest
25–50%	Bulgaria, Malta, Czech Republic, Hungary, Republic of Cyprus, Slovakia, Greece, Latvia, Italy, Romania, Croatia	Moderate
50–75%	Slovenia, Estonia. Poland, Lithuania, France, Austria, Belgium, Spain, Germany, Ireland, United Kingdom	Strong
>75%	Portugal, Denmark, Luxembourg, Finland, the Netherlands, Sweden	Very strong

Source: Based on the data in the Eurobarometer 469 "Integration of immigrants in the European Union"

Kingdom or Germany, where the pressure on migrants was most evident, considers that migrants have a positive effect on the social and cultural aspect in proportion of 75% and 69%, respectively. In Romania, a state that does not have a significant influx of immigrants, opinions are divided: 47% of respondents answered in the affirmative and 46%—negatively, a result that can be generated by the lack of tolerance towards migrants or it may mean that their low number hasn't managed to influence social and cultural life in any way.

Exchange of Traditions and Customs with the Migrant Population

Migrants contribute to the enrichment of cultural life by introducing new ideas, customs and traditions. Far from erasing the existing culture, they expand it. The clearest example is found in the United States, where hundreds of different ethnic groups live in harmony under the American flag, building a shared culture.

Another relevant example would be the borrowing of a holiday specific for the migrants' home country. For example, Mardi Gras is a holiday that originated in France but is celebrated worldwide in places such as Brazil, France, Germany and the Netherlands. The Christmas tree or Santa Claus are other elements borrowed by the natives from migrants, and today, they have come to be adopted globally.

Negative Effects at the Macroeconomic Level

Increase Spending on Education for Migrants Attending State-Subsidized Schools

Destination countries incur additional costs to ensure access to education for migrant children as well (Kivisto, 2020). These expenses are considered inefficient and unsustainable, especially due to the fact that the migrant family can be involved in circular migration and then the graduate will not generate productive effects which would contribute to economic growth. Another example of unsustainable spending may be the situation where the pupil/student decides to leave the education system and is neither in education nor in employment (NEET). In this case, the amounts spent are not being capitalized on employment based on the qualification obtained, and secondly, he or she becomes the recipient of social benefits.

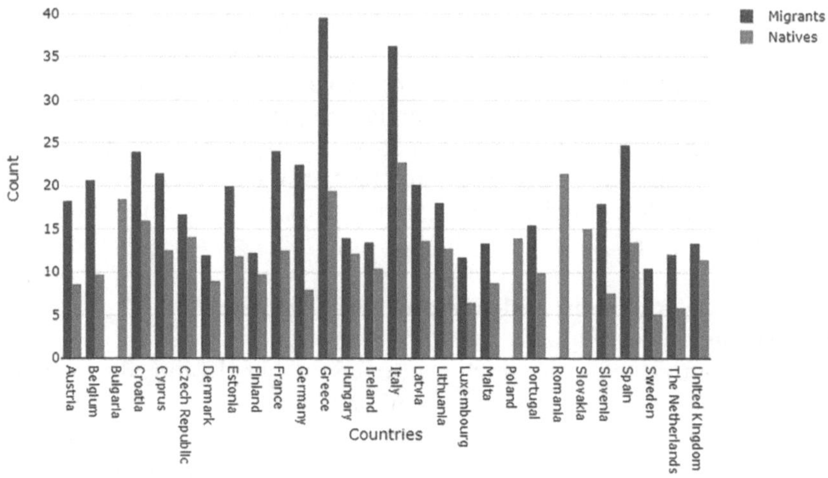

Fig. 7.4 Young people who are neither in education nor in employment in the European Union by country of origin in 2021, %. (Source: Based on Eurostat (2022) data). Note: No data are available on NEETs of migrant origin in Bulgaria, Romania, Poland and Slovakia, and for the UK the latest available data is from 2019

This risk is even higher, mainly due to the fact that in all countries, except Croatia and Hungary, the rate of NEET young people of foreign origin is higher compared to the natives, while Greece and Italy register values of about 35–40% (Fig. 7.4).

Increasing Spending on Access to Health Services

Due to the fact that developed countries are the preferred destination of migrants from poor countries, and they tend to have the highest fertility rate, once they arrive, they can benefit from prenatal and postnatal medical services, generating an increase in spending by destination countries. In Germany, for example, 1 in 4 children born in German cities has migrant parents (SPIEGEL, 2018). However, in the long run, these expenses have a positive impact on society.

At the same time, opponents of migrants believe that with their arrival in the country, expenses related to access to health services will increase due to the fact that migrants are more likely to be ill, but some studies (Neuman, 2014; Constant et al., 2015; Fox, 2018) have shown the opposite. Newly arrived migrants tend to be healthier compared to natives, and subsequent cases of illness occur after a certain amount of time spent in the destination country, as a result of either changing the diet, of working conditions or stress and others.

Increase State Spending on Providing Social Assistance to Unemployed Migrants
The granting of social aids and benefits generates the dissatisfaction of the local population and can lead to mass riots, a phenomenon that contradicts the objectives of sustainable development. However, there are papers (OECD, 2014; Jaumotte et al., 2016; Kancs & Lecca, 2018) according to which migrants generate higher fiscal benefits than expenses, paying taxes and fees which exceed the total aid received from developed countries.

Problems with the Availability and Distribution of Utilities as a Result of Changes in Geographical Distribution
The increase of the population in a certain area at a high rate and in a short period of time leads to the impossibility of providing all persons with utilities at the optimal quantity and quality. Therefore, the ability of local and central authorities to effectively manage such situations will depend on their ability to guarantee and ensure the provision of utilities, especially water and energy.

The Risk of Food Crises Due to Overcrowding in Urban Areas and the Reduction of the Rural Population Engaged in Agriculture
In recent years we tend to consume more than we produce. At the level of 2021, we consumed all the annual resources by July 28 (Global Footprint Network, 2022), at a faster pace than in previous years (in 2017 the annual resources were consumed by August 2). In addition, urban areas rely on adjacent ecosystem services to decompose biodegradable waste, but the capacity of ecosystems is not unlimited, and when overcrowded, downstream human settlements are endangered, as is agriculture, leading to the possibility of food crises.

Problems with Water Supply
As the population of cities increases as a result of migration, the amount of water for urban supply increases, which is redirected from the agricultural sector to consumption, thus affecting agricultural productivity (Kumar et al., 2020). According to studies, the amount of water

consumed by a person in an urban area is twice as high as the consumption of a person in a rural area (United Nations, 2015).

Negative Effects at Household and Individual Level

The Appearance of Health Problems
Studies show that migrants are more likely to have health problems than natives (Carballo & Nerukar, 2001; Brell et al., 2020). On the other hand, some studies point out that migrants can bring with them diseases that are unusual for the native population (Gushulak & MacPherson, 2004; Wilder-Smith et al., 2007; Brown et al., 2014).

Increasing Crime Rate
Opponents of immigration often argue that migrants contribute to higher crime rates, but research suggests that people tend to overestimate the relationship between immigration and crime (Nunziata, 2015; Hooghe & de Vroome, 2016). The literature (Bell, 2014; Papadopoulos, 2014; Vasile et al., 2019) provides mixed conclusions for the relationship between immigration and crime worldwide, but finds that immigration has no impact on the crime rate or can even help reduce it.

Migrants Tend to Import Their Culture
Migrants' thinking, norms, habits and customs expand and influence the culture of the destination country. Such extensions and influences may not be desired by the native population, for reasons that may include less civilized practices, restrictions and collisions with the rules, laws and values of the destination country in general (Adida et al., 2012; Chapman & Ciment, 2015).

The Emergence of Conflicts between Migrants and Natives
Distrust of neighbours and incrimination by local authorities mitigate viable forms of self-organization meant to fix the shortage of authorities protection, which over time can lead to significant conflicts with natives.

Short Appreciations

In the case of all the negative effects listed in the literature, the idea of the superiority of developed states over migrants from less developed countries is felt (Guma & Dafydd Jones, 2019). The attempt to keep their own culture and customs, the fear of the possibility of increased crime rate, although studies show no connection of migration to the phenomenon, the idea that migrants can bring new diseases, unusual for natives, are all elements of the superiority rich countries feel in relation to migrants, especially the low-skilled ones from the global economic periphery. The attitude of the native population and some policy measures adopted by the legislative authorities are aimed at reducing the number of migrants, but in the literature (Anderson, 2019) the notion of methodological denationalization has appeared, which considers that migration should not be reduced, this being one among the many ways in which human mobility has been guided and constrained over the centuries. Methodological denationalization implies that, globally and nationally, concepts such as citizens of a country and migrants should be abandoned, and the notion of the working citizen should emerge. This working citizen can originate from any country and should be treated equally. Anderson (2019) considers that the idea of the well-being of the citizens of one country should not persist to the detriment of others, but that there should be policies aimed at the well-being of all working citizens, regardless of origin.

References

Adams, R. H., & Page, J. (2005). Do International Migration and Remittances Reduce Poverty in Developing Countries? *World Development, 33*(10), 1645–1669. https://doi.org/10.1016/J.WORLDDEV.2005.05.004

Adida, C. L., Laitin, D. D., & Valfort, M.-A. (2012). Muslims in France: Identifying a Discriminatory Equilibrium. *Journal of Population Economics, 27*(4), 1039–1086.

Adunts, D., & Afunts, G. (2019). Seasonal Migration and Education of Children Left Behind: Evidence from Armenia. *SSRN Electronic Journal.* https://doi.org/10.2139/ssrn.3396383

Ambler, K., Aycinena, D., & Yang, D. (2015). Channeling Remittances to Education: A Field Experiment among Migrants from El Salvador. *American Economic Journal: Applied Economics, 7*(2), 207–232. https://doi.org/10.1257/app.20140010

Anderson, B. (2019). New Directions in Migration Studies: Towards Methodological de-Nationalism. *Comparative Migration Studies, 7*(1), 36. https://doi.org/10.1186/s40878-019-0140-8

Arango, J. (2017). Theories of International Migration. In: *Global Movement and Settlement* (pp. 25–45). Routledge.

Askarov, Z., & Doucouliagos, H. (2020). A Meta-Analysis of the Effects of Remittances on Household Education Expenditure. *World Development, 129*, 104860. https://doi.org/10.1016/J.WORLDDEV.2019.104860

Bell, B. (2014). *Crime and Immigration*. IZA World of Labor. https://doi.org/10.15185/izawol.33

Boboc, C., Vasile, V., & Todose, D. (2012). Vulnerabilities Associated to Migration Trajectories from Romania to EU Countries. *Procedia - Social and Behavioral Sciences, 62*, 352–359. https://doi.org/10.1016/J.SBSPRO.2012.09.056

Brell, C., Dustmann, C., & Preston, I. (2020). The Labor Market Integration of Refugee Migrants in High-Income Countries. *Journal of Economic Perspectives, 34*, 94.

Brown, D., Edwards, H., Seaton, L., & Buckley, T. (2014). *Lewis's Medical-Surgical Nursing: Assessment and Management of Clinical Problems* (4th ed.). Elsevier.

Carballo, M., & Nerukar, A. (2001). Migration, Refugees, and Health Risks. *Emerging Infectious Diseases, 7*(3 Suppl), 556–560. https://doi.org/10.3201/eid0707.017733

Chapman, R., & Ciment, J. (2015). *Culture Wars: An Encyclopedia of Issues, Viewpoints and Voices.* Accessed September 9, 2019, from https://books.google.ro/books?id=XO9nBwAAQBAJ&pg=PA330&redir_esc=y#v=onepage&q&f=false.

Cheianu-Andrei, D., Gramma, R., Milicenco, S., Pritcan, V., Rusnac, V., & Vaculovschi, D. (2011). *Specific Needs of Children and Elderly Left Behind as a Consequence of Migration*. CEP USM.

Constant, A. F., Garcia-Munoz, T., Neuman, S., & Neuman, T. (2015). A "Healthy Immigrant Effect" or a "Sick Immigrant Effect"? Selection and Policies Matter.

Dustmann, C., & Mestres, J. (2010). Remittances and Temporary Migration. *Journal of Development Economics, 92*(1), 62–70. https://doi.org/10.1016/J.JDEVECO.2008.12.002

European Commission. (2017). *Integration of Immigrants in the European Union. Special Eurobarometer 469.*

European Commission. (2019). *Standard Eurobarometer 91 Spring 2019 Public Opinion in the European Union.*

European Commission. (2022). *Standard Eurobarometer 96.*

Eurostat. (2022). Young People Neither in Employment nor in Education and Training by Sex, Age and Country of Birth (NEET rates) [edat_lfse_28] Last update: 11-05-2022. In: Eurostat Indicators. Accessed July 29, 2022, from https://appsso.eurostat.ec.europa.eu/nui/show.do?dataset=edat_lfse_28&lang=en.

Fassio, C., Montobbio, F., & Venturini, A. (2019). Skilled Migration and Innovation in European Industries. *Research Policy, 48*(3), 706–718. https://doi.org/10.1016/J.RESPOL.2018.11.002

Fox, M. (2018). *Migrants Don't Bring Disease. In Fact, They Help Fight It.* NBC. Accessed September 9, 2019, from https://www.nbcnews.com/storyline/immigration-border-crisis/migrants-don-t-bring-disease-fact-they-help-fight-it-n944146.

Gelb, S., & Krishnan, A. (2018). *Technology, Migration and the 2030 Agenda for Sustainable Development.*

Global Footprint Network. (2022). *Earth Overshoot Day.* Global Footprint Network. Accessed July 29, 2022, from https://www.overshootday.org/about/.

Guma, T., & Dafydd Jones, R. (2019). "Where Are We Going to Go Now?" European Union Migrants' Experiences of Hostility, Anxiety, and (Non-) Belonging During Brexit. *Population, Space and Place, 25*(2), 1–10.

Gushulak, B. D., & MacPherson, D. W. (2004). Globalization of Infectious Diseases: The Impact of Migration. *Clinical Infectious Diseases, 38*(12), 1742–1748. https://doi.org/10.1086/421268

Harder, N., Figueroa, L., Gillum, R. M., Hangartner, D., Laitin, D. D., & Hainmueller, J. (2018). Multidimensional Measure of Immigrant Integration. *Proceedings of the National Academy of Sciences of the United States of America, 115*(45), 11483. https://doi.org/10.1073/pnas.1808793115

Helliwell, J. F., Jeffrey, S., & De Neve, J.-E. (2021). *World Happiness Report 2021*, New York.

Hooghe, M., & de Vroome, T. (2016). The Relation between Ethnic Diversity and Fear of Crime: An Analysis of Police Records and Survey Data in Belgian Communities. *International Journal of Intercultural Relations, 50*, 66–75. https://doi.org/10.1016/J.IJINTREL.2015.11.002

Jaumotte, F., Koloskova, K., & Saxena, S. C. (2016). *Impact of Migration on Income Levels in Advanced Economies.* International Monetary Fund.

Kancs, d.' A., & Lecca, P. (2018). Long-Term Social, Economic and Fiscal Effects of Immigration into the EU: The Role of the Integration Policy. *The World Economy, 41*(10), 2599–2630. https://doi.org/10.1111/twec.12637

Katseli, L. T., Lucas, R. E. B., & Xenogiani, T. (2006). *Effects of Migration on Sending Countries: What Do We Know?* OECD.

King, R. (2012). *Theories and Typologies of Migration: An Overview and a Primer.* Malmö University.

Kivisto, P. (2020). Blaming Immigrants: Nationalism and the Economics of Global Movement. *Contemporary Sociology: A Journal of Reviews, 49*(3), 274. https://doi.org/10.1177/0094306120915912x

Kumar, P., Avtar, R., Dasgupta, R., Johnson, B. A., Mukherjee, A., Ahsan, M. N., Nguyen, D. C. H., Nguyen, H. Q., Shaw, R., & Mishra, B. K. (2020). Socio-Hydrology: A Key Approach for Adaptation to Water Scarcity and Achieving Human Well-Being in Large Riverine Islands. *Progress in Disaster Science, 8*, 100134. https://doi.org/10.1016/j.pdisas.2020.100134

Lam, T., & Yeoh, B. S. A. (2019). Parental Migration and Disruptions in Everyday Life: Reactions of Left-Behind Children in Southeast Asia. *Journal of Ethnic and Migration Studies, 45*(16), 3085. https://doi.org/10.1080/1369183X.2018.1547022

Lu, Y., Zhang, R., & Du, H. (2021). Family Structure, Family Instability, and Child Psychological Well-Being in the Context of Migration: Evidence from Sequence Analysis in China. *Child Development, 92*(4), e416–e438. https://doi.org/10.1111/cdev.13496

Matano, A., & Ramos, R. (2018). Remittances and Educational Outcomes: A Regional Investigation for Moldova. *The Annals of Regional Science, 60*(3), 451–471. https://doi.org/10.1007/s00168-016-0757-6

Medina, C., & Cardona, L. (2010). The Effects of Remittances on Household Consumption, Education Attendance and Living Standards: The Case of Colombia. *Lecturas de Economia, 72*, 11–43.

Neuman, S. (2014). *Are Immigrants Healthier than Native Residents?*

Nunziata, L. (2015). Immigration and crime: evidence from victimization data. *Journal of Population Economics, 28*(3), 697–736. https://doi.org/10.1007/s00148-015-0543-2

OECD. (2010). *Open for Business: Migrant Entrepreneurship in OECD Countries.* OECD Publishing.

OECD. (2014). *Is Migration Good for the Economy?* OECD.

OECD, ILO, World Bank. (2015). *The Contribution of Labour Mobility to Economic Growth.* OECD, ILO, World Bank.

Papadopoulos, G. (2014). Immigration Status and Property Crime: An Application of Estimators for Underreported Outcomes. *IZA Journal of Migration, 3*(1), 12. https://doi.org/10.1186/2193-9039-3-12

Rotariu Traian. (2009). *Demografie şi sociologia populaţiei: structuri şi procese demografice.* Polirom.

Smita, S. (2008). *Distress Seasonal Migration and its Impact on Children's Education.*

SPIEGEL. (2018). *Germany and Immigration: The Changing Face of the Country.* SPIEGEL. Accessed September 9, 2019, from https://www.spiegel.de/international/germany/germany-and-immigration-the-changing-face-of-the-country-a-1203143.html.

Stănculescu, M., Stoiciu, V., Alexe, I., & Motoc, L. (2011). *Impactul Crizei Economice Asupra Migraţiei Forţei De Muncă Româneşti.* Friedrich-Ebert-Stiftung.

Taylor, E. J. (1999). The New Economics of Labour Migration and the Role of Remittances in the Migration Process. *Internation Migration, 37*(1), 63–89.

United Nations. (2015). *International Decade for Action "Water for Life" 2005–2015.* Water and Cities.

United Nations. (2019). *World Population Prospects 2019.*

United Nations. (2020). International Migration 2019. In: *Department of Economic and Social Affairs. Population Division*. Accessed June 7, 2022, from https://www.un.org/development/desa/pd/sites/www.un.org.development.desa.pd/files/files/documents/2020/Feb/un_2019_internationalmigration_wallchart.pdf.

Valette, J. (2018). Do Migrants Transfer Productive Knowledge Back to Their Origin Countries? *Journal of Development Studies, 54*(9), 1637–1656. https://doi.org/10.1080/00220388.2017.1333109

Vasile, V., Bunduchi, E., & Ciuhu, A.-M. (2019). Immigrants' Economic and Social Integration in Host Country-from Preconceived Ideas to Real Life. Case Study on the Romanians'. *Challenges of the Knowledge Society*, 1143–1150.

Wilder-Smith, A., Schwartz, E., & Marc, S. (2007). *Travel Medicine: Tales Behind the Science*. Elsevier.

World Economic Forum. (2013). *The Business Case for Migration*.

Yoshino, N., Taghizadeh-Hesary, F., & Otsuka, M. (2017). *International Remittances and Poverty Reduction: Evidence from Asian Developing Countries*.

CHAPTER 8

Migration Policies and Remittances, as a Support Factor for Development in the Origin Country

Elena Bunduchi and Daniel Stefan

The Migration Strategy

Mobility and Migration Strategy at EU Level

One of the fundamental principles of the European Union is free movement mentioned in the Treaty on the Functioning of the European Union (TFEU) (European Union, 2012). The rules of the Treaty on the free movement of persons initially applied only to economically active persons. Since 1993, European Union (1992), through Articles 20 and 21, has changed the EU rules on the free movement of persons, so that all EU citizens have obtained the right to move and reside within the EU, without restrictions. EU citizens who have the status of "worker" in another EU country have the same rights as working citizens in that country. These legal provisions are in line with the non-discrimination universal principle based on the nationality of individuals (European Union, 2010; European Union, 2012). Likewise, Directive 38 (European Union, 2011) was implemented, which aims to apply measures on respecting the right to free movement.

The principle of free movement also relates to non-EU countries, members of the European Free Trade Association (EFTA) as well as Switzerland.

V. Vasile et al., *International Labour Mobility*,
https://doi.org/10.1007/978-3-031-18683-7_8

At the EU level, the status of the posted worker[1] is also regulated by the European Union (2018), which ensures equal rights in relation to the citizens of the host Member State.

On 13 March 2018, the European Commission presented a legislative proposal on the creation of a European Labour Authority, which seeks to guarantee that EU legislation on labour mobility is applied in a fair, transparent and efficient way. Its role is to resolve the various situations that have arisen between Member States with regard to labour market issues, including the management of labour mobility disputes caused by disparities between labour market systems.

Millions of EU citizens have benefited from free movement, but its consequences have been the subject of intense public and political debate in many EU countries, especially after the 2008 economic crisis.

In addition to worker mobility, the EU is also facing migration from third-country nationals. The EU's goal is to establish a stable approach to handling regular migration and preventing the illegal one. Appropriate supervision of migration flows means guaranteeing decent treatment of third-country nationals legally residing in the EU, improving methods to prevent illegal migration and fostering stronger cooperation with third countries in all areas. EU's goal is to create a set of rights and obligations for legal migrants, similar to that for EU citizens.

In order to manage the flow of people from the EU Member States and third countries, the European Union has established a number of policies.

Global Approach to Migration and Mobility

In 2011, the European Commission approved the "Global Approach to Migration and Mobility" (GAMM), which sets out general rules on EU relations with third countries in the field of migration, with human rights being a transversal area of GAMM. The main areas of regulation are set on legal and illegal migration, human trafficking prevention, asylum policy and the impact of migration flows on economic growth.

Strategic Orientations Starting with 2014

An area of freedom, security and justice serving the citizen—Stockholm programme (AFSJ) was implemented in December 2009 as a continuation

[1] The posted worker is an employee sent by the company where he works to provide certain services in another Member State for a limited period of time.

of the multiannual programmes adopted in Tampere (1999) and The Hague (2004) and ended in 2014. In March 2014, the European Commission issued a statement, entitled "An open and secure Europe". In agreement with Article 68 of the TFEU, the European Council defined the "strategic guidelines for legislative and operational planning in the area of freedom, security and justice" for the period 2014–2020. These are not a programme and focus on the purpose of transferring, applying and consolidating current legal tools and procedures. The guidelines emphasize the importance of adopting a universal approach to the phenomenon, which could make the best use of legal migration, thus providing safety, preventing illegal migration and effectively controlling borders.

European Agenda for Migration

The European Agenda for Migration (European Commission, 2015) proposes prompt actions to deal with the situation in the Mediterranean, which are to be taken in the coming years in order to deal more effectively with all aspects of immigration.

Regarding long-term actions, the Commission recommends:

- Combating illegal migration
- Securing borders through effective management of migrant flows
- The development of a common and effective asylum policy
- The modernization of the "blue card" system and creation of an effective model for legal immigration into the EU by evaluating the existing framework and boosting cooperation with key origin countries in order to ensure legal remedies for the EU

A new Strategic Agenda 2019–2024

This Agenda provides a general framework for promoting the interests of citizens and centres on:

- Protecting citizens and their freedoms
- Building a strong and vibrant economic base
- Building a green, fair, social and climate-neutral Europe
- Promoting European values and interests

In addition, the EU negotiates readmission agreements with origin countries for the transit and for the return of illegal migrants and collaborates with them to prevent human trafficking. The readmission agreements intend to deliver the required inducement for readmission negotiations in the concerned third country, without encouraging clandestine migration.

An analysis of the current provisions of the EU acquis suggests that, for stays longer than three months, there is a fundamental difference between mobility rights for EU citizens and migration rights for third-country nationals, with more limited conditions for the latter.

EU directives on the migration of third-country nationals give freedom to the national laws of the Member States. Thus, these can limit or encourage migration from third countries in accordance with national policies and priorities; there are, thus, differences in rules and practices at EU level.

New Pact on Migration and Asylum

This Pact consists of nine legislative and non-legislative initiatives. Its aim is to create stronger governance at the Member State level on migration and asylum, balancing the principles of shared responsibility and solidarity within the EU; to develop legal migration routes and liquidate illegal ones; to implement integrated and rapid procedures for establishing migrant and asylum status, together with efficient management of borders and the Schengen area in order to increase resilience to possible crises, regardless of their nature; and to improve cooperation among EU and the main third origin countries. This Pact was even more necessary with the COVID-19 pandemic, which led to a violation of the basic principle of the European Union—free movement. In an effort to control the spread of the new virus, authorities have decided to impose travel restrictions. These had effects on both EU and non-EU citizens and had consequences for migrant flows, especially for migrant labour. However, for certain categories of workers, such as those in key sectors (health, transport, agriculture, etc.), there were certain facilities in order not to block the development of activities and the transformation of the pandemic crisis into an economic one. These workers had the status of critical/ essential/ key workers, regulated by European Commission Guidelines (European Commission, 2020). Their mobility was thus possible within the European Union. The details of their status, including the policy measures carried out by the Member States to facilitate access, are discussed in Chap. 10.

Migration Strategy in Romania

Migration is a phenomenon that Romania is facing, both from the perspective of immigration and emigration. Although Romania's role as a country of origin for migrant labour is well known, it is gradually beginning to become attractive from the perspective of the destination country, especially for migrants from Asian countries (Popovici, 2021). This attractiveness is due both to the increase in the level of economic development of Romania and to the volatility registered in the Black Sea basin. Due to the increased emigration, Romania is starting to face a labour shortage; hence, attracting new workers, especially from non-EU countries, was an action to reduce this deficit. At the insistence of employers, the number of foreigners admitted to the labour market increased from 5500 to 100,000 people in 2021 compared to 2016 (Ofițeru, 2022). In addition to the fact that there are more legal migrants, the official data of the Border Police indicate 91,014 attempts to cross the border illegally (Border Police, 2022) twice as many compared with the previous period. And the number of asylum seekers has increased to 9591 (36% more than compared to 2020). With the outbreak of the military conflict on the Romanian border, their number is constantly increasing, so it is important to manage as efficiently as possible the flows of people who want to transit or stay in Romania.

In this sense, the integration of foreigners in the economic and social life of Romania puts significant pressure on the policy and strategies for efficient management of the phenomenon. As an EU member state, Romania must take into account European legislation and directives in the field of migration, but these are adjusted depending on the directions of national policy.

Therefore, in 2021, the National Strategy on Immigration was elaborated, targeting the period 2021–2024 (Romanian Government, 2021). The aim of the Strategy is to offer a normative framework on the efficient migration management and includes strategic and specific objectives and directions of action in the field of migration.

The first objective of the Strategy refers to the efficient management of the migration phenomenon, through a better information made available to the responsible institutions from the migrants' origin countries; the adapting of national legislation to the European one concerning the development of legal migration channels for third-country nationals; and the facilitation of the migrants' access to the labour market and the education system.

The second objective aims to align the national asylum system with the European and international one, in order to streamline the process of granting asylum or refugee status, to ensure optimal conditions for the assistance of applicants, as well as the relocation of asylum seekers and refugees.

The third objective concerns preparedness measures for a high influx of migrants, which could occur in crisis situations in their country of origin.

The last general objective includes the measures necessary for the successful implementation of policies in the field of migration, asylum and integration of foreigners in Romania.

Therefore, in the objectives of the National Immigration Strategy, a special emphasis is placed on the flows of migrants and their efficient management, and a very vague mention is made of the mobility of EU citizens; there is a very clear delimitation between the two categories of flows of people.

In addition to the National Strategy on Immigration, Romania also applies the National Strategy for Romanians Abroad (Ministry for Romanians Abroad, 2017), which addressed all Romanians living in diaspora communities and in the historical/traditional ones in Romania's neighbouring states. The purpose of this strategy was to promote respect for the rights and interests of Romanians abroad; however, the objectives of the strategy were focused more on Romanians in historical and traditional communities than on Romanians in the diaspora (Table 8.1).

Although in the National Strategy for Romanians Abroad for the period 2017–2020 were mentioned measures for the integration of Romanians returned in Romania, we consider that they were not enough, as measures to develop entrepreneurial relations not only with Romanians returning home, but also with those who are in the destination country, but remit in Romania, are necessary. The management of efficient relations between state institutions and the diaspora can promote the development and economic growth of Romania, if the money sent home is directed to investments, and not only in consumption.

At the level of 2022, there is no Strategy for the efficient management of relations with Romanians in the diaspora, so that, since 2021, citizens from other destination states have been called upon to contribute by completing a questionnaire to develop a new strategy, but this has not yet entered into force.

Table 8.1 Implications of the National Strategy for Romanians Abroad on Romanians in the diaspora for the period 2017–2020

General objectives	*Specific objectives*	*Implications for the diaspora*
Preserving, developing and affirming the identity of Romanians abroad.	Promoting the Romanian language in the educational field, social environment, media; and Romanian culture in Romanian communities.	These directions of action target exclusively the persons of Romanian origin located in the communities from the neighbouring states with Romania, as there is no reference to the diaspora within this objective.
Consolidation of the Romanian associative environment abroad.	Formation of representative organizations of Romanians in the host countries.	The intention to elaborate the measures for informing the Romanians from the destination countries regarding the observance of the legislation of the respective countries is mentioned; and supporting the formation of associations of associations abroad, but there is no mention on the concrete directions in which these actions will be carried out.
Supporting the integration processes and defending the rights of Romanians abroad.	Defending the rights of Romanians; supporting their integration in the country of destination; supporting return migration.	Supporting the diaspora by pursuing respect for their rights under EU regulations or bilateral agreements in the case of Romanians in non-EU countries. Assistance regarding the integration in the Romanian society of the returned migrants through business opportunities, of accessing European funds; and recognition of seniority in work.
Institutional consolidation and efficiency in the field of Romanians everywhere.	Harmonization of legislation at national level regarding Romanians everywhere; ensuring transparency and a dialogue between institutions and Romanian citizens.	Establishing a dialogue between the diaspora and government institutions on the definition of public policies aimed at them.

The lack of well-targeted measures to keep the population employed, as well as to attract through policies the return of Romanians already involved in migration, was felt most in the pandemic context, when Romanians once seen as supporting poor families were suddenly accused and treated with contempt for bringing home new cases of COVID-19 (aspect dealt with in Chap. 9).

Policies on Migration and Remittance Dynamics, as a Support Factor for Development in the Origin Country

The role of diaspora on the entrepreneurship in the destination country began to be highlighted as early as the 1970s. Studies have shown the positive impact of migrants in the destination country, as a result of setting up small and medium-sized enterprises (SMEs), as a result of creating and expanding niche markets in migrant communities and creating jobs for both natives, as well as for other migrants (Kloosterman & Rath, 2003).

Research shows that entrepreneurship among migrants is growing (Wadhwa et al., 2009; Lofstrom & Wang, 2019; Brzozowski et al., 2021; Marques et al., 2022). According to a study by the American Immigration Council (2022), migrants and their children founded 44% of Fortune 500 companies in the United States, generating revenues of 7.2 trillion dollars in 2021. At the same time, the study found that Fortune 500 companies founded by migrants and their children employed 14.8 million people in the United States. Nearly 3.2 million migrants run their own businesses, including SMEs, and they are more likely to be entrepreneurs than Americans (American Immigration Council, 2022). Thus, these new entrepreneurs have an important role in the development of the US economy, because the increase in the number of jobs in the United States is attributed to new companies and start-ups. Within the European Union, entrepreneurship among migrants is becoming more widespread, but their share in total entrepreneurs differs in the Member States, from 1% in Poland to over 20% in the UK and Cyprus (OECD, 2017). Due to the fact that many migrants' businesses are in areas such as retail, restaurants and catering (Jennings et al., 2013), they sell products from the country of origin to diaspora members and even the natives of the destination country (Khojasteh & Raja, 2017). In this way, there is a win-win situation; in the origin country there is an increase in exports and the promotion of domestic products, and in the country of destination migrant business contributes to economic growth by creating new jobs and increasing budget revenues.

Due to the impact of diaspora entrepreneurship in the destination country, we consider that it can also generate benefits in the country of origin, as follows:

- It contributes to business and career development and innovation. Considerable investments by diaspora members, if successful, create jobs and stimulate competition.
- It establishes economic, political and social capital due to global networks. Less developed countries are more likely to be isolated from global trade, capital and knowledge flows. Diaspora members have the opportunity to create connections with potential partners in the destination country. These can lead to opportunities for joint investment, trade and the encouragement of strategic partnerships; through which they can accelerate the transfer of technology from richer to poorer countries.
- It increases human capital by transferring the knowledge gained in the destination country. The human capital that entrepreneurs in the diaspora can bring to their country of origin is reflected not just in new knowledge and abilities, but as well in the skills needed to identify and explore investment opportunities overlooked by local entrepreneurs as a result of their ability to switch between different cultural perspectives.
- Diaspora entrepreneurship is transformed into social capital, as a result of cultural and linguistic identities. Diaspora has benefits compared with other foreign entrepreneurs who invest in their country of origin: knowledge of cultural and social customs, the business environment and the local language.

The development of entrepreneurship in the country of origin from migrants' financial sources is supported in many states by state institutions and various organizations, which have created programs to promote investment amongst migrants. Initiatives differ from private funding to those managed by the home government or mixed funding, but most involve a public-private partnership. Some initiatives are strictly aimed at migrants from different countries of destination, others have open access, their purpose being the contribution of migrants through remittances to the economic development of the origin country.

Networking Organizations

Networking organizations are institutions whose purpose is to stimulate diaspora entrepreneurship by providing prospects for meetings between local professionals and migrants in order to initiate potential business in the origin country. Certain of these organizations encourage partnerships between locals and diaspora members, and others facilitate the creation of partnerships between diaspora professionals from different destination countries.

RePatriot

Repatriot is a Romanian community that aims to provide tools for support, counselling, entrepreneurship education and opportunities for partnerships between the diaspora and the Romanian population. During the first three editions of the RePatriot Summit, over 700 participants were involved, and as a result of these meetings, businesses were established in areas such as IT, tourism, technology, agriculture, construction, etc. (RePatriot, 2019).

BiD Network

The growing business network provides assistance to migrant and native entrepreneurs in raising funds for business projects in 12 underdeveloped countries such as Uganda, Mexico, Argentina, Bolivia, Tanzania, Colombia, Peru, Kenya, Rwanda, the Philippines, Jordan and Ecuador. Network assistance consists of posting the business plan developed by entrepreneurs on the network's website, where experts and investors can contact potential entrepreneurs in order to implement business plans. The network is successful, with 237 partnerships, attracting more than $ 34 million to East African countries (BiD Network, 2019).

Mexican Talent Network

The Mexican talent network was initiated in 2005 by the Secretariat for External Relations in partnership with the National Council for Science and Technology and the Mexican Institute of Foreigners, being financially supported by the United States-Mexico Foundation for Science. It facilitates the transfer of knowledge of highly qualified Mexican professionals who are abroad, in the fields of business development, education and entrepreneurship, and promotes the image of Mexico as a favourable business destination for international shareholders. The Mexican Talent Network facilitates the creation of internship programs for teachers, researchers and students, in companies suggested by the network members; it provides expertise through network members in areas such as the automotive and aerospace industry, creative industry; and develops strategies to increase the impact of Mexican businesses that could offer outsourcing services. Currently, the Network comprises over 6500 Mexican professional members, located in 28 countries worldwide, carrying out over 180 projects in research, science and technology; innovation; creative industries; and social responsibility (Uribe & Vizcaino, 2018).

Mentoring Organizations

Compared to network organizations, mentoring organizations show greater involvement in promoting entrepreneurship among returned migrants, due to the fact that they try to build partnerships between business people who want to expand their business in different states and experts or business leaders from the diaspora of those countries. Mentoring organizations provide assistance in conducting feasibility studies and market research, internships and employment opportunities within them.

GlobalScot

GlobalScot is a diaspora-based mentoring organization in Scotland that promotes economic development. In 2001, Scottish Enterprise (funded by the Scottish government) released GlobalScot as a worldwide network comprising Scottish businessmen encouraging the growth of the Scottish economy. The purpose of the GlobalScot organization is to increase the attractiveness of Scotland's investment climate (Global Scot, 2018).

The organization has over 600 members, who perform on average over 1000 contracts in various economic fields in over 50 states (Global Scot, 2018). GlobalScot helps entrepreneurs to identify business opportunities abroad, by conducting market research, negotiating business offers, making business plans and developing business migrants' networks. Moreover, GlobalScot has given lectures in schools and universities, providing professional development instruction and opportunities for internships or even employment within the organization.

Armenia 2020

Armenia 2020 is a mentoring organization launched in 2001, which aimed to train the Armenian diaspora in finding various training scenarios for the Republic of Armenia by 2020. Across its conferences and dedicated posts, it aims to provide guidance in the process of developing internal and external migration management policies, leading to the economic development of Armenia. Several members of the organization are also members of the National Competitiveness Council of Armenia, which assists the Prime Minister in establishing investment attraction policies in Armenia. Armenia 2020 has been expanded to 2031, continuing to focus on strategic analyses of finding Armenia's long-term economic growth opportunities (Initiatives for Development of Armenia, 2019).

Training Organizations

Training organizations help potential entrepreneurs in the diaspora gain the expertise and abilities needed to run a profitable business. These training organizations facilitate the transfer of knowledge from diaspora experts to home or diaspora entrepreneurs, provide business management lessons and guidance on how to finance a business.

Programme Solidarité Eau

The programme for economic projects and migration was initiated by the Programme Solidarité Eau (a non-profit organization) in 2001. The aim of this programme is to assist African migrants in France to apply for business projects in France and in their origin countries. The programme is funded by the French Ministry of Foreign Affairs, the French Ministry for Employment, Labour and Social Cohesion, Programme Solidarité Eau, along with the European Commission and the Catholic Committee against Hunger and for Development. Micro Enterprise Support Group, in 1996, started to coordinate the Programme Solidarité Eau, a network of public authorities, development organizations and migrant associations, which advocates business projects initiated by migrants residing in France. The Micro Enterprise Support Group provides migrants with business assistance in their home countries. The network provides annual support to nearly 1000 African entrepreneurs (Program Solidarite Eau, 2019).

IntEnt

IntEnt, based in the Netherlands, was established in 1996 in the Netherlands by (SEON),[2] FACET BV[3] and Triodos Bank,[4] at the request of the Dutch Ministry of Foreign Trade and Development Cooperation. Its aim is to take measures to promote entrepreneurship amongst migrants.

The organization provides assistance in creating businesses to stimulate economic growth in Morocco, Turkey, Suriname, Ghana, Ethiopia, Afghanistan and the Antilles. Among the benefits it offers to potential entrepreneurs, there are: orientation sessions and training courses; counselling; consulting; market research; mediation; assistance during and after the establishment of the business; management training; and additional funding opportunities. Between 1998 and 2007, IntEnt contributed to the establishment of 236 companies, concluded 194 business plans, qualified 1176 participants and accepted 1693 customers. The total value of the investments exceeds EUR 14.5 million, at the same time, almost 900 new jobs have been created, which proves their sustainability (Newland & Tanaka, 2010).

Investment Organizations

Investment organizations offer funds and capital infusions to potential entrepreneurs in the diaspora who have innovative business concepts that will promote the economic growth of their origin countries. Some of these investment organizations are more involved in overseeing different types of expenses which occur at different stages of business project implementation, and others are interested in the final results. Due to the fact that these organizations cannot provide business consulting and mentoring, they provide financial entrepreneurs with financial resources, which allow them to carry out their business plans.

Start-up Diaspora in Romania

Under the 2014–2020 human resources programme, measures have been developed to attract investment from the diaspora. Released in 2016 and

[2] SEON is an organization that offers consulting to SMEs, as well and trainings in the Netherlands.

[3] FACET BV is an organization that offers consulting to SMEs of states in transition and development from Central and Eastern Europe.

[4] Triodos Bank is a Dutch bank, with branches in over 30 countries.

managed by the Romanian Ministry of Foreign Affairs, the programme seeks to stimulate diaspora entrepreneurs to invest in Romania. The programme is dedicated to all Romanian regions, except Bucharest-Ilfov, and received EUR 30 million funding from the European Structural and Investment Funds 2014–2020. It financed the formation of innovative and non-agricultural enterprises in the urban areas of Romania and was dedicated to Romanians who had emigrated for at least one year in the previous three years and had the experience of entrepreneurship abroad, specific work experience and professional training in the investment area (Ministry of Foreign Affairs, 2019). Thirty-two projects worth over RON 76 million (approximately EUR 16 million) were approved under the diaspora start-up program (CilvConsulting, 2019). Most of the chosen projects target Romanian migrants from Italy, Greece and Spain, and the feedback received suggests that there is a high demand among all Romanian migrants for support in setting up businesses back home.

1 × 1 Program in Mexico
On 1 January 2009, the Mexican government started an investment program called 1 × 1, which involves providing financial resources from government funds to finance the business projects of Mexican migrants. Migrants can apply for a loan of up to 300,000 Mexican pesos (nearly $ 25,000). The loan is exempt from interest. The distinctive characteristic of the 1 × 1 program is that the loan is not repaid to the government, but becomes a payment to a social investment through the Tres por Uno (3 × 1) remittance-based program (Migration News, 2009). In this way, in fact, migrants indirectly invest in social projects authorized by associations in his Mexican hometown (modernization of schools, housing for the poor, etc.), and the amount of repayment is covered by other federal or state funds. As a result, the 1 × 1 program helps both the small business projects of migrant entrepreneurs and the collective investments of the community.

African Diaspora Marketplace
USAID and Western Union launched a competition in 2009 in which American members of the African diaspora proposed business ideas for SMEs that would promote economic growth in Sub-Saharan Africa. Applicants need to be in partnership with an organization in Africa and to hold at least 25% of the capital of that organization. The goal of the African Diaspora Marketplace is to stimulate job creation, earn revenue and

produce goods and services by providing appropriate grants to potential entrepreneurs in the African diaspora living in the United States (African Diaspora Marketplace, 2019). The winners of the competition received grants of up to $ 100,000. The main winning areas are the establishment of medical institutions, a franchise business that would provide healthcare to people living in rural Ghana, establishment of a materials for students used at school. The term of execution of business plans is 18 months (International Diaspora Engagement Alliance, 2019).

Crowdfunding

With the involvement of the diaspora community, crowdfunding platforms lead to connecting people from different regions in order to support entrepreneurship, increasing the standard of living and the economic level in the country of origin, through remittances and diaspora investments.

LelapaFund

LelapaFund is a crowdfunding platform whose purpose is to promote investment opportunities in previously untapped areas on the African continent. Focusing exclusively on SMEs, Lelapa reduces costs for its customers by combining investment preparation for SMEs with high-precision, data-based tools. Lelapa has operations in Nairobi, Kenya and Paris, France (LelapaFund, 2019).

Government24

Guvern24 is a crowdfunding platform in the Republic of Moldova, launched in 2016, aiming to create a community of people willing to provide the necessary resources for the development of the country. It supports projects in areas such as business development, science and technology, culture and public infrastructure. By the end of 2016, about 23 projects from different localities were financed, totalling over 2 million MDL, the equivalent of approximately 100,000 euros, collected from over 5000 Moldovan migrants (Vasilache et al., 2017). The funded projects focused on road repair and maintenance, drinking water supply, local economic development, road infrastructure development, public lighting, etc. So far, over 400 projects have been registered on the crowdfunding platform (Guvern24, 2019).

Instead of Conclusions

Migration is a phenomenon that requires the establishment of rules, measures and policies for the effective management of its causes and consequences. At the European Union level, migration policies must be in line with the principles of solidarity and responsibility shared by all Member States. The European Migration Strategy makes a clear delimitation between the term EU worker and migrants from third countries, as well as refugees and asylum seekers. Due to the fact that Romania is not a state of interest for the last category of migrants, we did not refer to them regarding the measures in the Immigration Strategy.

In addition to immigration strategies, state institutions need to develop policies for migrants.

The issue of managing the effects of migration and of appropriate policy measures to optimize the effects is an open and quite controversial issue in the literature and in decision-making.

Migration policy, naturally, aims to maximize the effects of human mobility. The policy of the individual is the main divergence of the objectives and expectations of the country of origin and is increasingly subject to complex restrictions from the perspective of the country of immigration, at a time when free movement is a fundamental right. The open question is to what extent we can create a balance of policy, starting from the principle of freedom and pursuing the aspects of sustainable development, human, social, economic and environmental protection. Policies promoted at the national level in recent decades focus mainly on immigrant management, and the emphasis, through regulatory measures, is varied, from freedom, respectively, non-regulation and acceptance of the dynamics of social development through multiculturalism, to policy measures aimed at social assimilation, and tackling conditions that may lead to immigrants' limitations of access (conditions, language, level of education, professional profile, etc.).

From a policy perspective we have:

- Migration management policies, which mainly lead to multiple restrictions
- Lack of emigration management policies or acceptance of an aggressive international recruitment policy (head hunter), international recruitment agencies, online platforms for managing demand versus labour supply for geographical areas that exceed the national territory (e-jobs)

- Diaspora policies aimed at repatriation in order to address chronic deficits in countries of origin (structural demographic deficit in the labour market, often chronic)

In most cases, these return policies have yielded far too poor results (the repatriation policy in times of crisis), which raises the question of the usefulness of often significant financial efforts made by the country of origin for return versus policies of remaining home and integration into the labour market of the young generation and solving the NEETS problem.

References

African Diaspora Marketplace. (2019). African Diaspora Marketplace. http://www.diasporamarketplace.org/.

American Immigration Council (2022). New American Fortune 500 in 2022: The Largest American Companies and Their Immigrant Roots. https://data.americanimmigrationcouncil.org/en/fortune500-2022/

BiD Network. (2019). Facilitating Investment for East African SMEs. https://www.bidnetwork.org/page/121645/.

Border Police. (2022). *Activity Report 2021.* Border Police. https://www.politiadefrontiera.ro/files/docu/1646123974382-sintezabilantpfr2021final.pdf.

Brzozowski, J., Šimić Banović, R., Alpeza, M. (2021). Overcoming constraints to immigrant entrepreneurship in Croatia: the role of formal and informal institutions. *Post-Communist Economies, 34*(8), 1–28. https://doi.org/10.1080/14631377.2021.1928825

CilvConsulting. (2019). *Planul de afaceri - Romania Diaspora Start Up.* https://planul-de-afaceri.ro/plan-de-facere-finantare-fonduri-europene/romania-diaspora/

European Comission. (2015). A European Agenda on Migration. *Brussels, 13.5.2015 COM (2015) 240 Final.*

European Commission. (2020). *Communication from the Commission.* Guidelines Concerning the Exercise of the Free Movement of Workers during COVID-19 Outbreak (2020/C 102 I/03). Official Journal of the European Union. https://ec.europa.eu/esco/portal/how

European Union. (1992). *Treaty on European Union.* https://eur-lex.europa.eu/legal-content/RO/TXT/?uri=celex:11992M/TXT.

European Union. (2010). *Carta drepturilor fundamentale a Uniunii Europene.* Jurnalul Oficial al Uniunii Europene.

European Union. (2011). Directiva 2004/38/CE A Parlamentului European și a Consiliului.

European Union. (2012). *Consolidated version of the Treaty on the Functioning of the European UNION*. Official Journal of the European Union.

European Union. (2018). *Directiva (UE) 2018/957 a Parlamentului European și a Consiliului din 28 iunie 2018 de modificare a Directivei 96/71/CE privind detașarea lucrătorilor în cadrul prestării de servicii*. PE/18/2018/REV/1. https://eur-lex.europa.eu/legal-content/RO/TXT/?uri=CELEX:32018L0957

Global Scot. (2018). *Unlocking Your Growth Potential*.

Guvern24. (2019). *Conectăm oamenii – Guvern 24*. https://guvern24.md/categories/

Initiatives for Development of Armenia. (2019). *Armenia 2020*. https://www.idea.am/armenia-2020

International Diaspora Engagement Alliance. (2019). *The African Diaspora Marketplace*. http://www.diasporaalliance.org/african-diaspora-marketplace/.

Jennings, J., Bryant, M. L., Chawla, C.-H., Jankie, A., & Lawrence, J. (2013). *Immigrant Entrepreneurs Creating Jobs and Strengthening the U.S. Economy in Growing Industries*. Immigrant Learning Center, ILC & The ILC Public Education Institute.

Khojasteh, M., & Raja, S. (2017). Agents of Change: How Immigrant-Run Ethnic Food Retailers Improve Food Environments. *Journal of Hunger & Environmental Nutrition, 12*(3), 299–327. https://doi.org/10.1080/19320248.2015.1112759

Kloosterman, R., & Rath, J. (2003). *Immigrant Entrepreneurs: Venturing Abroad in the Age of Globalization*. Berg.

LelapaFund. (2019). *LelapaFund*. https://www.lelapafund.com/about

Lofstrom, M. W. & Wang, C. (2019). Immigrants and entrepreneurship. *IZA World of Labor*. https://wol.iza.org/articles/immigrants-and-entrepreneurship/long

Marques, C. S., R Galvão, A., Mascarenhas, C., Pinto, D. (2022). The importance of immigrant and return migrant entrepreneurship in the development of a low-density region. *Strategic Change, 31*(2), 259–268.

Migration News. (2009). Mexico: Migrants, Remittances, 3×1 - Migration News | Migration Dialogue. https://migration.ucdavis.edu/mn/more.php?id=3548.

Ministry of Foreign Affairs. (2019). *Diaspora Star-Up*. http://diaspora-start-up.ro/detalii-finantare/.

Ministerul pentru Români de Pretutindeni. (2017). *Strategia Națională pentru Românii de Pretutindeni pentru perioada 2017–2020*.

Newland, K., & Tanaka, H. (2010). *Mobilizing Diaspora Entrepreneurship for Development. Diaspora Development and Policy Project*. Migration Policy Institute. https://doi.org/10.4324/9781315646763

OECD. (2017). *The Missing Entrepreneurs 2017*. OECD. https://doi.org/10.1787/9789264283602-en

Ofițeru, A. (2022). De ce a aprobat România cu 400% mai mulți muncitori străini decât anul trecut: „E o soluție de avarie". Europa Liberă. https://romania.europalibera.org/a/muncitori-straini-romania/31676022.html.

Popovici, O. C. (2021). *Impact of Immigration and Population Change on Economic and Social Development in Romania.*

Program Solidarite Eau. (2019). *The Economic Initiatives and Migration Programme.*

RePatriot. (2019). *Repatriot.* https://repatriot.ro/despre/

Romanian Government. (2021). 2021–2024 National Strategy for Immigration. https://igi.mai.gov.ro/wpcontent/uploads/2021/10/strategia_nationala_din_19_august_2021.pdf

Uribe, D. O., & Vizcaino, B. (2018). 15 years Connecting Mexico Around the World: The Institute for Mexicans Abroad (IME) | LinkedIn. https://www.linkedin.com/pulse/15-years-connecting-mexico-around-world-institute-ime-oliva-uribe/.

Vasilache, A., Bunyan, D., & Tejada, G. (2017). Ghid de planificare strategică locală cu integrarea migrației, principiilor drepturilor omului și egalității de gen | PNUD în Moldova.

Wadhwa, V., Saxenian, A., Freeman, R., Gereff, G., & Salkever, A. (2009). *America's Loss is the World's Gain: America's New Immigrant Entrepreneurs, Part IV.*

CHAPTER 9

COVID-19 Boomerang Effect on the Migration Policies of the Country of Origin

Elena Bunduchi and Daniel Stefan

Introduction

The new coronavirus (2019-nCoV), or severe respiratory syndrome virus (SARS-CoV-2) as it is now called, has spread rapidly from Wuhan city in Hubei Province, China, to the rest of the world (Wang et al., 2020).

Massive Chinese migration during the Chinese New Year was thought to have fuelled the epidemic, and cases in other provinces in China and other countries (Thailand, Japan and fast-growing South Korea) were reported in people returning from Wuhan (Singhal, 2020).

From this perspective, it was considered that population migration is the key factor in the spread of the new virus (Jia et al., 2020). Most of the differential space transmission of SARS-CoV-2 (COVID-19) in China is due to migrants returning from the affected regions. The population that emigrated from Wuhan was the main source of infection in other cities and provinces. The long-distance transmission of COVID-19 from cities such as Harbin and Wenzhou happened due to the large number of migrants from Wuhan to these cities, and to the likelihood that migrants have engaged in long-distance travel (Fan et al., 2020).

V. Vasile et al., *International Labour Mobility*,
https://doi.org/10.1007/978-3-031-18683-7_9

During the outbreak of the COVID-19 pandemic, government officials and researchers were concerned that mass movement of humans could contribute to the spread of the disease (Nikolaenko, 2021). Hence, pandemic control policies had as their central element measures of social distancing. This proved an effective tool in managing past epidemics, limiting human-to-human transmission and reducing morbidity and mortality (Hatchett et al., 2007; Caley et al., 2008). Social distancing can reduce the spread of the epidemic, but it has generally been applied in combination with other actions—including more restrictive measures such as isolation and quarantine.

In some countries, although the authorities imposed methods to mitigate COVID-19 transmission, these led to precarious situations that even caused adverse effects, leading to the intensification of the transmission of the new virus. For example, imposing social distancing led, in many countries, to a stop of the main economic activities and the almost general lockdown of the economy, leading, in turn, to an increase in the number of people left without jobs. The most vulnerable employees were migrant workers who were engaged in medium- or low-skilled economic sectors and areas, and who had low incomes. These people decided to return to their countries of origin, as a result of losing their job and revenue and fearing the infection with the new virus. Their return to congested and loaded means of transport led to the infections of some healthy individuals, and consequently to the spread of the virus (Pulla, 2020).

High unemployment and return migration are similar effects to those that occurred during the 2007–2008 financial crisis. Migrant workers are often the underdogs, the parties that have the most to lose when economic crises occur—because of short-term contracts, their vulnerable status or the sectors in which they work. Therefore, because the world economy was gradually slowing down and migrants were returning home or were prevented from going abroad, a decrease in remittances was foreseen, reducing the vital support they offered to the communities in their origin countries. On the other hand, the return of migrants at the time when people previously engaged in the labour market were in technical unemployment (defined as a situation in which the employee's individual employment contract is suspended as a result of the temporary interruption or reduction of the activity, without termination of employment, for economic, technological, structural or similar reasons). This generated additional pressure for their home countries.

Romania, being one of the countries with a high number of labour migrants (3rd place within EU countries—see Annex 9.1), and which has benefited from migration through remittances, has been forced to identify effective policies for managing the return flows of the migrants back home, both in terms of social distancing and from an economic point of view.

The present chapter aims to highlight the boomerang effect of the encouraging migration policy that Romania had, in the context of the global COVID-19 pandemic.

Evolution of COVID-19 in Romania

In Romania, the first case of infection with COVID-19, detected on 26 February 2020, was a man who had been in contact with an Italian citizen visiting Romania between 18 and 22 February 2020. The evolution of COVID-19 cases was generally slow in Romania, so in the first two weeks after the first case of infection, less than 50 people were tested positive (see Fig. 9.1).

However, on 16 March 2020, the state of emergency was declared in Romania, initially for a period of 30 days. Along with the state of emergency, Military Ordinances were adopted, according to which traffic restrictions were imposed, air travel was suspended, public places were closed, sports gatherings and competitions were banned and social distancing was encouraged. The number of cases of infection continued to show an upward trend. The largest increase in the number of people tested positive for SARS-CoV-2 occurred on 23 March 2020. For this reason, the authorities adopted on Tuesday, 24 March 2020, the Military Ordinance no. 3, which drastically restricted the movement of all persons.

The cause that led to the rapid increase in the number of positive cases with the new virus (in spite of the restrictions imposed by the Emergency

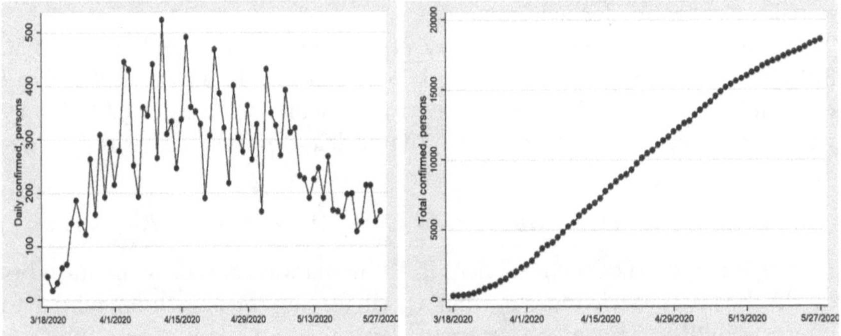

Fig. 9.1 The number of daily and total confirmed cases with SARS-CoV-2, 18 March–27 May 2020. (Source: Based on Date La Zi (2020) data)

Table 9.1 Romanian migrants by destination countries in 2020, persons

Main destination countries	*Persons*
Italy	1,048,862
Germany	654,822
Spain	613,336
United Kingdom	393,569
Hungary	214,514
United States	170,469
France	138,550
Austria	121,355
Israel	100,679
Canada	97,253
Total Romanian migrants	*3,987,093*

Source: Based on (United Nations, 2022) data

Ordinances) originates in the large number of Romanian labour migrants who returned home from the destination countries in which they had been working before the global health crisis. The most pressing problem was the fact that most Romanians returned from the countries most affected by the pandemic—Italy and Spain.

Therefore, the main cause of the virus spread rate was closely linked to the destination routes of the Romanian labour migrants. Table 9.1 presents the main preferred destination countries of Romanian migrants.

Although various hypotheses were debated in the press regarding the actual number of Romanians returning home, from over 200,000 to more than 1 million persons based on official data provided by the Border Police (2020), they can be considered at most as a proxy, due to the fact that it is not known exactly how many of those entered the country as tourists, in transit or cross-border workers.

However, according to a survey conducted by Sociopol, more than 800,000 people returned to Romania between 7 and 23 March 2020, out of which more than 50% referred to the "fear of the new COVID-19 virus" as the reason for their return (Tudorică, 2020).

Phases of Infection with the New COVID-19 Virus in Romania

Initially the spread of the new virus in Romania was caused by the mobility of the business environment, that is, of foreign businessmen who had interests in Romania and vice versa, Romanians with business interests abroad. Therefore, because of patient zero—the Italian businessman—the first case of infection of a Romanian with the new virus was recorded. The spread was also connected to the movement of persons for personal gain or tourism. Among the highly publicized cases were that of a former employee of the Ministry of Internal Affairs, who had travelled abroad in early February 2020. Because he hid his travel and continued his activity, having contact with more than 120 people at the workplace alone, over other 30 people were infected.

The second and largest factor in the infection and spread of the new virus was the return home of Romanian labour migrants, especially from countries such as Italy, Spain, Germany or France. These persons returned not because of their distrust in the destination countries' medical systems or their confidence in the Romanian medical system, but because of the economic uncertainty of their stay in those countries. Those who have returned are people with low or medium levels of qualification and education, who had low-skilled jobs in their destination countries, and a large proportion of them were employed in the informal economy. As a result of the fact that in Italy a person can be the beneficiary of the social protection system only if that individual is a resident and/or if he has a long-term employment contract, people with temporary contracts and/or workers without legal contract have been left vulnerable and have decided to return to Romania. Official data (Romanian Government, 2020) confirm that 41.1% of all confirmed cases from that period have been recorded as a result of close contact with infected persons arriving in Romania or with their contacts. Thus, although international organizations, national authorities in origin countries as well as the literature consider labour mobility, expressed through remittances, as beneficial for the origin countries, in this situation of a health crisis, the negative impact of the migration phenomenon is highlighted both by the spread of the virus and by the negative impact on the economy. First, most of the individuals who entered Romania before the cancellation of flights and the closure of borders hid the fact that they came from "red zones", so as not to be placed in quarantine. Secondly, the health insurance budget and social security budget were put under pressure.

Most of the individuals who returned from labour mobility do not pay taxes and contributions to the health insurance system in Romania. The quarantine expenses (about 62 euro/capita/day for 15 days), both for the treatment of their infection, as well as for the people infected by them, were covered from public resources. Hence, the public health system was put under pressure, having to treat individuals regardless of whether they had paid health contributions or not. In Romania, the average cost of treating a patient infected with COVID-19 was 2313.77 euros (Monitorul

Cluj, 2020). Therefore, the total expenditure on the treatment of patients with COVID-19 up to 27 May 2020 amounted to more than EUR 43.02 million (EUR 2313.77 per capita for 18,594 persons), which means that it takes 383,716 employees to earn an average salary to support the cost of this treatment through health contributions. Although these amounts represent only 0.24 per cent of the Health Insurance Budget (Romanian Parliament, 2020), the pressure was felt much more intensively as a result of the fact that, with the establishment of the State of Emergency, economic activities were stopped, employed persons either lost their jobs or were placed in technical unemployment, i.e. budget receipts have decreased significantly, for example by 82% in the case of added tax.

The third wave of infections was due to the migration due to the Easter holidays, an annual phenomenon, and was not due to fear of the new virus, but to Romanian customs and culture.

In parallel with these waves of infections, which were imported, there was a phenomenon of community spread of the virus through the medical system and due to non-compliance with the conditions of social distancing. The most eloquent example is the case of the city of Suceava, where over 20% of all cases of infection in Romania were located and more than 5.55 ‰ per 1000 inhabitants (Date La Zi, 2020). The reason why hospitals in Suceava became outbreaks of infection was poor management and non-compliance with social distancing measures among the medical staff. At the same time, many people did not inform authorities that they had returned from "red zones", and started to seek different medical services in order to cure their unsolved medical issues at home rather than abroad, due to high costs of treatment in the destination country.

Migration of Romanian Critical Workers During COVID-19

The epidemic caused by the new COVID-19 shocked the world, as well as European and Romanian economies alike. Thus, states have been forced to adopt budgetary policy measures in order to increase the capacity of their health systems, to provide aid and support to particularly affected economy sectors and to citizens, especially those without a job due to redundancy, or those who have recently returned from abroad.

Having acquired the right of free movement of citizens, Romania has adopted a policy encouraging labour mobility and remittances. The latter are considered beneficial for the economy, not only as a result of rising living standards but also as a result of their redistribution in the form of investments (Bursa, 2018). Thus, at the level of 2019, remittances constituted 3% of GDP, the 4th place at EU level by absolute value, with 3.57 million migrants (Table 9.2).

However, an average reduction of more than 27% of remittances as a result of the COVID-19 crisis was expected in Eastern European countries for 2020 (World Bank, 2020). This phenomenon will have a significant impact in the countries dependent on these flows, as is the case of Romania.

All the benefits of labour mobility and remittances discussed in the literature and at the authorities' level (such as balancing of the labour market by reducing the pressure that over three million Romanians would have

Table 9.2 Share of remittances in GDP in 2016–2020, %

EU countries	*2016*	*2017*	*2018*	*2019*	*2020*
Croatia	5.77	6.10	6.12	6.48	6.95
Latvia	4.4	4.19	3.59	3.33	3.22
Romania	3.15	3.10	2.89	3.26	3.00
Luxembourg	2.79	2.91	2.94	2.91	2.92
Belgium	2.27	2.28	2.29	2.28	2.43
Cyprus	1.87	1.97	2.04	1.70	2.34
Hungary	3.24	2.88	2.73	2.88	2.34
Malta	2.15	2.04	1.87	1.74	1.92
Slovakia	2.37	2.27	2.09	1.98	1.79
Czech Republic	1.59	1.64	1.58	1.53	1.71
Estonia	2.02	1.89	1.88	1.75	1.65
Lithuania	2.98	2.73	2.58	2.38	1.40
Bulgaria	3.09	3.71	3.63	3.40	1.39
Slovenia	1.01	1.04	1.19	1.24	1.20
Poland	1.43	1.32	1.21	1.10	0.99
France	0.97	0.96	0.94	0.96	0.96
Austria	0.73	0.71	0.68	0.67	0.71
Sweden	0.55	0.57	0.55	0.60	0.57
Italy	0.51	0.50	0.47	0.52	0.51
Germany	0.44	0.43	0.42	0.47	0.47
Denmark	0.40	0.40	0.40	0.42	0.42
Greece	0.22	0.20	0.23	0.33	0.32
Finland	0.36	0.36	0.31	0.30	0.30
Netherlands	0.28	0.27	0.27	0.25	0.26
Portugal	0.21	0.22	0.23	0.26	0.26
Spain	0.21	0.23	0.24	0.23	0.23
Ireland	0.19	0.18	0.16	0.15	0.09

Source: Based on World Bank (2022) data

put on it) represent, in fact, a loss of Romania's labour resources. This phenomenon has occurred as a result of the fact that not only the unemployed have migrated, but also qualified and employed people, who were employed in important sectors of the economy.

It is essential to note that highly skilled migrants in highly qualified jobs in destination countries do not aim to remit the amounts expected by the authorities in the origin countries, which could have generated positive effects in the economy. A study by Sechet and Vasilcu (2015) points out that more than 72% of the Romanian doctors who migrated do not take into consideration the option of returning to Romania. Hence, these individuals tend to leave for professional development and career and have no tendency to return to their home country. In this context, we can no longer highlight the benefits of migration materialized through remittances, as there is a massive exodus of skilled labour, which generates long-term deficits difficult to cover.

Even during this pandemic period, Romania continued to export critical workers to developed countries, which depend on them (Papademetriou & Hooper, 2020), in fields such as agriculture, construction and even medical staff, while the Romanian medical system was already overloaded (Table 9.3), even before the emergence of the new virus.

According to Table 9.3, the small number of almost 318 medical doctors per 100,000 inhabitants in Romania registered in 2019 was determined by the migration of medical staff to other destination countries, such as France (where they exceed 17% of all foreign medical doctors) or Germany (representing over 10% of all foreign medical doctors), where there are approximately 10,000 Romanian doctors (Annex 9.2). Regarding Romanian nurses in destination countries, this category represents, for example, over 50% of all foreign nurses in Italy (OECD, 2021a) and according to preliminary data in 2020, over 20,000 nurses work in another destination country (Annex 9.3).

Therefore, the lack of measures to retain medical staff in the country before the outbreak of the new virus led to a deficit of about 40,000 persons, equivalent to 17.5% of the medical staff needs in public hospitals (Rotilă, 2018).

This shortage of doctors has increased even more as a result of the large number of over 1000 infections with COVID-19 among medical staff (Romanian Government, 2020). Besides poor management of hospitals by politically appointed managers and the lack of coordination of actions between hospitals and the Public Health Directorates, the advanced age of many doctors (who remained in the country) was a key factor contributing to the registration of many infected healthcare professionals. However, Romania continues to export medical personnel, even during this global

Table 9.3 The number of practicing doctors per 100,000 inhabitants

Countries	*2011*	*2012*	*2013*	*2014*	*2015*	*2016*	*2017*	*2018*	*2019*
Belgium	291.55	293.36	295.71	297.55	301.75	307.41	308.29	312.96	316.33
Bulgaria	385.41	387.43	395.24	397.75	404.04	410.66	418.40	421.71	423.60
Czech Republic	363.67	367.47	368.79	:	:	:	:	403.76	406.67
Denmark	378.92	383.76	384.94	387.74	392.93	399.82	410.89	419.44	:
Germany	387.70	394.64	403.50	410.82	413.93	418.65	424.88	431.09	439.39
Estonia	329.36	328.34	333.46	335.88	341.49	345.65	346.82	348.34	346.90
Ireland	266.70	270.68	267.46	301.20	311.91	319.18	325.75	327.94	331.68
Spain	383.52	382.34	381.09	380.08	384.54	382.35	387.68	402.08	440.36
France	305.70	307.30	308.50	309.21	310.62	312.14	314.12	314.44	317.03
Croatia	291.62	299.18	303.35	314.02	319.15	323.65	336.21	344.06	351.89
Italy	389.83	387.34	390.01	388.04	383.83	395.27	398.95	397.71	405.07
Cyprus	297.22	301.64	319.51	337.83	359.34	376.84	386.84	407.32	427.23
Latvia	313.44	314.40	319.13	321.60	319.79	321.25	320.50	330.38	326.73
Lithuania	409.73	421.85	427.70	430.74	433.92	446.69	455.63	459.78	456.96
Luxembourg	277.81	280.63	283.05	288.14	290.73	288.45	298.49	:	:
Hungary	296.22	308.87	320.91	332.35	309.72	321.12	332.48	338.37	349.37
Malta	316.86	328.79	344.16	360.37	367.60	382.78	396.37	397.21	402.53
Netherlands	:	:	:	342.50	349.14	353.68	360.33	367.22	371.51
Austria	484.22	489.54	498.85	504.61	509.12	512.96	518.28	524.14	531.81
Poland	221.27	223.38	224.09	230.68	232.81	241.58	237.75	:	:
Romania	*246.46*	*261.05*	*264.36*	*269.83*	*276.58*	*284.10*	*292.68*	*304.70*	*318.67*
Slovenia	249.46	254.14	262.92	277.02	282.53	301.40	310.11	317.81	326.19
Finland	298.61	306.87	314.69	320.63	:	:	:	:	:
Sweden	388.93	396.83	404.39	410.98	417.52	423.33	426.80	431.74	:
Iceland	350.46	356.08	360.76	364.40	377.55	385.17	387.30	389.26	389.39
Liechtenstein	305.68	316.45	324.47	319.48	320.05	328.77	363.52	352.98	373.42

(*continued*)

Table 9.3 (continued)

Countries	*2011*	*2012*	*2013*	*2014*	*2015*	*2016*	*2017*	*2018*	*2019*
Norway	418.81	423.19	430.62	442.92	445.28	458.23	473.49	485.78	496.87
Switzerland	383.28	391.57	404.00	412.58	419.71	425.06	429.78	433.86	434.97
United Kingdom	268.61	269.62	271.29	274.53	277.11	278.20	281.10	284.05	:
Montenegro	200.14	202.55	213.46	217.11	235.63	255.34	265.11	276.41	272.98
Albania	123.16	127.43	128.11	:	:	:	:	:	:
Serbia	:	:	:	:	:	295.44	295.88	298.23	:
TOTAL	**9624.4**	**9776.7**	**9948.5**	**9980.6**	**9788.3**	**10,295**	**10,504**	**10,522**	**9257.6**

Source: Based on Eurostat (2021) data

health crisis, with 231 medical staff leaving to Austria at the end of March 2020 (Euractiv, 2020).

In addition to the departures of the medical staff, we also witnessed during this period the seasonal migration of critical workers in agriculture, especially in Germany, with to the so-called Asparagus operation. Although, at European level, recommendations have been made for actions aimed to reduce the number of new COVID-19 infections (European Commission, 2020), especially regarding the transportation of critical workers, where increased hygiene and social distancing measures were needed, more than 40,000 Romanians went to Germany during that period. Many of them were crammed into the airport or coaches (Wienand, 2020), and one of the departed individuals died in the host country being tested positive for COVID-19. Besides endangering those individuals' lives, all critical workers infected were sent back home, exerting new pressure on the Romanian medical system.

Although labour mobility is determined by the wage differential between Romania and the destination countries of Romanian migrants, and although it is generally considered beneficial due to remittances, the consequences felt during the pandemic crisis show the precariousness of public policies that support migration and the boomerang effect created at the level of the origin country.

Conclusions

The emergence of the new virus has taken the whole world by surprise, since neither the medical system nor the economic and social ones were not prepared for it. As a result of the scale of the globalization phenomenon, the new COVID-19 virus has spread at a significant speed, reaching almost all countries of the world, regardless of geographical, climatic or economic position.

Population migration and labour mobility have become a key factor in the spread of the new virus. Romania, being a state heavily affected by labour mobility, has come to suffer from its own policy of encouraging migration. The negative impact of return migration has been felt both in the resulting contagion and increased local cases, and in the resulting high pressure on the health insurance budget, which, in turn, also suffers from a lack of contribution from employees who no longer have a job or from migrants returned who did not contribute recently (or even never) to the National Health Insurance Budget.

The case of Romania shows a different perspective of the migration policies that have as their central element remittances, calling into question these policies and how they are applied. The current pandemic situation offers new perspectives which have not yet been drawn up on migration policies, and brings to the forefront the need to assess the boomerang-type effects to which a country can be subjected following social or economic policies based solely on cost and immediate efficiency reasoning. The current pandemic status implies a massive rethinking not only of the policies to relocate production capacities to low-cost areas (such as China) but also to rethink migration systems and policies.

In our chapter, we identified some preliminary key findings that place Romania on a position of national and international interest in this current epidemiological context, but which could not be measured at this time due to the lack of public information available, thus being the subject of future research. In the economic context, Romania will face major negative effects as an emerging economy, due to national measures taken during the pandemic and, therefore, there is a need to develop efficient public policies to revitalize the Romanian economy. From a social point of view, the Romanian state had to adopt public strategies and policies through which to support the reintegration of workers on the labour market and through which to help social reintegration.

Our analysis aims to identify the impact of labour migration and the encouraging migration policies on the spread of the new virus, but the data availability does not allow us to analyse the scale of the whole phenomenon. In future research we will analyse the impact of migration and the effectiveness of policies adopted by the authorities in order to manage the pandemic situation.

Annexes

Annex 9.1 Top EU 10 countries classified by migrants stock in 2020, persons

EU countries	*Persons*
Poland	4.8
United Kingdom	4.7
Romania	3.9
Germany	3.8
Italy	3.3
France	2.3
Portugal	2.1
Bulgaria	1.7
Spain	1.5
Greece	1.1

Source: Based on United Nations (2022) data

Annex 9.2 Romanian doctors by destination countries, persons

Country	*2010*	*2011*	*2012*	*2013*	*2014*	*2015*	*2016*	*2017*	*2018*	*2019*	*2020*
Austria	16	22	23	31	51	53	51	55	62	60	
Belgium	566	744	866	975	1064	1172	1247	1300	1319	1371	1411
Chile					12	12	12	12	12	12	5
Czech Republic		1	2	1	1	6	8	8	8	11	11
Finland	38	44	46								
France		2697	3099	3410	3705	3993	4272	4497	4697	4911	
Germany	1269	1840	2559	3042	3363	3503	3661	3857	3978	4058	
Hungary	1701	1652	1624	1623	1683	1630	1699	1819	1870	1963	
Ireland		226	286	341	487	625	723	733	715	709	710
Israel	1206	1245	1252	1263	1308	1388	1445	1538	1635	1754	1913
Italy										266	335
Netherlands	43	47	43	45	46	57	60	64	57		
New Zeeland	18	18	20	23	20	19	19	19	19	25	
Norway	56	65	73	85	96	120	138	159	169	172	182
Poland					4	4	6	6	7	17	26
Slovenia	2	2	4	4	4	4	3	3	3	3	4
Sweden	421	485	564	628	735	569	729	814	921		
Switzerland	148	156	178	204	230	248	276	305	334	365	395
Turkey	4	4	4	4	4	4					
United Kingdom	435	582	639	764	852	872	949	1037	1129	1274	1347
US	2141	2324	2430	2457	2446	2457	2455				
TOTAL	***8064***	***12,154***	***13,712***	***14,900***	***16,111***	***16,736***	***17,753***	***16,226***	***16,935***	***16,971***	***6339***

Source: Based on OECD (2021) data

Annex 9.3 Romanian nurses by destination countries, persons

Countries	*2010*	*2011*	*2012*	*2013*	*2014*	*2015*	*2016*	*2017*	*2018*	*2019*	*2020*
Belgium	298	421	690	888	1068	1224	1329	1431	1598	1713	1791
Canada	430	448	472	508	515	520	527	524	518	513	
France	68	115	147	164	179	193	203	221	238	250	
Greece	22	22	22	22	22	22					
Hungary				431	530	576	591	603	626	621	
Israel	98	92	86	82	79	77	71	63	59	55	50
Italy	10,570	11,215	11,531	11,731	11,820	12,159	11,714	10,969	10,690	10,635	11,253
Netherlands						9	12	14	13		
New Zeeland		20	17	16	13	13	14	12	14	14	12
Norway	34	34	42	46	57	76	88	99	81	88	92
Sweden	2	4	8	17	24	30	49	58	73		
Turkey	2	3	3	3	3	3					
United Kingdom	1272	1909	2254	2606	3739	5997	8115	7725	7542	7407	7421
TOTAL	**12,796**	**14,283**	**15,272**	**16,514**	**18,049**	**20,899**	**22,713**	**21,719**	**21,452**	**21,296**	**20,619**

Source: Based on OECD (2021b) data

References

Border Police. (2020). *Open Data*. Accessed July 29, 2022, from https://www.politiadefrontiera.ro/ro/main/n-date-deschise-17/.

Bursa. (2018). *Banii trimişi de românii din străinătate încep să vizeze investiţii productive*. Bursa.ro. Accessed July 29, 2022, from https://www.bursa.ro/mugur-isarescu-banii-trimisi-de-romanii-din-strainatate-incep-sa-vizeze-investitii-productive-68508438.

Caley, P., Philp, D. J., & McCracken, K. (2008). Quantifying Social Distancing Arising from Pandemic Influenza. *Journal of the Royal Society Interface, 5*(23), 631–639. https://doi.org/10.1098/rsif.2007.1197

Date La Zi. (2020). Official Data about COVID-19. In: *Romanian Government' Project*

Euractiv. (2020). *Austria Imports Workers from Bulgaria, Romania to Plug Gaps in COVID-19 Care*. Accessed July 29, 2022, from https://www.euractiv.com/section/economy-jobs/news/austria-imports-workers-from-bulgaria-romania-to-plug-gaps-in-covid-19-care/.

European Commission. (2020). *Communication from the Commission*. Guidelines Concerning the Exercise of the Free Movement of Workers during COVID-19 Outbreak (2020/C 102 I/03). Official Journal of the European Union.

Eurostat. (2021). *Health Personnel (Excluding Nursing and Caring Professionals)*. European Commission. Accessed December 21, 2021, from http://appsso.eurostat.ec.europa.eu/nui/show.do?dataset=hlth_rs_prs1&lang=en.

Fan, C., Cai, T., Gai, Z., & Wu, Y. (2020). The Relationship between the Migrant Population's Migration Network and the Risk of COVID-19 Transmission in China—Empirical Analysis and Prediction in Prefecture-Level Cities. *International Journal of Environmental Research and Public Health, 17*(8), 2630. https://doi.org/10.3390/ijerph17082630

Hatchett, R. J., Mecher, C. E., & Lipsitch, M. (2007). Public Health Interventions and Epidemic Intensity during the 1918 Influenza Pandemic. *Proceedings of the National Academy of Sciences of the United States of America, 104*(18), 7582–7587. https://doi.org/10.1073/pnas.0610941104

Jia, J., Ding, J., Liu, S., Liao, G., Li, J., Duan, B., Wang, G., & Zhang, R. (2020). Modeling the Control of Covid-19: Impact of Policy Interventions and Meteorological Factors. *Electronic Journal of Differential Equations, 2020*(23), 1–24.

Monitorul Cluj. (2020). *Cât costă tratamentul unui pacient vindecat complet*. Monitorul Cluj. Accessed July 29, 2022, from https://www.monitorulcj.ro/actualitate/79491-coronavirus-cat-costa-tratamentul-unui-pacient-vindecat-complet.

Nikolaenko, D. (2021). *Explanation of Pandemics: Hypotheses & Verification* (1st ed.). Lambert Academic Publishing.

OECD. (2021). Health Workforce Migration: Foreign-trained doctors by country of origin - Stock. *OECD.Stat.* https://stats.oecd.org/index.aspx?queryid=68336.
OECD. (2021a). *Health Workforce Migration: Foreign-Trained Doctors by Country of Origin - Stock.* Accessed April 21, 2021, from https://stats.oecd.org/index.aspx?queryid=68336.
OECD. (2021b). Health Workforce Migration: Foreign-Trained Nurses by Country of Origin - Stock. In: *OECD Statistics.* Accessed December 21, 2021, from https://stats.oecd.org/Index.aspx?QueryId=68336.
Papademetriou, D. G., & Hooper, K. (2020). How is COVID-19 Reshaping Labour Migration? *International Migration, 58*(4), 259–262. https://doi.org/10.1111/IMIG.12748
Pulla, P. (2020). Covid-19: India Imposes Lockdown for 21 Days and Cases Rise. *BMJ, 368*, m1251. https://doi.org/10.1136/bmj.m1251
Romanian Government. (2020). COVID-19 Ştiri Oficiale. In: *Stiri Oficiale.* Accessed July, 29 2022, from https://stirioficiale.ro/informatii.
Romanian Parliament. (2020). Legea nr. 6/2020 a bugetului asigurărilor sociale de stat pe anul 2020 actualizată 2020. In: Monitorul Oficial al României.
Rotilă, V. (2018). Impactul migraţiei asupra salariaţilor din sănătate.
Sechet, R., & Vasilcu, D. (2015). Physicians' Migration from Romania to France: A Brain Drain into Europe? *Cybergeo: European Journal of Geography*, 743.
Singhal, T. (2020). A Review of Coronavirus Disease-2019 (COVID-19). *Indian Journal of Pediatrics, 87*(4), 281–286. https://doi.org/10.1007/s12098-020-03263-6
Tudorică, I. (2020). Sociopol: 800.000 de români s-au întors în ţară în două săptămâni. 400.000 recunosc că au făcut-o de frica coronavirus . In: Economica.net
United Nations. (2022). International Migrant Stock | Population Division. In: *Population Division.* Accessed October 17, 2021, from https://www.un.org/development/desa/pd/content/international-migrant-stock.
Wang, C., Horby, P. W., Hayden, F. G., & Gao, G. F. (2020). A Novel Coronavirus Outbreak of Global Health Concern. *The Lancet, 395*, 470–473.
Wienand, V. L. (2020). *Erntehelfer entkamen Quarantäne-Region in Rumänien.*
World Bank. (2020). Migration and Development Brief 32 Migration and Development Brief 32 April 2020 Contents.
World Bank. (2022). Personal Remittances, Received (% of GDP). In: *World Bank Indicators.* Accessed Feburary 2, 2022, from https://data.worldbank.org/indicator/BX.TRF.PWKR.DT.GD.ZS.

CHAPTER 10

Migrant Critical Workers During and After COVID-19 Pandemic

Elena Bunduchi, Valentina Vasile, Calin-Adrian Comes, and Daniel Stefan

Since March 2020, as the new virus began to affect all countries in the world, millions of migrants felt the effects of the pandemic more than the natives. Some migrants remained stranded in their destination countries, others were forced to return due to mobility restrictions and economic bottlenecks and some were forcibly expelled. And with the mutations suffered by the virus and the possibility of new waves of illness, there have been several episodes of migrants returning to their countries of origin.

In order to cope with the mobility of people, the authorities of the host and home countries have adopted all kinds of measures aimed at reducing the rate of spread and infection of the population. The host countries quickly closed their borders to foreign citizens and chaotically imposed travel restrictions both inside and outside the country, even if this meant migrants lost their jobs or even left the countries where they lived. And while some states did not resort to forced relocation, others put pressure on countries of origin to accelerate the return of migrants (le Coz & Newland, 2021). But migrant-dependent countries like Germany, the United States or the United Kingdom (United Nations, 2022) were affected because of the return of migrants to their country of origin,

V. Vasile et al., *International Labour Mobility*,
https://doi.org/10.1007/978-3-031-18683-7_10

especially because their jobs were in the essential areas, such as the medical system, agriculture or services (Fasani & Mazza, 2020).

On the other hand, the countries of origin faced the challenge of receiving their citizens back, in the context of health crises they did not expect and faced with difficulty. An important problem in the reception of migrants was determined by the need to ensure adequate quarantine and/or isolation conditions and to cover the subsequent expenses. Simultaneously, there were problems concerning the reintegration of migrants into society and the labour market, given that unemployment rates have risen considerably (World Bank, 2021), leaving citizens previously employed in the country of origin without a source of income. The difficulty or sometimes even the impossibility of finding a job due to the economic crisis led to increasing poverty (IOM, 2020) and lack of subsistence sources, especially in the case of remittance-dependent families, where the person who remitted money had to return home, thus reducing the volume of remittances received by the beneficiary families. A summary of the World Bank estimates that due to the global economic contraction caused by COVID-19, remittance flows to poor countries will decrease by about 20% (World Bank, 2020). This reduction could not only contribute to an increased poverty rate, but would also negatively affect the ability of households to access much-needed health services during the pandemic.

Status of Migrants at EU Level

The COVID-19 pandemic has generated sudden and major changes in all spheres of the economic, political, social or cultural life. Unprecedented measures have been reintroduced at the level of EU Member States, contrary to the ideas and principles that underpinned the consolidation and formation of the European Union (EU). One of the changes brought about by the new virus was the reintroduction of controls at customs points and the restriction of the free movement of European citizens. Restrictions imposed due to reasons of public health and/or safety are justified in order to keep the pandemic under control, but they must be objective and comply with non-discriminatory principles. To this end, directives have been developed at EU level to protect health and further guarantee the safe movement of goods (European Commission, 2020a) and people (European Commission, 2020b).

Free movement of people is all the more important, as many European countries depend on migrant workers who hold positions in key sectors of the economy. Thus, to reduce the negative impact of the pandemic crisis and to avoid its transformation into an economic one, exceptions were implemented for cross-border workers, posted workers and essential (critical) migrants. According to the European Commission (European Commission, 2020b), the category of essential workers includes people who have a job in one of the following fields: healthcare, social services, pharmaceutical industry, technology and communications, energy and electrical engineering, infrastructure, civil protection, food industry, transport, public administration. At the same time, seasonal agricultural workers are included in the same category.

During the COVID-19 pandemic, the attitude of the native population and the media in general changed significantly compared to 2004–2014, when several Central and Eastern European states joined the EU. From the offences brought against migrants from Romania, Poland or Bulgaria as "invaders", whose numbers—of over 700,000 people—would increase the crime rate (Daily Express, 2006; Dawar, 2013) things that did not come true (Vasile et al., 2019) and from the fear of the idea of them taking over natives' jobs, migrants have become desirable workers, essential for the functioning and maintenance of the economy of the destination countries (Spencer, 2020). Although during the pre-accession and accession of Romania and Bulgaria plans were designed for negative advertisement and for convincing Romanians and Bulgarians not to go to work in the United Kingdom, "a country where it always rains and wages are low" (Hope, 2013), in 2020 special charter flights were organized to allow Romanian essential agricultural workers to return or go to work for the first time in the United Kingdom (O'Carroll, 2020), in order to reduce the crisis in agriculture generated by the exodus of migrants triggered by the COVID-19 pandemic. Paradoxically, some states imposed a 14-day quasi-quarantine (Hurst, 2020) on migrants, which meant banning contact with other people, especially locals, and restricting access to health services; however, during this time they had to work to support the economy of the destination country.

According to Eurostat (2020) data, we note that on average in the EU Member States the share of critical migrant workers in the total migrant workers exceeds that of essential natives (Table 10.1), and depending on the field of activity, such as cleaning services, almost a quarter of EU and non-EU migrant workers are concentrated.

A study by (OECD, 2020a) finds that, at EU level, 14% of all essential workers are migrants, regardless of the education level, while in the UK the share of migrants is 18%—care services, 20%—agriculture and 40%—food industry (Office for National Statistics, 2019). The contribution of migrant workers is even higher: about 23% of all doctors and 14% of all

Table 10.1 Share of migrant workers (EU and non-EU) and native workers in total workers by country of origin in the position of essential workers

Field of activity	*EU migrant workers*	*Non-EU migrant workers*	*Natives*
Cleaning workers	20.9	27.8	7.7
Personal care workers	12.6	16.6	9.7
Personal service workers	1.6	1.3	1.3
Market-oriented skilled agricultural workers	3.9	3.2	13.1
Construction, mining, production and transportation workers	5.1	5.7	3.2
Mobile installation operators	8.5	9.1	8.7
Machine and equipment operators	1.1	1.3	0.9
Health personnel	8.1	5.9	8.4
Food processing	2.9	2.6	2.2
Professionals in allied health professions	4.3	3.5	5.1
Professionals in fields associated with science and engineering	7.7	6	11.8
Forestry, fishing and hunting professionals	0.03	0.1	0.2
Professionals in science and engineering	4.2	2.6	4
Teaching professionals	11.1	7.8	15.4
ICT professionals	5.7	4.5	4.8
ICT technicians	1.9	1.4	2.4

Source: Based on Eurostat (2020) data

nurses at EU level are migrants, 68% of doctors and 22% of nurses in Luxembourg, 48% and 67% respectively in the UK, whereas in Belgium about half of the medical staff are of foreign origin (OECD, 2020a). Therefore, during the pandemic period, the paradigm of "invading" migrants was changed, the authorities of the destination countries realizing the importance of these types of workers.

In answer to the COVID-19 pandemic, a few measures have been taken by many states in order to enable migrant professionals to help cover labour shortages in areas that remain uncovered, in order to avoid a socio-economic collapse (Table 10.2).

The Impact of COVID-19 on the Mobility of Romanian Migrant Workers

The COVID-19 virus also reached Romania, and starting with 16 March 2020, the Romanian president declared a state of national emergency, because of the boost in the number of cases of infection with the new virus

Table 10.2 Facilities granted by destination states to migrant workers during the COVID-19 pandemic

Authors	*Analysed country*	*Areas essential workers*	*Facilities*	*Impact on migrants*
Berntsen and Skowronek (2021)	The Netherlands	Meat processing; agriculture; seasonal work	Introduction of a safety protocol for migrant workers, which includes regulation on safety measures at work, quarantine rules for sick people and the prevention of illness of those living with them, as well as increased access to medical services. At the same time, they are granted the right to health insurance for 30 days after the expiration of the work contract.	
Palumbo and Corrado (2020)	Germany	Agriculture	Elimination of travel restrictions on the open corridor to cover the shortage of workers for migrants from Romania, Poland and Bulgaria.	Failure to comply with the hygiene conditions and distancing measures imposed by the pandemic led to infection with the new virus and a growth in the number of import cases, as a result of sick people being sent back to their country of origin.

(*continued*)

Table 10.2 (continued)

Authors	*Analysed country*	*Areas essential workers*	*Facilities*	*Impact on migrants*
	Italy	Agriculture Care services	Granting an allowance of 600 euros for two months for people who were in the country until 8 March 2020. To reduce the staffing crisis, the authorities granted residence permits to seasonal workers for six months, with the possibility of extension in case of employment.	Failure to provide protective masks, as well as non-compliance with social distance measures, led to the dissatisfaction and illness of migrants, as was the case of a meat processing company in Bari or of Bulgarian Roma farmers.
	The Netherlands	Agriculture Meat processing	Removal of travel restrictions for essential workers in the field	Increasing the cases of COVID-19 infections of migrants and the risk of being fired if they reported risky working conditions.
	Spain	Agriculture	Extending the validity of migrants' residence permits by six months, and unauthorized workers were allowed to work in the agricultural sector. Providing temporary shelter and food for unemployed migrants from Catalonia, Fraga and Lleida.	Outbreaks of infections in various parts of Spain as a result of non-compliance with public health protocols adopted by the authorities.

(*continued*)

Table 10.2 (continued)

Authors	*Analysed country*	*Areas essential workers*	*Facilities*	*Impact on migrants*
	Sweden	Agriculture	€15 million investment in a program to encourage the employment of unemployed low-skilled migrant in services for public land and forest cleaning maintenance	The possibility of increasing incomes due to the increase in the number of hours worked, thus resulting in more remittances sent to the country of origin. Replacement of migrant workers from Asia with those from Central and Eastern Europe due to the removal of movement restrictions between Member States.
OECD (2020b)	United Kingdom	Medicine	Automatic extension of residence permits for one year.	
	France		Unauthorized medical staff may work as support staff in non-medical professions.	
	Spain		Immediate employment of foreign medical workers.	
	Germany, Belgium, Ireland and Luxembourg		Acceleration of the procedures for recognizing the certifications of migrant medical staff.	
	Italia		Granting temporary practice licenses for migrants.	

and the poor quality and training of the national health system. The state of emergency, which was subsequently extended until 15 May, led to an unprecedented violation of human freedoms and rights, from the right to movement, privacy, education, association, private property to economic freedom. Other measures aimed at reducing the intensity and rate of spread of the new virus consisted in isolating and quarantining people arriving in Romania from areas at high risk of infection, closing borders and restricting air, road, rail and maritime traffic and travel.

Romania is an emigration state, with approximately 4 million migrants at the level of 2020 (United Nations, 2022) having as objectives: higher wages (Bunduchi et al., 2019) based on the right to free movement in EU membership, pursue of an education, family reunification, either by bringing parents or children (second generation migrants), professional development, etc. As such, Romania has been affected by imported infections. Romanians prefer destinations such as Italy, Spain, Germany, the United Kingdom, and France (United Nations, 2022), countries strongly affected by the new virus: France—6.4 million infected, the United Kingdom—6.18 million infected, Spain—4.68 million, Italy—4.42 million and Germany—3.8 million infected, being all in the top 15 states with the most infections worldwide (Our World in Data, 2021). The number of Romanians who returned home during that time is not certain, depending on the source of information and ranging from 200,000 to 1,279,000 people (Agerpres, 2020; Pora, 2020). Even if the authorities urged the departed Romanians not to return to the country during the pandemic, this was not possible for many of them. The severe pandemic situation in the destination countries led the authorities to act promptly and introduce measures to stop the spread of the new virus. Romanians who were on vacation or in transit found themselves in extreme situations due to the suspension of flights between Italy and Romania in February 2020 (Ministry of Foreign Affairs, 2020a). Coaches with passengers or truck drivers remained stuck in Austria and Hungary for national reasons of public health security, and only after the intervention of the Romanian authorities and the negotiation of bilateral solutions was it possible for those people to return home. Since the beginning of March, the Romanian authorities began repatriation of Romanians who lost their jobs in Italy and did not have the financial resources to return home. The repatriation of Romanians had a significant social impact, polarizing public opinion and dividing society between supporters and opponents of the decision to repatriate and accept those who return home. The diaspora has been accused by some of being responsible for the spread of the new virus and for burdening a health system which already had problems and insufficient resources, without them having contributed financially to its formation (Eftimie, 2020). The indignation was even greater, as many of those who came back were of Roma ethnicity, and in addition to the fact that they had not contributed to the Romanian health system as migrants, they had not contributed to it even when they had been in Romania, the great majority having been beneficiary of unemployment benefits and social benefits, refusing any official job or occupying informal jobs (Fleck & Rughiniş, 2008).

These uncertainties arose due to the lack of a long-term employment contract. Romanians who had until the pandemic temporary employment contracts, zero hour contracts specific to Great Britain (Adams & Prassl, 2018) or did not have a legal contract were left vulnerable to the measures imposed by the authorities in the destination states.

Once back in Romania, migrants were forced not only to endure the criticism and accusations of being responsible for the spread of the virus, but also to spend the savings they had made over the years, as the possibility of finding employment was very low, with an unemployment rate rising from 3.8% in January to 5% since March 2020 (National Institute of Statistics, 2022).

Contrary to the dynamics of repatriation, the Romanian authorities have reached bilateral agreements with some EU countries, such as Germany (Gascon Barbera, 2020) or the United Kingdom (UK Government, 2020), which allow key agricultural workers to cross borders. Under these conditions, a change in the behaviour of Romanian workers was observed (Fig. 10.1); of the several thousands who chose to migrate for work for a short period of time as essential workers, not all had the same status before the pandemic. Some of those who left at that point were already migrants, with temporary or medium-term employment contracts, but not for seasonal work in the agricultural field, whereas others became migrants for the first time, due to the loss of their job in Romania as a result of the measures imposed by the authorities, which resulted in a lockdown in the Romanian economy.

The relaxation of the restrictions for the Romanian essential workers caused an increase of the number of their infections in the destination countries, due to the precarious working and living conditions, without compliance with the social distancing measures. Thus, the Romanian seasonal workers who went to work in Germany (Ministry of Foreign Affairs, 2020b), the Netherlands (Ministry of Foreign Affairs, 2020c) and the

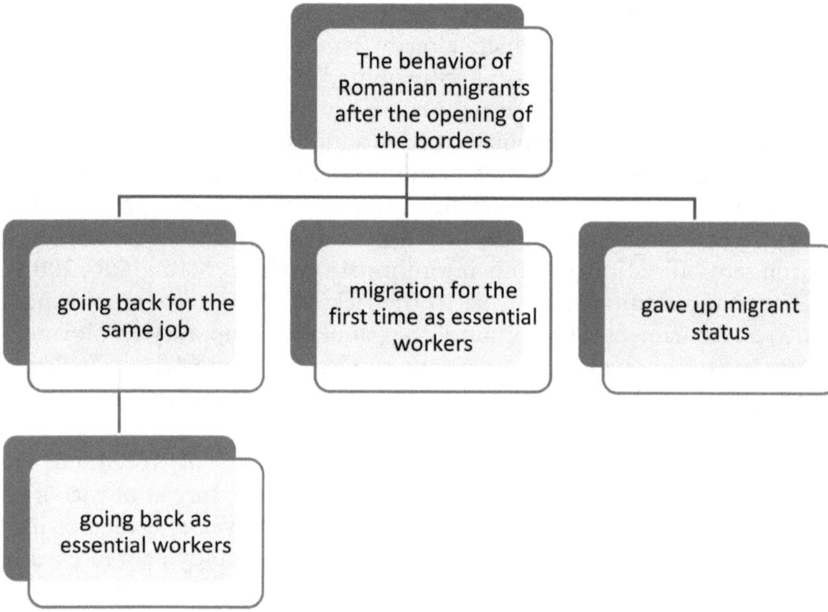

Fig. 10.1 Behaviour of Romanian migrants returning during the COVID-19 pandemic

United Kingdom (Ministry of Foreign Affairs, 2020d) were infected with the new virus. As a result of the situation, the Romanian authorities took a stand and engaged in bilateral discussions with their counterparts in order to develop measures to guarantee the protection of Romanian workers both during their transportation and during their stay in the destination country, with adequate working and living conditions.

The lack of protection measures during the transportation of Romanian workers had significant impact at EU level, with the European Parliament (2021) adopting a resolution on essential seasonal workers, while the European Commission (2020b) approved a series of recommendations meant to reduce vulnerabilities, to make better working and living conditions of these workers, to implement the existing legislation, as well as to better inform migrants regarding their rights.

However, these recommendations do not explain why the existing rules have not been applied and also do not set out concrete actions to remedy workers' protection failures, which arose with the COVID-19 pandemic crisis.

How Does COVID-19 Affect Labour Migration Patterns?

The COVID-19 pandemic is not just a dilemma that affects the health system, but it also has a substantial impact on the migration of people, reshaping the traditional pattern of migration for work. This pandemic crisis will have long-term implications for the socio-economic inclusion, for the acceptance and integration of migrants in host societies and for the labour migration model. Disinformation, discrimination and stigma against migrants is a problem encountered in both the migrants' country of origin and that of destination, and they lead to increasing xenophobia (Bauomy, 2020). On the other hand, in some EU countries migrants are much more valued, while low- or medium-skilled workers who are engaged in jobs indispensable to the running of the economy are expected by the authorities and by the locals alike, thus changing the low skills-low added value paradigm (de Camargo & Whiley, 2020).

In addition to the attitude towards migrants, the COVID-19 pandemic has influenced the migration model as follows:

- Job mobility has been restricted. Even though more and more states have granted various exemptions and allowed the mobility of essential workers, the same has not happened for the rest of the migrants who have not been included in this category. Maintaining the restrictions has had economic, social and family implications. At the same time, the possibility of a new lockdown has led some companies to modernize and develop their automation abilities, so that they may no longer depend on human labour. Dismissals in most industries have also affected migrants, especially those with temporary work visas, who have been forced to either find another job or return to their origin country which is likely to have been even more economically affected. Authorities have increasingly encouraged companies to hire natives once they restart their activity (Martin, 2020; USCIS, 2020). Such decisions have an increasing and long-term impact on migrants and countries of origin.
- The creation of "mobility bubbles" involves the delimitation of "safe" areas in and from which the mobility of persons of a certain nationality is allowed, such as the trans-Tasmanian bubble between Australia and New Zealand (McClure, 2021) and the bubble between Latvia, Lithuania and Estonia (Sytas, 2020). Although the

Delta version of the virus has led to the temporary closure of their bubbles, there have been discussions about their reactivation (Wright, 2021). These "safe areas" are not only a risk of encouraging security rhetoric against migrants from countries more severely affected by the new virus, but they have also generated a form of economic isolation which can lead to a change in the location of production lines and supply chains in order to economically recover the affected areas. Consequently, these changes can strengthen existing inequalities and accentuate the global North-South divide.

- Increasing illegal migration. Irregular migration is a problem that global society has not yet been able to address, and at least 100 million people are subject to this type of illegal migration (Runde et al., 2019). Due to the economic, political, social, cultural situation, many people choose to move to another country, and if there are problems travelling by legal means, most migrants turn to traffickers, smugglers and other actors who, in exchange of financial or other benefits, facilitate the illegal crossing of borders. This phenomenon is particularly prevalent in developing countries with poor health systems, with corruption, bureaucracy and unenforced legislation (OECD/ILO, 2018). During the pandemic, the lack of resources for testing, the insufficiency of the vaccine or the simple opposition to the vaccine has led more and more people to choose illegal ways to migrate, without epidemiological controls. Thus, they endanger both themselves and those with whom they travel, as well as those with whom they come into contact later.
- Globally, disparity was at its peak level in history when the COVID-19 pandemic began. In January 2020, about 2153 people were richer than the world's poorest 4.6 billion people (Oxfam International, 2020). Due to the increase of the pandemic period and its impact on migration, global inequality increased in the medium and long term. Remittance-dependent countries with a high share of these financial flows in GDP, such as the Philippines, Bangladesh, Ghana and Honduras, are the hardest hit due to the economic shocks to which migrant labour abroad has been subjected to and due to the reduction of income sources for beneficiary families. This generates negative effects on these countries' economies and, consequently, it widens the gap between rich and poor countries.

- Worsening inequalities may lead to an even greater boost in the number of migrants with the end of the COVID-19 pandemic, due to insufficient or even lack of financial resources in their countries of origin.
- Maintaining post-COVID-19 traffic restrictions. The COVID-19 pandemic introduced changes and led in a new age of migration by introducing restrictions, limiting mobility and the need for medical testing of migrants. Even if all these measures are meant to be transitory, necessary only as long as there is a risk of infection, fear of new waves of COVID-19 or other diseases, such as monkeypox, or other crises of a different nature (economic, social-political, etc.) may make the reintroduction of these measures much easier.
- Although many migration routes have been reopened, some political leaders see these migration restrictions as a chance to strengthen the medium- and long-term governance agendas built over xenophobia and discouragement of migrants. In this way, some destination countries preferred by many migrants could become for them countries with limited access.

Conclusions

An inclusive approach regarding the management of any pandemic requires a broad approach and detailed information on the entire population, regardless of nationality, including their socio-economic and cultural-linguistic needs. As for essential workers, concrete measures are needed to ensure their protection against the possibility of contracting diseases, better working and living conditions, equity and equality in accessing health services. To this end, we consider it essential to disseminate public health information and messages in the language spoken by migrants. In addition to information campaigns, it is important that trade unions or NGOs carry out workplace inspections in order to analyse compliance with the conditions under which they must work.

It is also important to be aware of the potential benefits and costs of public health measures and to avoid mistakes of approach and discrimination, such as discouraging and/or limiting access to health services or the separation of migrant families due to border closures.

Last but not least, there is a need to develop internationally applicable legislation to reduce inconsistencies between the laws of different states, in line with Objective 6 on fair and ethical recruitment and safeguard conditions of the Global Compact on Migration, in order to protect migrant workers against all types of exploitation and abuse, so that both the origin and destination country benefit from their socio-economic contribution. The COVID-19 pandemic has shown us that maximizing socio-economic benefits is an option only when the rights of migrant workers are respected and they are provided with adequate and safe working conditions, especially in the case of essential workers.

References

Adams, A., & Prassl, J. (2018). *Conditions of Work and Employment Series No. 101.*

Agerpres. (2020). Orban: Din 23 februarie, s-au întors în ţară 1.279.000 de cetăţeni români | AGERPRES • Actualizează lumea. In: Conferinţă de presă susţinută de prim-ministrul Ludovic Orban. Accessed August 20, 2021, form https://www.agerpres.ro/politica/2020/05/04/video-orban-din-23-februarie-s-au-intors-in-tara-1-279-000-de-cetateni-romani%2D%2D498675.

Bauomy, J. (2020). COVID-19 and Xenophobia: Why Outbreaks are Often Accompanied by Racism. In: *Euronews.* Accessed August 21, 2021, from https://www.euronews.com/2020/03/05/covid-19-and-xenophobia-why-outbreaks-are-often-accompanied-by-racism.

Berntsen, L., & Skowronek, N. (2021). State-of-the-Art Research Overview of the Impact of COVID-19 on Migrant Workers in the EU and The Netherlands. Nijmegen Sociology of Law Working Papers Series 01.

Bunduchi, E., Vasile, V., Comes, C.-A., & Stefan, D. (2019). Macroeconomic Determinants of Remittances: Evidence from Romania. *Applied Economics, 51*(35), 3876. https://doi.org/10.1080/00036846.2019.1584386

Daily Express. (2006). *Get Ready for the Romanian Invasion.* Accessed August 6, 2021, form https://www.pressreader.com/uk/daily-express/20060823.

Dawar, A. (2013). Immigration Minister Says, "It Will Not Be Like Polish Invasion All Over Again" | UK | News | Express.Co.Uk. In: *Daily Express.* Accessed August 6, 2021, form https://www.express.co.uk/news/uk/444231/Immigration-Minister-says-It-will-not-be-like-Polish-invasion-all-over-again.

de Camargo, C. R., & Whiley, L. A. (2020). The Mythologisation of Key Workers: Occupational Prestige Gained, Sustained... And Lost? *International Journal of Sociology and Social Policy, 40*(9–10), 849–859. https://doi.org/10.1108/IJSSP-07-2020-0310

Eftimie, A. (2020). Senator din partidul lui Băsescu, atac la românii care vin din Diaspora: Sunt oameni care muncesc la negru. In: *Mediafax*. Accessed August 16, 2021, from https://www.mediafax.ro/politic/senator-din-partidul-lui-basescu-atac-la-romanii-care-vin-din-diaspora-sunt-oameni-care-muncesc-la-negru-18994392.

European Commission. (2020a). Guidelines for Border Management Measures to Protect Health and Ensure the Availability of Goods and Essential Services C(2020) 1753 Final.

European Commission. (2020b). Communication from the Commission. Guidelines Concerning the Exercise of the Free Movement of Workers During COVID-19 Outbreak (2020/C 102 I/03). Official Journal of the European Union.

European Parliament. (2021). Free Movement of Workers. In: *Fact Sheets on the European Union*. Accessed December 5, 2021, from https://www.europarl.europa.eu/factsheets/en/sheet/41/free-movement-of-workers.

Eurostat. (2020). EU Labour Force Survey (EULFS). In: *Eurostat*. Accessed August 23, 2021.

Fasani, F., & Mazza, J. (2020). *Immigrant Key Workers: Their Contribution to Europe's COVID-19 Response. IZA Policy Paper 155.*

Fleck, G., & Rughiniș, C. (2008). Vino mai aproape. Incluziunea și excluziunea romilor în societatea de azi.

Gascon Barbera, M. (2020). Western Demand Wins Romanian Workers Coronavirus Travel Waiver | Balkan Insight. In: *BalkanInsight*. Accessed August 20, 2021, from https://balkaninsight.com/2020/04/14/western-demand-wins-romanian-workers-coronavirus-travel-waiver/.

Hope, C. (2013). "Don't Come Here, It's Not Very Nice" - Ministers Plan Campaign to Put Off Romanians and Bulgarians Migrants. In: *The Telegraph*. Accessed August 6, 2021, from https://www.telegraph.co.uk/news/politics/9830428/Dont-come-here-its-not-very-nice-Ministers-plan-campaign-to-put-off-Romanians-and-Bulgarians-migrants.html.

Hurst, L. (2020). Germany flies in seasonal workers with strict coronavirus precautions. In: *Euronews*. Accessed August 21, 2021, form https://www.euronews.com/2020/04/10/germany-flies-in-seasonal-workers-with-strict-coronavirus-precautions?fbclid=IwAR3DlzAeb-ps3_IyQmr0mVttqzf8sT_qN982fEj4l2tj6EWw7ndL4ULzp3w.

IOM. (2020). *COVID-19 Analytical Snapshot #54: Returning Migrants UPDATE. Understanding the Migration & Mobility Implications of COVID-19.*

le Coz, C., & Newland, K. (2021). *Rewiring Migrant Returns and Reintegration after the COVID-19 Shock*. Migration Policy Institute Policy Brief.

Martin, A. (2020). Coronavirus: What is the Impact for New Zealand's Migrant Workforce? In: *Scoop Business*. Accessed August 21, 2021, from https://www.scoop.co.nz/stories/BU2003/S00295/coronavirus-what-is-the-impact-for-new-zealands-migrant-workforce.htm.

McClure, T. (2021). Jacinda Ardern Says Start of Trans-Tasman Travel Bubble is 'Truly Exciting' | New Zealand. In: *The Guardian*. Accessed August 21, 2021, from https://www.theguardian.com/world/2021/apr/19/jacinda-ardern-heralds-very-significant-day-as-trans-tasman-travel-bubble-begins.

Ministry of Foreign Affairs. (2020a). Press Releases Regarding the Situation of Romanian Citizens in Italy in the Context of Measures Adopted to Manage and Prevent the Spread of COVID-19 Infection. In: Precizări de presă din 11.03.2020. Accessed August 13, 2021, from http://www.mae.ro/node/51878.

Ministry of Foreign Affairs. (2020b). Precizări de presă din 18.06.2020. In: *Romanian Government*. Accessed August 21, 2021, form http://www.mae.ro/node/52863.

Ministry of Foreign Affairs. (2020c). Precizări de presă din 21.05.2020. In: *Romanian Government*. Accessed August 21, 2021, form http://www.mae.gov.ro/node/52578.

Ministry of Foreign Affairs. (2020d). *Precizări de presă din 21.07.2020 – alți 28 de cetățeni români au fost testați pozitiv pentru infecția cu COVID-19 în Regatul Unit al Marii Britanii*. In: *Romanian Government*. Accessed August 21, 2021, from http://www.mae.ro/node/53170.

National Institute of Statistics. (2022). *Populatia ocupata pe activitati, grupe de varsta si sexe*. AMIGO. Accessed February 5, 2022, from https://insse.ro/cms/files/publicatii/Statistica%20teritoriala/Forta%20de%20munca_ind_JudLoc.htm.

O'Carroll, L. (2020). Romanian Fruit Pickers Flown to UK Amid Crisis in Farming Sector | Coronavirus | THE GUARDIAN. In: *The Guardian*. Accessed August 6, 2021, from https://www.theguardian.com/world/2020/apr/15/romanian-fruit-pickers-flown-uk-crisis-farming-sector-coronavirus.

OECD. (2020a). *COVID-19 and Key Workers: What Role do Migrants Play in Your Region?* OECD.

OECD. (2020b). *Contribution of Migrant Doctors and Nurses to Tackling COVID-19 Crisis in OECD Countries*. OECD.

OECD/ILO. (2018). *How Immigrants Contribute to Developing Countries' Economies*. OECD/ILO.

Office for National Statistics. (2019). *International Migration and the Healthcare Workforce*. Accessed August 6, 2021, from https://www.ons.gov.uk/peoplepopulationandcommunity/populationandmigration/internationalmigration/articles/internationalmigrationandthehealthcareworkforce/2019-08-15#data.

Our World in Data. (2021). *COVID-19 Data Explorer*. Accessed August 13 2021, from https://ourworldindata.org/explorers/coronavirus-data-explorer?zoomToSelection=true&time=2020-03-01..latest&facet=none&pickerSort=asc&pic

kerMetric=location&Metric=Confirmed+cases&Interval=New+per+day&Relative+to+Population=false&Align+outbreaks=false&country=GBR~ITA~ESP.

Oxfam International. (2020). *World's Billionaires have more Wealth than 4.6 billion People*. Oxfam International. Accessed July 19, 2022, from https://www.oxfam.org/en/press-releases/worlds-billionaires-have-more-wealth-46-billion-people.

Palumbo, L., & Corrado, A. (2020). *COVID-19, Agri-Food Systems, and Migrant Labour: The Situation in Germany, Italy, The Netherlands, Spain, and Sweden*. Open Society Foundations.

Pora, A. (2020). Între 200.500 și 950.500 de persoane intrate în România au "scăpat" de carantină și izolare. Testați între 0,82%- 3,29%. In: Europa Liberă. Accessed August 16, 2021, from https://romania.europalibera.org/a/%C3%AEntre-200-500-%C8%99i-950-500-de-persoane-intrate-%C3%AEn-rom%C3%A2nia-au-sc%C4%83pat-de-carantin%C4%83-%C8%99i-izolare-testa%C8%9Bi-%C3%AEntre-0-82%2D%2D-3-29-/30499768.html.

Runde, D. F., Yayboke, E. K., & Gallego, C. G. (2019). *Out of the Shadows Shining a Light on Irregular Migration*, Washington, DC, USA.

Spencer, D. (2020). Coronavirus Shows We Can – And Must – Change How We Work. In: *The Conversation*. Accessed August 6, 2021, from https://theconversation.com/coronavirus-shows-we-can-and-must-change-how-we-work-135905.

Sytas, A. (2020). Coronavirus: Latvia, Lithuania and Estonia Create 'Travel Bubble' to Ease Restrictions. In: *World Economic Forum*. Accessed August 21, 2021, from https://www.weforum.org/agenda/2020/05/baltic-states-to-create-travel-bubble-as-pandemic-curbs-eased/.

UK Government. (2020). Coming to the UK for Seasonal Agricultural Work on English Farms. In: *Department for Environment, Food & Rural Affairs*. Accessed August 20, 2021, from https://www.gov.uk/guidance/coming-to-the-uk-for-seasonal-agricultural-work-on-english-farms.

United Nations. (2022). International Migrant Stock | Population Division. In: *Population Division*. Accessed October 17, 2021, from https://www.un.org/development/desa/pd/content/international-migrant-stock.

USCIS. (2020). Employment-Based Immigration: Third Preference EB-3. In: *US Citizenship and Immigration Services. US Government*. Accessed August 21, 2021, from https://www.uscis.gov/working-in-the-united-states/permanent-workers/employment-based-immigration-third-preference-eb-3.

Vasile, V., Bunduchi, E., & Ciuhu, A.-M. (2019). Immigrants' Economic and Social Integration in Host Country-from Preconceived Ideas to Real Life. Case Study on the Romanians'. *Challenges of The Knowledge Society*, 1143–1150.

World Bank. (2020). *Phase II: COVID-19 Crisis through a Migration Lens Migration and Development Brief 33*.

World Bank. (2021). *Unemployment, Total (% of Total Labor Force) (Modeled ILO Estimate)*. Accessed August 13, 2021, from https://data.worldbank.org/indicator/SL.UEM.TOTL.ZS.

Wright, H. (2021). Baltics Planning to Revive "Travel Bubble". In: *ERR News*. Accessed August 21, 2021, from https://news.err.ee/1608228552/baltics-planning-to-revive-travel-bubble.

CHAPTER 11

Conclusions

Valentina Vasile and Elena Bunduchi

The importance of the migration phenomenon and remittances is recognized worldwide, representing a very relevant issue, especially that its effective management is a challenge for society in general.

Money flows associated with international labour migration represent an important source of income for more and more households in the less developed countries of the world.

If, in the past (eighteenth and nineteenth) centuries, work abroad was also associated with a permanent change of residence, starting with the last decades of the twentieth century, migration for work, with temporary residence abroad, even multi-year, became an increasingly used form of employment, being preferred by workers for the comparative financial advantages. Remittances supplement the incomes of migrant households from the country of origin, contributing to the growth of consumption and entrepreneurial activities, but also to support investments in living conditions (housing conditions), access to health services and education.

This chapter, which focuses more on the impact of mobility for work and remittances for the country of origin, analyses the externalities as a whole, respectively beyond the positive net effect, beyond the surface and short-term positive effects.

The COVID-19 pandemic also identified the important role of essential workers, causing host countries to change their policies regarding foreign workers faster and to a greater extent, encouraging immigration for work.

V. Vasile et al., *International Labour Mobility*,
https://doi.org/10.1007/978-3-031-18683-7_11

Working abroad has multiple effects, demographic, economic, social, cultural, but with adverse effects for the country of origin. Among them we mention:

- A job abroad means less pressure on unemployment in the country of origin but also an increase in the employment deficit in areas essential for development—construction, transport, health, education and so on.
- Working abroad for a longer period leads in more and more cases to the relocation of the household in the host country with important effects for the country of origin—from the demographic decline to the accentuation of the aging of the population; from the labour force deficit to the reduction or even the cessation of remittances, so the decrease in demand for consumption, investments and so on.
- The free movement of people in the European space has proven that migrant workers, when unfavourable conjunctural economic situations appear (such as the financial crisis of 2008–09 or the pandemic of 2020–21), choose migration to another more developed state over the alternative of returning to the country of origin, or the return is short, temporary, only until a new opportunity for (re) occupation abroad is identified.
- The opening of developed states to the acceptance of migrant workers to reduce the employment deficit stimulated migration flows for work even in pandemic conditions, for new contingents of workers, the first two motivations for migration being (a) the advantage of higher earnings from work; (b) the employment opportunity for graduates, in the professions associated with the fields of initial education—that is, qualified and highly qualified staff in the health sector and beyond.
- Remittances continue to represent for the countries of origin, less developed, an important financial source in the short term and become increasingly volatile in the medium and long term.

Thus, this book aimed to identify the positive and/or negative effects of remittances and migration from an economic, financial and social point of view. Following the application of the research methods stated in the introduction, we find that the research hypotheses have been validated and we conclude the following:

- The concept of migration has evolved a lot lately, but, although it is analysed from the perspective of different approaches (social, demographic, historical, geographical, anthropological, economic, political), there is still no universally accepted definition, which to include all the defining elements as a whole.
- The notion of remittances also creates confusion at the time of registration, quantification and comparison at the level of beneficiary countries, as a result of the existing methodological differences, although the International Monetary Fund has come up with clarifications, which should reduce the existing uncertainties.
- An important amount from remittances is from informal employment and are sent to the origin countries using informal channels. The lack of data on the real value of remittances worldwide is explained by the high cost of transferring to countries of origin through official channels, thus allowing the influence of unofficial channels to increase. Although the issue of reducing these costs was included in the UN Sustainable Development Goals, the results are below expectations. Thus, there is a need for measures adopted at national level, in the first instance, to reduce transfer costs.
- The increase in the number of migrants worldwide has registered accelerated rates since the 1990s, and in the last ten years, with different patterns of migration, but mainly looking for better work opportunities. At the level of the European Union, the formation of main areas of attraction for both EU citizens and migrants from third countries is registered, and in the countries of Southern and Eastern Europe, the population is decreasing as a result of a negative net migration rate. Following the application of the same methodology for determining the indicators of the migration phenomenon at the EU level, we find that Croatia, Romania and Portugal are the most affected countries by the migration phenomenon, even in the conditions where the share of remittances in GDP does not exceed a few percent.
- The econometric analysis of the impact of remittances and FDI on economic growth by using fixed and random effects OLS for panel data shows us the difference in the behaviour of the two sources of external financial flows in the case of EU-28 member states + Republic of Moldova, Ukraine and Serbia. Thus, there is a significant influence of remittances on the level of economic growth in countries with a high rate of external mobility and a more modest GDP/

capita, and the higher the economic level of the states, the more the impact of remittances loses its intensity. In the case of FDI, there is a lack of any effect on economic growth, the exception being the less developed states.
- Analysis of remittances from a multidimensional perspective at the macroeconomic level demonstrates their negative impact on labour market indicators. Thus, in the case of Romania and the Republic of Moldova, there is a decrease in the active population and the employment rate along with the increase in remittances and the lack of any influence on the unemployment rate, which implies that individuals migrated from the position of employed person and not from the unemployed. So, it can be seen that remittances do not balance the labour market of the two states, having, as a whole, negative effects. At the same time, remittances contribute to the increase in import consumption, generating imbalances in the balance of payments in Romania and the Republic of Moldova. Instead, remittances have positive effects at the microeconomic level reflected in the increase in the disposable income of households, thus allowing them to increase their current consumption expenditures, with health and education, endowment with durable goods and technologies.
- In addition to the economic and financial effects, remittances also generate positive and negative social effects in the country of origin and destination, at the macro- and microeconomic levels, and depending on them, the migration policies adopted by the authorities of those states are shaped.

The work brings original information and contributions regarding the analysis of the effects of migration from the perspective of remittances entered in the country of origin. It approaches remittances as an economic-financial factor but also as one that affects the consumption model, social behaviours, quality of life, the sustainability of household development, the migrant's professional career and so on.

We consider the following as elements of originality and personal contribution:

- Developing a classification of remittances from an economic perspective
- Proposing an indicator for quantifying the impact of migration and remittances in the countries of the world and making a ranking of

the countries at the world level, European and in the space of the former socialist states
- Comparing the concept of official registration of remittances in the balances of payments in Romania and the Republic of Moldova according to the indications of the International Monetary Fund
- Proposing measures to reduce the costs of transferring remittances to the countries of origin
- Cluster analysis of the states depending on the rate of external labour mobility with subgrouping according to GDP/capita level, in order to determine the impact of remittances/FDI on economic growth
- Extensive analysis of the impact of remittances at the macro and microeconomic level, highlighting the negative effects of remittances on the increase in import consumption

Summarizing, the results of the analyses carried out in this book reveal the fact that there is a significant, but strongly differentiated influence of remittances on the country of origin, with a net positive impact in the short term but which, in the medium and long term, turns into a net loss, on multiple plans not only from the financial perspective, respectively demographic, of using the human capital created in the national education system, in terms of the standard of living of the household associated with the multi-year migrant turned into emigrant, of local economic development, of social problems and of the alteration of the cultural model.

The research aspects are current and present importance for the further development of the subject, both from a theoretical and practical point of view; offers useful results and conclusions to local and national decision-makers, and not only, regarding economic, social and behavioural effects, on the consumption model and the investment potential of remittance savings for entrepreneurial activities.

The conclusions of the analyses and the comments presented are contributions to the knowledge in the field of remittances and labour migration and can be useful for the foundation of mobility management tools for work—attractive factors for retaining labour resources, the development of policies for the adequacy of the professional training profile to the demand of the national market, to support entrepreneurship and so on.

Proposed future research directions are found in:

- Identifying the extent to which we can transform remittances into sustainability factors at the level of individuals and households; this aspect is all the more important because, during the pandemic, it proved to be the most resilient external financial source for many less developed states. That is why we propose to analyse the resilience of remittances in the new post-pandemic context in which the policies of the host states have changed significantly.

- Finding instruments aimed at achieving a macroeconomic balance between facilitating the transfer of income (remittances) through official channels in the largest proportion (minimizing the cost of the transfer).
- Promoting tools and mechanisms to increase collaboration between the diaspora (second and third generations) and the country of origin.
- Identifying the advantages/disadvantages of the social inclusion of emigrants in the country of destination. A multi-year emigrant has a certain degree of economic inclusion in the labour market, but ensuring the sustainability of employment and social inclusion must be analysed in detail in order to reduce the inequalities and inequities inherent in the current situation of globalization of markets and covering the employment deficit through foreign labour (immigrant).
- An important aspect that we propose to analyse as a continuation of the analyses presented in this volume is the effect of digitization and the increase in remote or hybrid employment on the amount of remittances and their sustainability, from the perspective of the country of origin.

The problem of analysing remittances and their impact on the country of origin remains open, the change in host countries' policies raising new challenges for less developed countries of origin. Although remittances, through the annual flows, represent a source of stimulating consumption and, partially, domestic production, they also represent a risk for increased migration, therefore for the loss of labour resources, so necessary for economic and social development of the origin countries.

Kolibri 360 GmbH
Ferdinand-Jühlke-Straße 7
99095 Erfurt, Deutschland
produktsicherheit@kolibri360.de